Messianic Ethics

Messianic Ethics

*Jesus' Proclamation
of the Kingdom of God and
the Church in Response*

HERALD PRESS
Waterloo, Ontario
Scottdale, Pennsylvania

Canadian Cataloging-in-Publication Data
Wiebe, Ben, 1942-
  Messianic ethics

Includes bibliographical references and index.
ISBN 0-8361-3585-7

1. Kingdom of God—Biblical teaching.
2. Christian ethics—History—Early church, ca. 30-600. I. Title.

BT94.W54 1992   231.7'2   C92-093294-0

The paper used in this publication is recycled and meets the minimum requirements of American National Standard for Information Sciences—Permanence of Paper for Printed Library Materials, ANSI Z39.48-1984.

Scripture quotations are used by permission and unless otherwise indicated are from the *New Revised Standard Version Bible*, copyright 1989, by the Division of Christian Education of the National Council of the Churches of Christ in the USA; those marked RSV are from the *Revised Standard Version Bible*, copyright 1946, 1952, 1971 by the Division of Christian Education of the National Council of the Churches of Christ in the USA; those marked KJV are from *The Holy Bible, King James Version*.

MESSIANIC ETHICS
Copyright © 1992 by Herald Press, Waterloo, Ont. N2L 6H7
  Published simultaneously in the United States by Herald Press,
    Scottdale, Pa. 15683. All rights reserved
Library of Congress Catalog Card Number: 91-58984
International Standard Book Number: 0-8361-3585-7
Printed in the United States of America
Book and cover design by Paula M. Johnson

00 99 98 97 96 95 94 93 92 10 9 8 7 6 5 4 3 2 1

To Patti
with gratitude
for our partnership in life
in the service of the kingdom

Contents

Foreword by Willard M. Swartley 11
Preface 13

Introduction 15
    The Non-Eschatological Reduction of Ethics • 16
    Imminent Eschatology and Suspension of Ethics • 17
    Existential Interpretation and the
        Elimination of Ethics • 18
    A Way Forward • 19
    A Word on Method • 21

1. The Historical Background of the Question 25
    The Importance of Ritschl and Weiss • 26
        Kingdom in the Thought of Ritschl • 28
        The Kingdom and the Ethical Response • 30
        The Kingdom and Jesus' Destiny • 34
    From Weiss to Wilder • 36
        Harnack and Ethics Without Eschatology • 36
        Albert Schweitzer and Consistent Eschatology • 38
        C. H. Dodd and Realized Eschatology • 40
        Bultmann and Existential Eschatology • 44
        Wilder and the Ethics of Realized Eschatology • 47
        Evaluation • 49
    Elements for a New State of the Question • 51

2. Resources for Jesus' Proclamation and Teaching....55
**God's Kingship for Israel and the Nations
According to the Scriptures** • 56
God's Kingship and Israel • 57
God's Kingship and the World • 60
The Messiah and the Restoration of Israel • 63
God's Reign in Daniel and Postbiblical Judaism • 73
**Eschatology and Ethics in the Scriptures
and in Postbiblical Judaism** • 82
Eschatology and Ethics in the Scriptures • 82
Eschatology and Ethics in Daniel
and Postbiblical Judaism • 85
Conclusion • 89

3. The Kingdom of God and the Proper Response.....93
New State of the Question • 93
John the Baptist and Jesus • 99
Jesus' Proclamation, Acts, and Teaching • 102
**Response to Proclamation, Action,
and Teaching** • 107
The Beatitudes • 108
The Proclamation • 111
The Issue of Repentance • 112
Accepters Versus Rejecters • 116
Proper Response to Jesus' Initiative
Toward Sinners • 120
**Eschatological and Social Dimensions
of Jesus' Ethics** • 121
A Community Intent on God • 126
Servant of All • 127
The Way of Liberation • 128
The End of Domination • 129
A Community of Reconciliation • 131
The Community and the Ethic of Love • 132

4. Jesus' Messianic Mission...135
Authenticity and Purpose of Jesus' Esoteric Teaching • 136
The Content of the Esoteric Teaching • 143
- Peter's Confession at Caesarea Philippi • 144
- Messiahship and the Ethics of Discipleship • 149
- Self-Giving Service • 154
- The Primacy of Love • 156
- The Practice of Love: Forgiveness • 157
- The Willingness to Bear Suffering • 158
- Death as Victory • 158

Ethics for the Messianic Community • 160

Conclusion... 167

Notes 175
Bibliography 201
Index of Ancient Sources 209
Author Index 218
Subject Index 220
The Author 224

Foreword

One of the most debated issues in New Testament studies over the last century has been the relation between ethics and eschatology in Jesus' self-consciousness, and the significance of this for our understanding of his teachings and deeds. Did Jesus expect an imminent end to history and life in this world? Albert Schweitzer argued that he did. Johannes Weiss had earlier regarded Jesus' eschatological proclamation of the kingdom of God as a transcendental expectation which made human achievement of its demands impossible. This contrasted with Albrecht Ritschl, who had urged just such human effort.

In Schweitzer's view, Jesus' radical ethics were intended for a brief interim—until the end came. They were "cut" primarily for individualistic appropriation, since no long-term community, the church, was envisioned. Because the outcome has differed—history has continued for two thousand years—eschatology has thus often been viewed as a liability to ethics (so Jack T. Sanders and Richard Hiers in recent literature).

Ben Wiebe argues against these notions, while at the same time accepting Jesus' proclamation of the dawning kingdom of God as a central feature of Jesus' mission. He contends that Jesus knew himself to be the long-expected messianic King and thus came heralding the inbreaking kingdom of God. Through mighty deeds and casting out unclean spirits, Jesus brought signs of the kingdom's inauguration. He came to restore Israel to be a faithful community of God, and to enlarge that community to include Gentiles as well, thus fulfilling the promises to Abraham (Gen. 12:1-3).

Jesus' ethical teachings are thus best understood as ethics for the repentant, restored people of God. They are for a people and its communal life, a people later known as the church.

Hence, Jesus' ethics are comprehensible only within this dual context of Jesus' self-consciousness as messianic King and his intent to restore a faithful peoplehood. For then the radical shape of his teaching makes sense: the King models and calls his followers to humble service in contrast to the way the world's kings rule; the King leads the way to liberation from domination and inaugurates a community in which love and reconciliation are its hallmarks. Jesus' own death consummates his ethics, demonstrating that the way of suffering love is God's way to victory over evil. In the midst of that suffering, Jesus forgives those who crucified him, thus releasing power that can convert enemies to become reconciled to God and to fellow humans.

The reader may wonder why Wiebe gives so much attention to "historical Jesus" questions, including the chapter on history of research. However, in the end it becomes clear that the authorization for the ethic of Jesus is Jesus' own intentions as well as the Scripture, which speaks forth his word. Certainly, many New Testament scholars will not be as optimistic as Wiebe that so much of the Jesus tradition can be established by historical critical investigation. Yet all readers must consider anew whether eschatology has the effect of putting ethics on discount or whether instead it actually functions positively for ethics—as the muscle for the gospel's distinctive ethic. The proclamation of the kingdom coming is thus the empowering possibility for a new way of living, loving, and hoping.

I commend Wiebe's book for study in the college, university, and seminary classroom. It will also stimulate energetic Sunday school classes and study groups. But the greater and more important challenge is for the church to live the ethic which the book sets forth with new clarity and fresh appeal.

—*Willard M. Swartley*
Professor of New Testament
Associated Mennonite Biblical Seminaries
Elkhart, Indiana

Preface

The centrality of *the kingdom of God* for Jesus is confirmed in the crucible of criticism. It was at the center of his proclamation and the determining ground for his mission. Yet scholarship remains obscure on the nature of the kingdom of God.

What did Jesus presuppose and what resources did he draw upon in making his proclamation of the kingdom? What for Jesus was the interaction between his aims and the responses he expected? In carrying out his mission, was he concerned with the individual in general or with Israel? What was the link between eschatological renewal and community?

If the kingdom of God and positive ethical response to Jesus have an integral correlation in the teaching of Jesus, it follows that they can be clearly understood only in relationship. Concretely, the meaning of kingdom and of response depend on a recovery of the purposes of Jesus for the people, Israel, to whom he came. The aim of this book is to provide opportunity for giving attention to Jesus' proclamation and the intended response.

I wish here to recognize the people who have supported me by sharing my interests and encouraging me. I want to acknowledge the generous stimulation and guidance which Ben Meyer provided over the period of my studies and in supervising my Ph.D. thesis at McMaster University. The high standards of his criticism have been a challenge for me to think and write more clearly.

Finally, I want to express thanks to my family: To my wife, Patti, for her part, of which typing the several drafts is only the most apparent contribution. To our children, Paul, Carrie, and Stephen, whose presence and encouragement also was important in the completion of this work. And to S. David Garber and the staff at Herald Press for their interest and effort in bringing this work to publication.

—Ben Wiebe
Hamilton, Ontario

Introduction

Following upon the work of Johannes Weiss and Albert Schweitzer, all New Testament scholars of the twentieth century have been compelled to deal with the problems attendant on the recovery of early Christian eschatology. They have searched for the coherence between Jesus' eschatological proclamation and the response he intended to elicit, and this has inevitably raised the more general question of the relation between eschatology and ethics. Those who rediscovered early Christian eschatology did not make the issue of eschatology and ethics their highest priority. They nevertheless did glimpse the startling implications of eschatology for ethics.[1]

In the interpretation of Jesus' kingdom-of-God proclamation, attention for the most part has been directed either to eschatology or to ethics: at one time the primary focus was on the human ethical response (e.g., Ritschl and Harnack), at another time on the activity of God (e.g., Johannes Weiss). This set up a critical divergence. On the one hand, without a larger understanding of reality, ethics and the language of ethics lose their meaning or authority.

A case in point is the history of "situation ethics." As "ethics" designed for everybody in general, simply to be determined in the situation, it swiftly became so abstract that talk about ethical response lost all determinate meaning. On the other hand, such ethicists reduced the significance of connection between Jesus' teaching and the issues confronting disciples living in the world until the Gospels only provided a "sort of atmosphere of ethical concern but little more."[2]

Or, if Jesus' ethical teaching was seriously considered, this divergence resulted in a moralization of Jesus' teaching: ethics was reduced to rule keeping. But the kingdom as God's initiative is not revealed without the beauty of his grace. Response then has the character of *doxology* or trust. Behavior is an effect and not only self-determined action; it is a reflection of the gracious initiative of God as much as it is action toward future achievement. Living is an act of praise rather than one of servile obedience.[3] The ethical response thus emerges from and embodies a specific understanding of God and his purposes for the world.

We need to examine the assumption that Jesus directed his mission exclusively to the individual (parties to this assumption included T. W. Manson, at one end of the spectrum, and Rudolf Bultmann and his school on the other) and that he was indifferent to the wider issues of justice and community. Is Norman Perrin right in asserting that "the individual had become the significant religious unit"? I maintain that Perrin overlooks important aspects of Jesus' proclamation and teaching.

In reply to the individualistic interpretation of Jesus' ethics, we observe that the division between religion (individual) and politics (community) was alien to the setting in which Jesus carried out his mission. It is possible, to be sure, that Jesus' teaching transcended this setting, but that specific hypothesis would need to be demonstrated, not simply asserted. Second, it is questionable to assume that sin is the act of the individual alone and that Jesus came to deal only with sin. How Jesus fulfilled his mission among and for his people, and how he stood with respect to conflict, poverty, liberation, and justice—these are issues not without relevance for understanding his ethics.

The Non-Eschatological Reduction of Ethics

According to a common assumption, Jesus' message was ahistorical by definition, focused on eternal religious and moral principles and accordingly divorced from the conflicts and power struggles that conditioned his time. Yet it is strange that Jesus' mission should be presented as if Jesus had to choose between two options: the politics of revolutionary nationalism, or a wholly suprapolitical stance of noninvolvement. Was there no range of possibilities between violent revolution and unqualified allegiance to the existing order?

In 1900, Adolf von Harnack argued that for Jesus "the kingdom of God comes by coming to the individual"; what mattered for Jesus was "God and the soul." Accordingly, beyond providing a general direction of regard for the neighbor, the gospel provides no help for life in community.[4] More recently E. F. Scott offered the judgment that Jesus made it his aim to keep a safe distance from the "stormy politics of his age," and labored under the burden of carrying on "a purely religious work in a heated political atmosphere."[5]

More important for the neglect of the ethical dimension in Jesus' teaching are the factors inherent in two influential contexts for New Testament interpretation.

Imminent Eschatology and Suspension of Ethics

Weiss and Schweitzer have been credited with the view that a relation between history and ethics was not a basic concern for Jesus. The conviction that the coming of the kingdom meant the imminent end of all things left room only for an "ascetic ideal" without history or ethics.[6] If the kingdom is identified as otherworldly reality, and with the destruction of this world in imminent cosmic cataclysm, concern about the historical character and destiny of Israel would not register on the scale for Jesus. Hence, for Schweitzer, the ethical teaching of Jesus, to the extent that he attended to it at all, could only be interpreted as "world-negation."[7]

What this means in concrete terms is evident in Schweitzer's treatment of the question of tribute to Caesar. Schweitzer asks how, if one took Jesus' perspective, "could one be concerned at all about such things?" The institution of the state was in any case to come to an end within months; the question of whether to pay tribute or not was therefore irrelevant. "One might as well submit to it, its end was in fact near." According to Schweitzer, such issues had no significance for Jesus and were first posed by history through the delay of the parousia (coming of Jesus).[8] The same held for questions about the place and meaning of the Torah. For Jesus, he affirmed, these questions were of no significance. Eschatology, identified simply as an end-of-the-world event, excluded all such questions.[9]

However this understanding of Jesus' mission is evaluated, further developments precisely in the area of eschatology mean that the assessment of Jesus' teaching offered by Weiss and Schweitzer cannot serve as a blanket invocation for the suspension of ethics. On this we will consider two groups of Jesus' sayings: (1) those that point to the presence of the kingdom (which even Weiss could not altogether ignore); and (2) those showing that Jesus refused to set dates or times for the coming of the end. The idea that the kingdom is to be exclusively identified with the end is open to serious question. One may well ask whether "time" was a factor at all in Jesus' view of the coming of the kingdom. Finally, and most important, what is to be made of the body of Jesus' ethical teaching in the Gospels?

Existential Interpretation and the Elimination of Ethics

The individualistic and ahistorical character of existentialist interpretation has now been widely recognized.[10] It is beyond our scope to explore the issue of whether the existentialist approach is a viable hermeneutic; it is often used to convey not only the meaning of Jesus' teaching in contemporary terms, but also as the framework for historical understanding of this teaching itself.[11] Rudolf Bultmann affirmed on the one hand that Jesus identified eschatology with the coming to pass of certain events. Yet at the same time he claimed that the kingdom of God did not "in any sense depend on these events."[12] He wanted to insist that Jesus himself understood the kingdom of God in existential terms, apart from any relation to events in time.[13]

The proclamation of the eschatological kingdom of God places the person in the crisis of decision. Bultmann took this crisis to be the final meaning of Jesus' announcement of the kingdom.[14] To the extent that there could be talk of ethics, Bultmann identified it with the decision for or against God. He did include the call to love the neighbor within the scope of decision for God. He spoke of *radical obedience*, the controlling question of authenticity, which ruled out specific ethical content. Thus the point of Jesus' teaching was not to illuminate and inform ethical decisions, according to Bultmann. Each person was to discover in the particular, concrete situation what it is to love one's neighbor.[15] Jesus did not explain how this process was to work. Neither the available choices nor the reasons why one choice would be preferable to another could be properly considered ahead of time. That would destroy the hearing of God's word in the moment.

Thus the transposition of eschatology into existential terms in effect eliminates ethics. Indeed, for Bultmann the kingdom of God provided no light for making plans or taking action within this world.[16]

There is no reason to question the propriety of the search for Jesus' understanding of existence; but the point and the limitations of this interpretation need to be clearly identified. What is illegitimate is the exclusion of dimensions of Jesus' teaching because they do not fit into the existentialist frame of reference. The eschatological teaching of Jesus anticipated coming events. This same teaching anticipated a renewed community, and the kingdom itself has a corporate significance. If the limits set by existential interpretation for eschatology evaporate, this itself means the ethical dimension of Jesus' teaching cannot be set aside.

A Way Forward

It is evident that the relation between eschatology and ethics continues to be a vital, if still unsettled, question. Further, it is apparent that a successful answer to this question will turn on one's grasp of eschatology, ethics, and their reciprocal relationships. The aim of this study is to offer such an answer. What ethical response was called for by Jesus' proclamation of the kingdom of God? This study deals in turn with the character of the intended response to Jesus' public proclamation (chapter 3), and with the character of the intended response to the renewed call to discipleship that Jesus made to the twelve when he announced his destiny to them (chapter 4). Both investigations call for a fairly full account of Jesus' eschatological perspectives of the kingdom of God. But our primary interest is in the intended correlation between Jesus' eschatology and ethics; our aim is to illuminate the character of Jesus' ethics.

This work can be aptly located in the larger field of Christian biblical ethics. In the Christian community the Scriptures serve as a source of ethical insight and moral authority. There is an interdependence between Scripture and the people of God: Scripture came into being as the record of God's saving and guiding activity with his people Israel and through Jesus Christ with the church. This is enough warning about the inadequacy of a naively direct appropriation of the Scriptures. The messianic ethics of Jesus is not the whole of New Testament ethics.

Moreover, it takes acts of recovery to grasp Jesus' messianic ethics and to grasp the whole of New Testament ethics. There can be no doubt about the immediacy of the impact of these ethics on all who share in and profit from these acts of recovery. But the contemporary Christian community is not fully and adequately served by limitation to this kind of direct and immediate impact. We need a more massive and reflective mediation of all New Testament ethics to influence the present. Studies such as this one accordingly seek to serve two purposes: first, to recover ancient meaning with its original form and force; and second, thereby to provide theology with data indispensable for the task of mediating to the Christian community today a fully rounded and wholly contemporary Christian ethics.

Scripture does not come in the form of a timeless moral code. Covenant and commandment are given in history as God relates himself to particular persons and groups (e.g., Abraham, Israel). At the same time the biblical emphasis is on the continuity of God's purpose, which includes a great variety of people and concrete situations. Within such continuity there is a consistency of purpose from the past to the anticipated future (cf. Deut. 30:11, 14; Mic. 6:6-8; Mark 10:6-9; Rom. 12:2).[17] To use Scripture as a resource in moral discernment, we need to have an awareness of the meaning or intention expressed in the text and of the kind of question that may be appropriately asked. For example, just because Scripture speaks with authority about nature does not mean that it will answer any or every kind of question in this area. The basic reference in Christian biblical ethics is to Scripture as integrally involved in the very process of the formulation and development of the ethics.[18]

Our purpose here is to consider the teaching and mission of Jesus and his significance for ethics. Thus the center of attention is on the place and meaning of "messianic ethics," grounded in the eschatological mission of Jesus Christ. This messianic ethics is both old and new. It reflects the purposes of God from the beginning and it anticipates the triumph of those purposes at the end. In this context we can properly ask and answer questions about the place of creation, the Old Testament Scriptures, or tradition as sources of moral insight. Whatever light they shed on identity and behavior must cohere with and pass through the eschatological event of Jesus Christ.[19]

Jesus' mission was addressed to the people of God, and it envisaged the eschatological restoration of the people of God. The meaning of participation in the kingdom of God was therefore mediated in and through this community. The interpretation and discernment of the appropriate response to God's initiative in Jesus could not take place as an intellectual operation by the lone individual. The promise of Jesus to actualize his will had as its context the community gathered in his name (cf. Matt. 18:18-19). The witness of the gospel was to be interpreted and appropriated anew in the future, from the perspective of the teaching Jesus gave the disciples. In this perspective the community was not envisioned without the Scriptures (including the oral or written witness of the apostles) or the Scriptures without the community. The fulfillment of the promise of guidance was to be claimed in the assembly of those gathered around this Word to converse and understand together the will of God with respect to some specific moral issue (cf. Acts 2:42; 15:6-21, 28-29).

A Word on Method

It is important that, taking account of the range of evidence on Jesus in the Gospels, we begin with what can be more securely established before dealing with what is less certain. This involves the question of the framework in which particular data find their proper meaning. Certain types of information are directly helpful in establishing this framework: basic facts known about Jesus (such as baptism by John, crucifixion as "king of the Jews"); a knowledge of the basic character of first-century Judaism; and knowledge of the early church as outcome of Jesus' life and destiny. If we then examine sayings and accounts in their different forms and sources, we will discover certain common characteristics, such as Jesus' proclamation of the kingdom, his position on the Law, and his attitude toward the various groups in society. Within the larger whole, the perplexing parts can become intelligible.

But agreement on how to proceed in order to achieve this is not easy to find. One of the reasons for the difficulty and consequent confusion, I believe, is that studies have tended to take up one aspect of Jesus. The focus may be on Jesus as teacher, or Jesus as storyteller (in the parables), or Jesus as miracle worker. Here we intend to take account of Jesus in the context of his public ministry (e.g., eating with tax collectors and sinners, teaching the crowds, calling the twelve disciples) and his destiny (in relation to the outcome that is the church). This requires the regular consideration of two or more lines of evidence in seeking to ascertain and establish key points.

Much of the detailed discussion on evidence for authenticity will be taken up in the notes in order to proceed in a more direct and intelligible way with the development of the argument. Yet there is a concern throughout with answering questions on the basis of evidence. Even when indexes are not specifically referred to, the way evidence is presented is done with an awareness of them (e.g., the use of more than one line of evidence to establish a point or the prevalence of multisource and multiform citations from the Gospels). To some this measure of attention to questions of history and authenticity will appear as a distraction; to others this will appear as not sufficiently critical or rigorous. I will try to disappoint both!

Here the issue of criteria in the historical criticism of the Gospels arises and must be addressed. The view, which has largely prevailed for at least 150 years, has been that the proper formulation and use of criteria would yield objective results.[20] There is wide agreement on their usefulness. Yet there is confusion about their application in particular cases and about the extent of their importance in making judgments on what is so or not so. With "objective results" as the goal, some interpreters exalt the criterion of dissimilarity, that Jesus must have been different from Judaism, or from the early church. But none of these criteria are standards invariably relevant to ascertaining historicity.

That Jesus called disciples, affirmed the authority of the Scriptures, shared in the worship of the synagogue and temple, understood God as the God of Abraham, of David and Isaiah, of Israel, and of all creation—all this is without question historical even though all in accord with Judaism. Again, that Jesus proclaimed the kingdom of God, regularly taught in parables, healed the sick, ate the Passover supper with his disciples before his death, and was crucified under Pontius Pilate—all this is similarly historical, though it all is in accord with the faith of the church.[21]

Thus the confusion has centered around the question of presupposition in criticism and interpretation of the Gospel accounts. How shall we take account of subjectivity as a component and as a condition of objectivity? The disagreement has been in part about which criteria are cogent or pertinent, and in part about whether in fact they are adequate to the task.

The list of criteria (or, more accurately, indexes) for historicity normally includes the following:
- Discontinuity with early Christianity.
- Originality vis-à-vis Palestinian Judaism.
- Distinctive and personal idiom (e.g., "amen," "abba").
- Coherence with material shown by other means to be authentic (e.g., if a saying in a new setting bears the stamp of the same inner logic of material already acknowledged to be authentic).
- Multiple attestation (in relatively independent strands of tradition).
- Multiform attestation (e.g., in narrative material, or sayings material).

Of these indexes, discontinuity with the transmitting church is regularly the most convincing. For example, if (as seems clear) the tendency of the transmitting church was to present Jesus as independent of John the Baptist, the historicity of the tradition of Jesus seeking baptism by John is established with high probability. The index of originality vis-à-vis Palestinian Judaism can be relevant for certain cases in weighing the authenticity of a saying or tradition. A saying that stands in discontinuity with the early church but with roots in Judaism is not thereby rendered unhistorical. In the Gospel record we meet with the words and deeds of a distinct and original person; the evidence for the originality of Jesus is both more extensive and compelling than the evidence for the originality of the early Christian community. At the same time, multiple attestation will normally be the most useful to establish a reasonable degree of certainty about what was characteristic of Jesus and about the main lines of his mission and teaching.[22] Although each index may not have the force of independent cogency, all the indexes have their own importance as part of the cumulative evidence for determining historicity.

Since the task of criticism depends on human judgment in the discernment of what is or is not so, matters will hardly ever be settled by a single decisive question. Rather, what is normally involved is a range of considerations depending on relevant indexes and cumulative evidence. The pertinence and the application of particular indexes must be established from case to case (otherwise criticism becomes merely arbitrary and superfluous). The presence, for instance, of discontinuity or originality is positive evidence for historicity, but their absence is not positive evidence against historicity. For example, the early Christian community saw itself as responsible to Jesus, evidenced most clearly by traditions preserved counter to the tendencies of the church. If this is so, it certainly would preserve traditions in accord with existing patterns and tendencies.

Thus the task of Gospel study is not only a question of sources or evidence but often even more a challenge to awareness and judgment. In our situation, we are confronted with an array of evidence. By it we are compelled to seek answers to questions of history and meaning.

1

The Historical Background of the Question

What was the meaning of Jesus' kingdom-of-God proclamation, and what response to it did Jesus seek? In the history of scholarship, answers to this question have varied widely. This is evident in the set of contrary views we see in that history. For some, the kingdom of God is to be realized *in* the human (ethical) response; for others, the kingdom is wholly the eschatological deed of God, and human response can only be described as preparation for its coming in the future. In the view of some scholars, Jesus was concerned with the absolute future or the end; in the view of others, Jesus was concerned with what was to happen in the course of history. Again, according to certain scholars, the kingdom of God in Jesus' proclamation is the rule of God in the human heart; but others insist that the kingdom of God in Jesus' proclamation is to be effective in history and as the end of history.

In this chapter it is not my purpose to present my own efforts to answer this question: What was the meaning of Jesus' kingdom-of-God proclamation, and what response to it did Jesus seek? The immediate issue, rather, is how critical scholarship up to the present has answered this question. Therefore, to clarify the matter, I shall review the work of major scholars who have contributed to the discussion, from Albrecht Ritschl to Amos Wilder. Thus I shall pick out of more recent scholarship the elements that seem to me to offer promise of a new state of understanding on the ethics called for by Jesus.

We begin our survey with a fairly full account of Albrecht

Ritschl. Johannes Weiss inaugurated a new era in the discussion of Jesus and the kingdom of God, and yet Weiss also defined his own position precisely vis-à-vis that of Ritschl. Further, it was Ritschl who first clearly related Jesus' proclamation and his ethical teaching. We begin, then, with Ritschl's 1889 work, *Die christliche Lehre von der Rechtfertigung und Versöhnung*.[1]

The Importance of Ritschl and Weiss

Briefly stated, Ritschl's view was that the kingdom of God is realized in Christian ethical action in the present. The decisive reaction to this thesis was from his student and son-in-law, Johannes Weiss. Weiss's *Die Predigt Jesu vom Reiche Gottes* (1892) subjected Ritschl's thesis to a partly positive but also negative critique. The question of the nature of the kingdom of God and the appropriate response to it came into critical focus for the first time.

Under the influence of the Enlightenment, Ritschl had developed a synthesis on the basis of Kant, Schleiermacher, and Rothe. A section in the first volume of Ritschl's major work, *Rechtfertigung und Versöhnung*, is a discussion of Kant's ethics and theology.[2] In it Ritschl recognized that, for Kant, the "kingdom of God" was the goal of all ethical activity.[3] Jesus was the archetype of humanity pleasing to God, an example of the moral reason within us all by which we make the kingdom the goal of this activity.

Ritschl also devoted a section in the first volume of his work to discussion of Schleiermacher,[4] who understood the kingdom as the corporate life of Christians in fellowship with God.[5] Schleiermacher saw redemption as the influence of Jesus (sinless perfection), and from this he derived the "teleological character of Christian piety."[6] That is, the kingdom is to be realized and becomes the goal of the person under the influence of Christ. Jesus' life of sinless perfection is the beginning of the kingdom, and his influence is the power by which he leads people to live and act for that kingdom.

Richard Rothe, rarely mentioned by Ritschl, had nevertheless strongly influenced him at certain points. This is most clearly evident in his conception of the kingdom of God. For Rothe, the kingdom was also the enacting of the highest good, but Rothe set this in the framework of the Hegelian speculative method and of the historical process of thesis interacting with antithesis leading to synthesis, and so to the final goal.[7]

A key to understanding Ritschl is seeing behind him the preeminent emphasis on ethical activity in the work of Kant, Schleiermacher, and Rothe. All three related the kingdom of God to the highest good; they further argued that the highest good found realization through the ethical task. The concept of "the highest good" was at once the organizing perspective for ethics, the goal of action, and the result of this goal-directed action.[8] On one hand, the kingdom of God was the establishment of the highest good by God himself. On the other hand, it was to be realized by ethical action and was already present in human ethical accomplishment.

To hold that there was a close relation between ethics and the kingdom of God led to a further question: What is the nature of this relationship? The answer finally depended on how the kingdom was understood. Both Kant and Schleiermacher ignored the eschatological dimension of the kingdom and concentrated instead on the kingdom as present and developing in human ethical striving and accomplishment.[9] Kant purposely avoided reference to eschatological consummation; he emphasized the role of ethical activity in the development of "the highest good" in history. For Schleiermacher, the center of attention was not the ethical duty or the good disposition of those involved but the concrete "goods" that contribute to "the highest good."[10]

In his speculative explication of the kingdom, Rothe considered the relation of the kingdom to the eschaton. But he failed to show how the kingdom is at once the goal and accomplishment of human ethical activity and God's action. However their attempt might be evaluated, these three—Kant, Schleiermacher, and Rothe—forged a bond between the kingdom of God and ethics. This construction was determinative for the thought of Ritschl.

Ritschl presented his central perspective in the form of a thesis: Christianity can only be properly described with reference to two focal points. The first point is the redemption wrought by Jesus Christ, which brings freedom from guilt and spiritual freedom of the individual "over the world." The second point is the kingdom of God, which arises out of redemption, for it is the moral organization of people in community through love. For Ritschl, this described the reciprocal relation between the religious and the ethical character of the Christian life.[11]

In accord with Reformation theology, Ritschl was interested in upholding the distinction between (religious) faith toward God and (ethical) works of love toward the neighbor. Accordingly, justification restored the relationship of the sinner to God and was at the same time an essential condition for moral activity toward people.[12] The aim of Ritschl was to clarify the relation between redemption as means to the divinely determined end of the kingdom. That is, the (ethical) kingdom of God was the "goal and content of religion and of the redemption accomplished through Jesus."[13]

Kingdom in the Thought of Ritschl

For Ritschl, the intimate relation between the kingdom and ethics was epitomized in his view of the kingdom of God as the highest good. He attempted to express this through a distinction between redemption and the Christian ethical task. Redemption was the removal of the guilt that separated the sinner from God and prepared the ground for participation in the kingdom of God.[14] The emphasis was upon redemption as an inner spiritual experience without reference to freedom from social evils or economic deprivation. Redemption, as the religious dimension, itself entailed no corresponding human action.

The kingdom of God, however, represented not only the highest good of God for humanity (the religious dimension), but also the human ethical task. Redemption was therefore distinct from response in ethical action but set the stage for such response. The realization of this highest good was the goal toward which people were to strive. Through their righteous conduct, members of the Christian community "share in effecting the kingdom of God."[15] The kingdom as the highest good was the goal set by God. The redemption wrought by Jesus and effective through the church served this goal. This gave to Christianity its teleological and ethical character. Therefore, the highest good was no longer simply identified with God and his gracious action but became "the positive ethical task of man as well."[16]

Although Ritschl depended on his predecessors in his conception of the kingdom of God, he also differed from them in his extensive efforts to base his views on Scripture. Not only did he make the kingdom central in his systematic thought, but he also did so with the claim that this was demanded by the significance that the kingdom had in Jesus' teaching.[17] Weiss, as noted above, took up the investigation of this claim in *Die Predigt Jesu vom Reiche Gottes*.[18] He was pleased to accept from Ritschl the insight into the central importance of the kingdom; but he early reached the disturbing conclusion that Ritschl's conception of the kingdom and of the kingdom in Jesus' proclamation "were two very different things."[19] Weiss's concern was that in the interpretation of a theme like the kingdom of God, the original historical meaning might have been supplanted by an alien point of view.[20]

The work of Weiss, always with a critical eye on Ritschl's position, brought to center stage the thoroughly eschatological character of Jesus' proclamation of the kingdom of God. According to Weiss, the kingdom comes into being wholly at the initiative and by the action of God: "The actualization of the kingdom of God is *not* a matter for human initiative, but entirely a matter of God's initiative. The kingdom of God in Jesus' view, is never an ethical ideal, but is *nothing other than the highest religious Good*, a Good which God grants on certain conditions."[21]

Jesus' transcendental conception of the kingdom of God stood in complete contrast to any notion of human "actualization" of this kingdom.[22] This corresponded to the fact that in Jesus' proclamation the kingdom is imminent but wholly future. What its coming would mean, Jesus did not need to explain at length. The people understood that God's coming kingdom was the antithesis of all present conditions of sorrow, or of oppression from enemies.[23]

Because of the work of Weiss, the context for interpretation of the kingdom became a crucial issue. The expectation of God's coming kingdom has a variety of different forms or emphases in the Old Testament prophets and Jewish apocalyptists. Weiss took Jewish apocalyptic to be the context for Jesus' kingdom-of-God proclamation, particularly the dualistic conception of the coming of the kingdom expressed in terms of the opposition between the power of Satan and the power of God. This dualistic view, in which the world was sharply divided between the realms of good and evil, divine and Satanic powers, was the basis, in Weiss's opinion, for Jesus' proclamation of the imminent coming of the kingdom of God.[24]

The Kingdom and the Ethical Response

Central to the debate on the relation between the kingdom of God and proper ethical action has been the question of whether the kingdom is present or future. Many held, with Ritschl, that it was to be realized in the present and still remained a goal for the future; this raised the question of whether or how the kingdom could be both present and future. How one understood the role of Jesus was crucial at this point.

For Ritschl, Jesus had a central place in the coming of the kingdom. He surpassed all his prophetic predecessors by revealing himself as the Son of God and the messianic king. Therefore, he did not first prepare the way but established the kingdom of God.[25] This meant that Jesus exercised his messianic role "through his morally effective teaching and by his readiness to engage in the action of a servant—not by the compulsion of legal judgment."[26] Jesus was the exemplar and founder of the kingdom of God. It was his special vocation to establish the kingdom of God. He did this by faithful preaching of the truth and by loving action in the face of opposition from the leaders of Israel. Jesus was the first to actualize in his own life "the final purpose of the kingdom of God." At the same time, the establishment of the kingdom required Jesus to call the disciples. In this way the kingdom found its proper correlative in ethical action through a distinct community.[27]

Ritschl had closely identified the kingdom and ethics. Accordingly, the kingdom was a reality only insofar as there were people who lived as obedient subjects, directing their wills toward the highest good, the kingdom of God. Ritschl emphasized love as the comprehensive ethical content of the kingdom. Hence, the righteousness of the kingdom was action motivated by the universal law of love (of God and the neighbor). This action of love was carried out in the "naturally conditioned communities" (i.e., marriage, the family, civic and social life, the state).[28] These "vocations in society" were to be taken up in order to "serve the common good." But the ethics of these vocations were determined by "the principles that govern each."[29]

Thus, according to Ritschl, the ethical response in a person's social setting was determined by the law inherent in that situation. Although Jesus was important for the kingdom, the requirements of response could be both known and fulfilled independent of any relation to him. To be sure, faith conditions the response in a general way by providing a direction to act unselfishly in the fulfillment of one's vocation. That was the meaning of Jesus' own example in the fulfillment of his vocation.[30] The ethical activity in one's vocation was to be motivated by and directed to the goal of realizing the kingdom of God, the highest good.[31] Only action directed toward that end could be properly described as Christian action.

There remains a question on which Ritschl offered no light: What action serves the ultimate end of the kingdom? This is a blind spot based on the assumption that appropriate ethical response can be identified simply with vocational conformity. It rests on an assumption of society as already "Christian" and overlooks the fact that structures of society are affected by "godless" or evil powers. For Ritschl, ethical action was determined by this goal (of the kingdom as highest good) and therefore not to be determined by any form of concrete ethical teaching (e.g., the commands of Jesus).

Since love was the correlative of the kingdom and the standard for moral judgment, in the concrete this meant the duty of love is the regular duty of one's vocation.[32] Yet Ritschl also insisted that love for the neighbor transcended the limits of these natural communities. In this connection, he identified love with regard for another as a person of infinite worth; it is love that binds the human race together.[33] Further, the kingdom present in the world through love-motivated action is at the same time above the world, beyond the natural divisions of humanity.[34] It is not surprising, then, that Ritschl defined both love and the kingdom as invisible, though effective in actions and relationships. The kingdom was an "invisible entity within the Christian community and as such is the object of faith."[35]

In contrast to Ritschl, and in accord with his own emphasis on the kingdom as wholly future, Weiss insisted that Jesus' mission was only preparatory to the coming of the kingdom. On this account Jesus, in announcing the kingdom of God, did not differ in principle from John the Baptist. Yet Weiss also noted that in his exercise of power over evil spirits, Jesus distinguished himself from John. But Weiss made little of this distinction. The ministry of both Jesus and John was preparatory and exactly the same. Therefore, Jesus' ministry as a whole did not bear messianic significance but had only a preparatory significance.[36]

Still, there were points at which a deeper meaning with respect to Jesus' mission and the coming kingdom seemed to break through for Weiss. Jesus understood himself to have a decisive role as "bearer of the Spirit of God against the kingdom of Satan."[37] Inasmuch as Jesus was moving victoriously against the strongholds of evil (Matt. 12:25-28), those opposing Jesus ought to have understood "that the kingly rule of God was already begun."[38] Thus, according to Weiss, Jesus had received the commission from God to represent the kingdom.

Weiss, however, took the words of Jesus at the Last Supper to signify Jesus' painful realization that the kingdom had still not been established. This was in accord with the basic premise of Weiss: the kingdom could only be the end-time eschatological event, established "solely by God's supernatural intervention."[39] But what if Jesus' words and acts themselves represent God's action or "intervention" (e.g., Mark 2:5-12; Matt. 12:28//Luke 11:20)? The path to this understanding of the kingdom remained closed for Weiss. Accordingly, Jesus himself waited for and at the same time was aware that he would be the "messiah" in the kingdom. Jesus' mission was that of a teacher or prophet who expected that he would *become* the Son of man.[40]

Weiss granted that there were some sayings of Jesus indicating that the kingdom was already present: "Though Jesus generally pictured the kingdom of God as still future, there are, on the other hand, statements in which the rule of God already appears actualized."[41] Again, on the basis of his casting out the demons (cf. Matt. 12:25-27), Jesus expected people to draw the conclusion that the kingly rule of God was already begun.

Yet the range of texts posed a question. Weiss responded with a sharp alternative: "Either the kingdom is here, or it is not yet here." He criticized the idea that the kingdom was to be realized in a particular community of people or in their obedience.[42] The strongest argument against this, Weiss believed, was in the words of the prayer: "Your kingdom come."[43] He argued that since the disciples were called to pray that the kingdom should come, it was for them in no sense present. They were rather called to "seek God's kingdom" (Luke 12:31).

Weiss rejected the idea that there could be different stages in the coming of the kingdom. When Jesus spoke of the presence of the kingdom, this was not to be understood in the normal sense.[44] Jesus could speak of the presence of the kingdom in connection with his miracles of casting out demons and healing, in which the power of Satan was already being broken. But, according to Weiss, for Jesus these were "moments of sublime prophetic enthusiasm."[45]

Against these sayings, Weiss referred to "the great profusion of sayings in which the establishment of the kingdom remains reserved for the future."[46] Weiss had his solution to the difference between the two sets of sayings: (1) the kingdom of Satan is already broken, the rule of God is already gaining ground; but (2) it is not yet historical event.[47] The Beatitudes depict the contrast between the present condition of the hearers and the transformed condition of the future life in the kingdom.[48] He concluded that the kingdom of God could only be a future eschatological reality.

This understanding of the kingdom on the part of Weiss then set its stamp on his view of appropriate ethical response. The imminence of the kingdom was "the motive for the new morality."[49] In the terms of Weiss, Jesus' expectations of his hearers were dramatic, demanding a decisive either-or response. The goods, relationships, and activities of this world had lost all value; indeed, now they could only be a hindrance. The old world was on the brink of destruction: "God himself must come and make everything new."[50] Therefore, appropriate response now meant waiting, as well as certain ascetic acts of preparation. To seek the kingdom was to prepare oneself by acquiring the righteousness that God commends. People were to free themselves from this world, its goods and bonds, in order to be worthy of the kingdom. These acts functioned as entrance requirements to the kingdom of God.[51]

Weiss perceived another strand in Jesus' ethical teaching. In the quieter periods of his ministry, when he was not thinking of the end of the world, Jesus spoke words of abiding ethical value. This was his teaching on the sanctity of marriage, on truth-telling, on love of God and neighbor.[52] On one hand Weiss was aware that there were sayings of Jesus on the presence of the kingdom. And on the other hand he was aware of ethical actions described in Jesus' teaching that were not simply deeds of preparation for the imminent end of the world. But he did not explore the relation between these two sets of sayings. Instead, he took such long-term ethics to be exceptions that had no place in the basic understanding of Jesus' teaching and mission.

The Kingdom and Jesus' Destiny

There was, for Ritschl, a clear connection between the death of Jesus and the kingdom of God. Jesus exercised his dominion "in his very readiness to suffer everything even unto death for the sake of his vocation."[53] The kingdom of God presupposed redemption. Redemption itself had a religious or spiritual significance. It referred to forgiveness of sins that separate the person from God. Forgiveness made it possible for sinners to participate in God's final purpose, the kingdom of God.

The obedience of Christ to his vocation could be interpreted as a "priestly offering."[54] According to Ritschl, the resurrection in the power of God was the consistent fulfillment "of the revelation effected through him" of the final will of God for humanity.[55] In the fulfillment of his vocation through love, Christ revealed at once the will of God and the meaning of the kingdom of God.⁵⁶ What this means for ethics is not developed, a point to which we must briefly return. The kingdom began with and was founded concretely upon the life of Jesus Christ. Humankind, in the form of the community founded by him, now has the responsibility of realizing the kingdom of God.

Weiss, however, had a quite different approach to the death of Jesus. Yet it is not clear how Weiss thought of Jesus' death in relation to the kingdom of God. According to Weiss, it was clear that what had been eagerly awaited did not happen. At a certain point Jesus became convinced that the end had been postponed. It became apparent to Jesus that the kingdom *could* not yet come because the people had not yet shown evidence of true repentance in ethical conduct.⁵⁷ The Jewish leaders aligned themselves in direct opposition to Jesus. Jesus' call for response was mostly lost through the indifference on the part of the people. Hence, Jesus reached the conclusion that "the establishment of the kingdom could not yet take place."⁵⁸

First, the guilt of the people had to be removed. Jesus did not expect to live to see this happen; instead, he had first to fall victim to death at the hands of his opponents. Jesus did not and could not understand this to mean failure; it must serve as a means in bringing about the final goal. Jesus seized upon the audacious idea "that his death itself should be the ransom for the people otherwise destined to destruction (Mark 10:45)."⁵⁹ Once the kingdom was established, Jesus expected to return on the clouds in glory, an event he anticipated within the lifetime of the generation that had rejected him.⁶⁰

Thus we see that Ritschl and Weiss had very different views of the kingdom of God. These differences shaped their understanding of the response that Jesus sought to his proclamation. The understanding of proclamation or response sheds light in reciprocal fashion on both these scholars. The differences between Ritschl and Weiss go to the heart of the understanding of the kingdom of God and of appropriate response to it. What interested Ritschl was the presence of the kingdom, its development en route to the goal, and the present possession of eternal life in the kingdom.⁶¹ He acknowledged that this was not to be equated with the eschatological teaching of Jesus or his apostles.

They expected divine judgment and the kingdom of God coming to and for this world, including the events of resurrection of believers and the return of Christ. In Ritschl's view, this form of eschatology is no longer credible in the church.[62]

The effects of this shift in perspective are evident. The limited form in which Ritschl recognized the eschatological future had no decisive significance for present life and action. According to his basic ethical-developmental conception, the love of God manifested itself in the present and in the continuing realization of the kingdom of God. That is, the kingdom of God was identified as the goal to be realized in the present through human ethical activity. This relationship of the kingdom of God with ethics involved a conception of the kingdom of God as both the religious and the ethical highest good.

Insofar as Weiss established the eschatological character of the kingdom of God, it became impossible to hold that this kingdom could be an ethical good, the result of ethical striving. Ascetic acts of preparation in the face of the imminent coming of the kingdom were all that remained for response. Only God could bring about his kingdom. Therefore, the kingdom of God as the eschatological future reality was by definition not to be realized through human ethical action.

From Weiss to Wilder

In the twentieth century, biblical and other scholars came increasingly to regard eschatology as an alien encumbrance. Even for Weiss, as he discovered anew the landscape of eschatology, it represented a crisis to be overcome. Following his historical reconstruction of Jesus' eschatology, he himself returned again to the liberal understanding of Jesus.[63] In the alienation from eschatology and in the concurrent effort to reinterpret the gospel, various options presented themselves.

Harnack and Ethics Without Eschatology

Adolf von Harnack, a notable representative of liberal thought, attempted to take account of the Weissian critique. But he owed much to Ritschl in his method as well as in his ethical conception of Christianity, his explication of the kingdom of

God, his emphasis on love as the meaning of ethical action.[64]

The Conception of the Kingdom. In Harnack's view the distinctive emphasis in Jesus' proclamation was the idea of "the inward coming of the kingdom of God." He knew there was no direct line from Jesus' teaching to this conclusion. According to Harnack, there were two distinct but related focal points in this teaching: (1) the kingdom was apparently a purely future event, the rule of God actualized in an external fashion; and (2) it was an inward reality, already present and coming into effect.[65] The ambiguity arose because Jesus made his proclamation in continuity with the religious traditions of his people and at the same time fundamentally changed the conception of the kingdom.

According to Harnack, Jesus discarded expectations of a worldly and political nature in his proclamation.[66] He agreed with Weiss in thinking that Jesus "was profoundly conscious of the great antithesis between the kingdom of God and that kingdom of the world in which he saw the reign of evil and the evil one."[67] Jesus saw himself engaged in a dramatic struggle between the two opposing powers that would culminate in his being raised to the right hand of God. Yet this conception of the kingdom, held in common with his contemporaries, was not the basic content of Jesus' message.

The truly unique and authoritative character of Jesus' proclamation, Harnack affirmed, was the idea that the kingdom had already come and was present as the rule of God in the human heart or soul. "The kingdom of God comes by coming to the individual, by entering into his soul and laying hold of it. True, the kingdom of God is the rule of God; but it is the rule of the holy God in the hearts of individuals; it is God himself in his power." He thus emphasized the actual presence and inward coming of the kingdom. What mattered was "God and the soul, the soul and its God." From this standpoint the future reference in Jesus' proclamation and "everything that is dramatic in the external and historical sense has vanished."[68]

The Ethical Response. Harnack forged a view of the kingdom that shaped his understanding of the appropriate ethical response. On the one hand, all the affairs and goods of the world were to be evaluated in terms of the primary value of the human soul. According to Harnack, this meant the world was not simply rejected; instead, life in the world was affirmed and all was to be related to God. The concept of being children of God (*Gotteskindschaft*), first emphasized by Weiss, was the key for understanding both the religious gift and the ethical task. Out of the certainty of being a child of the Father, a person was to do God's will.

What does this mean for concrete ethical action? The gospel called the person to love for the neighbor but beyond that offered no direct help to order life in community.[69] Still, Harnack insisted that the values and principles of Jesus' teaching "must remain the basis and guideline of our development."[70] Harnack understood that Jesus' preaching called for a definite response: "The distinction of good and evil—for or against God—he would make a life question for every man." Yet the response was related not to the eschatological kingdom of God but to the "glad message of mercy and the fatherhood of God."[71] In the end Harnack defined an ethics without eschatology.

Albert Schweitzer and Consistent Eschatology

Albert Schweitzer himself recognized that in the renewed understanding of eschatology, the work of Weiss represented the decisive breakthrough.[72] In certain respects the position of Weiss could stand for that of Schweitzer. Both discovered the eschatology of Jesus and on this basis provided a critique of contemporary liberal theology. But Schweitzer went beyond Weiss by offering a "consistent" or, as Schweitzer's English translator put it, "thoroughgoing" eschatological interpretation of the life of Jesus. Schweitzer criticized Weiss for failing to apply his findings consistently across the whole of Jesus' teaching and actions.[73] As Harnack took account of Weiss, he sought to emphasize the relevance of Jesus and his teaching for modern life. Schweitzer, however, moved in the other direction to emphasize Jesus as a stranger to modern life and thought. What highlighted the strangeness of Jesus was his eschatological outlook.

The Conception of the Kingdom. Schweitzer's view was that Jesus' life was completely determined by his apocalyptic-eschatological vision. Jesus' life was a "dogmatic history," a history determined by theological beliefs. It was determined not by the natural course of events but by the imminent eschatological coming of the kingdom of God.[74] He believed that Jesus combined eschatology with a doctrine of predestination and that this was the frame for understanding Jesus' reaction to people and the determination by him of his own destiny.[75] It was also the ground of Jesus' assurance that the kingdom must come within a period of months.

With the coming harvest would come also the kingdom of God.[76] Jesus sent out the twelve to call people to repentance, expecting that this would bring on the final tribulation and signal the end (cf. Matt. 10:1-23). But the disciples returned from their mission, and the end did not come. Schweitzer hypothesized that this was a major turning point for Jesus. The movement of repentance had not been sufficient to bring the kingdom. This nonoccurrence drove Jesus to change his strategy. Jesus now came to understand his own death as taking on himself the suffering that had been foreseen as the final tribulation before the end. "His death must at last compel the coming of the kingdom."[77]

Jesus expected that beyond death he would be exalted as the Son of man. But according to Schweitzer, because Jesus' life ended in death, instead of fulfilling eschatological hopes, he destroyed the very possibility of their fulfillment.[78] Through the conclusion of his life, Jesus shattered the possibility of eschatology and, in so doing, Jesus grounded a new "spiritual" basis for living (that is his real "reign").

The Ethical Response. Because the kingdom of God was for Jesus a purely future entity, there could be "no ethic of the kingdom of God."[79] The kingdom of God would be the end of all natural relationships (e.g., Mark 12:25-26); temptation and sin would no longer exist. Rather, what Jesus provided, in Schweitzer's terms, was an "interim ethic" as instruction for the elect in true repentance. In agreement with Weiss, Schweitzer held that this "penitential discipline" was intended only for that brief urgent interval between Jesus' proclamation and the actual arrival of the kingdom.[80] Finally, what Schweitzer called for was a spiritualization through and beyond the actual words and deeds of

Jesus. Not Jesus as historically known, but the spirit proceeding from him carried his meaning and influence.[81]

Schweitzer did not examine the ethical teaching of Jesus in detail, but merely asserted that it was a heroic ethics for the interim between "now" and the coming of the kingdom. The kingdom as an end-of-the-world event calls for a penitential discipline as entrance requirements.

Has Schweitzer adequately characterized this teaching? Merely to assert a correspondence between eschatology and the ethics is not yet to show that such a correspondence really existed. Schweitzer sought a connection between Jesus' eschatologically determined words and Christian existence and action in our present. But if this meaning and influence of Jesus is, as Schweitzer apparently thought, absolutely independent of historical knowledge, what can be known about Jesus? How is it still possible to speak at all of the spirit of Jesus? There is no intelligible basis for ethical action having an eschatological quality, if the real future of the kingdom is, in the end, denied. Schweitzer, by abandoning the reality of the kingdom, could not really retrieve the ethics of Jesus. What he called "the spirit of Jesus" was perforce Schweitzer's own invention.

C. H. Dodd and Realized Eschatology

Although the work of Schweitzer confirmed Weiss's eschatological understanding of the kingdom of God, important issues remained to be resolved. For many there was a question about the lack of coherence between sayings of Jesus that seemed to refer to the presence of the kingdom and sayings that appeared to refer to the future of the kingdom. As a whole, however, the eschatological understanding of the kingdom of God could not be denied.

The Conception of the Kingdom. C. H. Dodd began by accepting the discovery of Weiss and Schweitzer, namely, the "eschatological" character of the kingdom. But he broke with them by proposing, on the basis of his own analysis of the sayings of Jesus, that for Jesus the kingdom was already present. In the Jewish usage prior to Jesus there already existed the notion of God as king in the present. Dodd referred to the rabbinic saying about taking upon oneself "the kingdom (*malkut*) of heaven." By this the Rabbis meant the careful observance of the Torah.[82]

The kingdom of God was also the great object of future hope, although the reference in Jewish sources was more often to "the life of the age to come."[83] According to Dodd, certain cases in the teaching of Jesus on the "kingdom of God" fit within this framework of contemporary Judaism.[84] Therefore, the kingdom could be "accepted" in the present with the expectation of blessings to be enjoyed in the world to come.

But the Gospels give sayings of Jesus that do not fit within this framework. Dodd pointed to the statement of Jesus, "The kingdom of God has come upon you" (Matt. 12:18//Luke 11:20). The kingdom of God was present in a new and distinctive sense.

> Something has happened, which has not happened before, and which means that the sovereign power of God has come into effective operation. It is not a matter of having God for your king in the sense that you obey his commandments: it is a matter of being confronted with the power of God at work in the world. In other words, the "eschatological" kingdom of God is proclaimed as a present fact, which men must recognize, whether by their actions they accept or reject it.[85]

Dodd understood the summary in Mark 1:14-15 in the same sense. "The time is fulfilled, and the kingdom of God has come near; repent, and believe in the good news." Dodd emphasized the two verbs in the above passages "is near" (*eggizein*) (Mark 1:15) and "has come" (*phthanein*) (Matt. 12:28//Luke 11:20). He concluded that Jesus did not intend to proclaim the kingdom "as something to come in the near future, but as a matter of present experience."[86] Dodd emphasized sayings which declare the kingdom to be present. He regarded these as "the most characteristic and distinctive of the gospel sayings on the subject. They have no parallel in Jewish teaching or prayers of the period."[87] This meant that "the *eschaton* has moved from the future to the present, from the sphere of expectation into that of realized experience."[88] Therefore, "realized eschatology" became for Dodd the fundamental point of departure for the interpretation of the kingdom of God.[89]

Nevertheless, Dodd recognized that Jesus' teaching also includes reference to the future of the kingdom. He attempted to understand references to the future and to the present in relationship. He observed that there was no precise equivalent form, "the kingdom will come," to balance the direct statement, "the kingdom has come."[90] In any case, the key move on Dodd's part was to interpret the future eschatological references as symbolic of the spiritual and the timeless. Thus

> these future tenses were only an accommodation of language. There was no coming of the Son of man in history "after" his coming in Galilee and Jerusalem, whether soon or late, for there is no before and after in the eternal order.[91]

Sayings on the future coming of the kingdom did not refer to a further "coming" of the kingdom in the world. Instead, this was the kingdom of the "new heaven and new earth" of apocalyptic thought, which for Dodd was the transcendent order beyond space and time.[92]

Thus from the two sorts of references to the kingdom of God, Dodd understood the kingdom on two planes. There is the sense in which it was present in and through Jesus historically; the eternal meaning that gave reality to history had appeared in history so far as history could contain it. There are also those future references which, according to Dodd, are symbolic and refer to an eternal order lying beyond all history. According to Dodd, even the events of the parousia and the revelation of the kingdom and judgment were included in Jesus' ministry. However, Dodd thought it was possible to interpret eschatology to mean that the present earthly expression "of the kingdom of God will yield to a purely transcendent order in which it will be absolute."[93]

In accord with his perspective, Dodd emphasized that the kingdom was a matter of individual experience.[94] The coming of the kingdom was the individual awareness that in Jesus it had indeed come.[95] Even the language of glory and power related to the coming kingdom of God now had to do with human discernment and experience.[96] In his later work, Dodd gave a larger scope to the kingdom. He said that "it would be wrong to suppose that [Jesus] so 'spiritualized' the idea of the kingdom of God as to make it relevant only to the inner life of the individual."[97] In an important sense, Jesus identified his mission as a mission to his own people.

Jesus, for example, welcomed the repentance of the unpopular tax collector and referred to him as a "son of Abraham." Similarly, when he defied criticism to heal a crippled woman on the Sabbath, she is called a "daughter of Abraham." Dodd observed that they were important to Jesus as individuals, but he also recognized that they were part of a people. The plight of these persons concerned this community to which they, and he, belonged. Their "salvation" also "concerned the well-being of the community as a whole."[98] He believed that for Jesus there was a correlation between the kingdom of God and this community "in and through which [the] kingdom is to be realized."[99] It was the aim of Jesus "to constitute a community worthy of the name of a people of God."[100]

The Ethical Response. The position of Dodd on eschatology was in contrast to that of Weiss and Schweitzer. Therefore, "realized eschatology" for Dodd meant the exclusion of "interim ethics." Repentance, instead of being an act of preparation for the kingdom, was provoked by God's gracious initiative in the kingdom.[101] Dodd, like Weiss, perceived two seemingly diverse types of ethical sayings: one type appeared to assume "the indefinite continuance of human life under historical conditions," while the other type appeared to expect the imminent end of these conditions.[102] With the emphasis on "realized eschatology," Dodd described the ethical teaching of Jesus as eschatological, providing moral precepts for life in the kingdom of God.[103] Since he defined the kingdom of God as the eternal nature of God revealed in time (in Jesus' ministry), the ethics were a reflection of the nature of God thus revealed. The standard for the moral life was the love of God exemplified in Jesus and his ethical teaching.

Therefore, with all the differences between Dodd and Schweitzer, there was also a basic similarity. Schweitzer "spiritualized" and reinterpreted the ethical teachings, and so affirmed within this world a new kind of spiritual and "eschatological" existence for people of all times. Dodd emphasized that with Jesus a qualitatively new age began in human history. Every person must decide one way or another for or against the new life in the kingdom.[104]

Bultmann and Existential Eschatology

The answer of Bultmann to the apocalyptic-eschatological interpretation was existential eschatology. Something of this attitude toward time and the kingdom of God had already been suggested by Schweitzer. Jesus' teaching was "spiritualized," having a reference to matters above time and history. "Dialectical" or "crisis" theology took the same tack and developed it in its own way.[105] In reaction to eschatology conceived in an ethical developmental sense (cf. Ritschl), eschatology now was understood in a timeless existential sense. The foremost representative in this century of transformed eschatology was Rudolf Bultmann.

The Conception of the Kingdom. In the wake of Weiss and Schweitzer, Bultmann emphasized that "the kingdom of God is no 'highest good' in the ethical sense. It is not a good toward which the will and action of men is directed, not an ideal which is in any sense realized through human conduct. . . . Being eschatological, it is wholly supernatural."[106] It is not something to be "built" or realized in human history. We can only say it draws near, that it comes, that it is constituted by the power of God alone.

More specifically, what events were signified when the kingdom of God was proclaimed? For Bultmann there "can be no doubt that Jesus like his contemporaries expected a tremendous eschatological drama."[107] This included the events of the coming of the Son of man, the raising of the dead, the judgment. Jesus identified eschatology with these events. Yet he also refused all apocalyptic speculation; he did not engage in the calculation of times or in watching for signs (cf. Luke 17:20-21, 23-24).[108] Bultmann concluded that for Jesus the kingdom of God "does not in any sense depend on these events."

For Jesus, the kingdom set before a person the ultimate either-or and compelled one to make a decision.[109] The kingdom was imminent and already dawning, but not yet here. On one hand, in agreement with Weiss and Schweitzer, he insisted that the kingdom is wholly future.[110] On the other hand, the kingdom of God "is not something which was to come in the course of time." Jesus expected the kingdom to come as an imminent future event, but there is another "true" meaning for these words. That is, the kingdom of God is always future, and always determines the present. The kingdom as imminent is what determines the present because now, in the present, it compels the human person to decision.[111]

The Ethical Response. The imminence of the eschatological kingdom of God makes the present the last hour. This situates the human person before the impending kingdom of God and creates the crisis of decision. According to Bultmann, the coming of the kingdom of God has nothing to do with the course of time; instead, it has to do with the call for decision from the hearer. In this way the kingdom of God is conditioning the present and giving it eschatological character. Just this Bultmann took to be the final significance of Jesus' eschatological proclamation.[112]

In Bultmann's view, the ethical teaching of Jesus was closely bound up with his eschatological preaching. Bultmann emphasized that God's kingdom was not to be understood as his reign in the individual human soul or in human society. Rather, the kingdom confronts each individual with the necessity of choosing God or "the world." Jesus did not present an ethic designed to effect change in this world. Indeed, as an eschatological ethic, it had no vision for a future to be formed within this world by human plans and actions.[113] At the same time, fulfillment of the will of God was the condition for participation in the salvation of his kingdom. This condition was not an external set task but true readiness and earnest desire for the will of God. Accordingly, Jesus was not correctly represented as teaching an "interim ethics." This teaching was not a set of exceptional instructions but had an absolute validity independent of the temporal situation. The motive for ethical action was the will of God and not eschatological expectations.[114]

The decision set before the person, Bultmann equated with

repentance.[115] Most often he identified response simply by reference to "decision." In every situation of life, Jesus demanded a decision between God (and his will) and that which was not of God (and therefore evil). The decision thus was between the only two possibilities for a person, good and evil.[116] The willing obedience of the whole person that arose out of the present situation was "radical obedience." This was not an obedience attached to the law; Jesus completely separated obedience from the law. God demanded that each one give the whole person and "not merely specific acts."[117]

For Bultmann, Jesus' radical demand for love was the explication of the will of God. The love of neighbor was the ethical expression of the decision for God. Both aspects, the eschatological proclamation and the ethical demand, placed the person before God and both directed each one to the present as the hour of decision for God.[118] What a person was to do in order to love the neighbor was not specified.

> It is assumed that everyone can know that, and therefore Jesus' demand for love is no revelation of a new principle of ethics nor of a new conception of the dignity of man. . . . Love is simply the requirement of obedience and shows how the obedience can and ought to be practised in the concrete situation in which man is bound to man.[119]

In this situation of encounter with the neighbor, "no standard whatsoever from the past or from the universal is available. That is the meaning of decision."[120] In the concrete situation, the person in "the crisis of decision" knows what is *now* good and evil.[121] For Bultmann, the apparent consideration or fear was that any standards for action or reflection on response would result in a formulation of "general ideas about the highest good, about virtues and values," or else some form of legalism.[122]

Bultmann was unwilling to be as "consistent" as Schweitzer in holding that Jesus' ethical teaching was wholly provisional in view of the impending kingdom. He did not maintain with Schweitzer that Jesus' ethic had a lasting significance despite its original "interim" character and the failure of the parousia.[123] Instead, his view was that Jesus himself considered his ethical teaching to be absolutely and essentially valid apart from any relation to events in time or history. In other words, Jesus himself actually lived in terms of the existential futurity of God's coming kingdom, which determined the present existential moment and made it the last hour (and so eschatological).[124]

Wilder and the Ethics of Realized Eschatology

The Conception of the Kingdom. In Wilder's view, Jesus' proclamation of the kingdom of God involved both present and future. Accordingly, it was the mission of Jesus to represent the redemption God was enacting in his generation.[125] Wilder distinguished between prophetic expectation and apocalyptic eschatology. On one hand, Jesus saw his mission in terms of apocalyptic eschatology associated with the Son of man. Wilder held that Jesus' ministry marked the beginning of the eschatological process that was to culminate in the kingdom or the life of the age to come. This was Jesus' "dualistic" view of the future, the apocalyptic view.

On the other hand, Jesus also had a "non-dualistic" or prophetic-messianic understanding of the future. Here Wilder referred to the character of Jesus' ethical teaching, the promise to the disciples of sharing rule with him over the tribes of Israel, and the saying that he would rebuild the temple after three days.[126] In this way Jesus pointed to the coming new social-historical order or new Israel.[127] According to Wilder, Jesus did not make use of apocalyptic images to develop a timetable for the future. Jesus' made use of this language to indicate the power of God.[128]

The basic point for Wilder was that Jesus saw a social-historical process beginning with his ministry and moving toward a climax. Jesus called on people to recognize it and to make the appropriate response. This mission was first concretely directed to Israel. Therefore, "Jesus' typical eschatology," with its accent on the advent of the kingdom, could be "considered as symbolic of the historical crisis of his time and its outcome."[129]

The Ethical Response. It was axiomatic for Wilder that Jesus' ethical teaching was rooted in a new relation to God in the present time of salvation. In accord with Weiss, eschatology functioned, first, as a sanction of ethics. "Jesus made the coming eschatological event . . . the motive and sanction" for his ethical summons, a summons that was contained in the call to repentance.[130] The ethics in this case took the form of entrance requirements to that kingdom.[131]

Second, and more in accord with Dodd, since Jesus' proclamation of the kingdom signified the "historical crisis of his time," ethics was qualified by the gift of forgiveness and reconciliation of the new age. Jesus' ethical teaching was grounded in a new human relation to God in the present time of salvation.[132]

Third, Wilder distinguished a class of heroic demands in Jesus' ethical teaching that had led people to think of Jesus' ethics as interim ethics. Wilder concluded that they had their dramatic urgency not because of the expectation of the imminent end, but because the coming of the kingdom through Jesus represented a crisis. It was a period of challenge and conflict for the kingdom amid the powers of evil that opposed it.[133] This was the ethic in the eschatological situation "construed in terms of discipleship to Jesus."[134] Since Jesus was himself the embodiment of the kingdom, people could not reject him without rejecting it; they could not accept the kingdom without accepting him. Therefore, righteousness issued in the summons to follow Jesus and to confess him.[135] "In particular, the most exigent requirements of Jesus have to do with the following of him in the period of struggle of the kingdom."[136]

Wilder made a basic distinction, related to eschatology, in Jesus' ethical teaching: he differentiated between the "formal" and the "fundamental" grounds for this teaching.[137] Eschatology, and the imaginative language in which it was expressed, could have only a "formal" significance. The fundamental ground of Jesus' teaching was his experience and conception of the nature of God. This meant that "the ethics are conceived as responses to the nature of God."[138] Although the imminent coming of the kingdom was the dominant sanction for righteousness, it was, nevertheless, only a formal sanction.[139] Language about "eschatological culmination" so partook of myth (the language of "representation") that it only formally determined ethics.[140]

For Wilder, "the eschatological kingdom" referred to the God-determined future, a future that lent urgency to present moral responsibility. Yet these sanctions were subordinate and supplementary to the fundamental sanctions.[141] Indeed, this future eschatology was significant only as it was transposed into something else. According to Wilder, the "temporal imminence" of God in Jesus' eschatological proclamation "is but a function of his spiritual imminence." It is "the latter which really determines conduct."[142] In Wilder's terms, Jesus' ethical teachings set forth the appropriate response of those already participating in the kingdom of God. In short, the fundamental occasion for response is the experience of the nature of God (revealed by Jesus), not the coming kingdom of God proclaimed by Jesus.

Evaluation

Before moving on to discuss elements relevant to a new state of the question on Jesus' proclamation and the proper ethical response to it, I offer a succinct evaluation of the history we have just outlined.

It is to Ritschl's credit that he recognized the kingdom as central to Jesus' teaching and central to his ethics. But Weiss rightly showed the ahistorical character of Ritschl's conception of "kingdom." The kingdom was "not a matter for human initiative, but entirely a matter of God's initiative." The kingdom of God as Jesus proclaimed it was not some "spiritual" or ethical ideal; it was the gift of God.[143]

But Weiss's own definition of the kingdom as the end of all things vitiated the relationship of the kingdom to present Christian life and ethical action. To Weiss, Jesus' ethic was basically an emergency ethic, grounded in the urgency of the present moment. It functioned as an entrance requirement to the kingdom of God. Nevertheless, Weiss himself recognized that according to Jesus' teaching, the kingdom and the appropriate response to it bore precisely on the present.

The issue, crucial in the work of Harnack, found a resolution in the "spiritual" character of Jesus' proclamation. Harnack identified the kingdom as an inward experience. What was "external and historical" vanished from view. By this move Harnack tried to accommodate Weiss. The accommodation, however, was superficial. Harnack did not really retain eschatology; his "essence of Christianity" remained typically liberal.

Schweitzer, on the contrary, confirmed the fundamental eschatological character of the kingdom in Jesus' proclamation. But, we ask, was the coming kingdom in Jesus' proclamation simply to be identified with a future cataclysmic event? And how did Jesus understand his death in relation to the coming of the kingdom? Schweitzer did not provide satisfactory answers.

Dodd rightly directed attention to those sayings that seemed to refer to the presence of the kingdom and used them as the key to the interpretation of Jesus' kingdom-of-God proclamation. But Dodd retreated into a more sober variation on liberal theology. "Eternity" took the place of "parousia." The difficulty that has always dogged Dodd's "realized eschatology" is that it effectively denied the eschatological future by appeal to Platonic categories (time and eternity) to interpret the kingdom of God. Though Dodd retained the language of the "kingdom of God," what mattered was the "nature of God." Ethics then was a reflection of the nature of God as revealed in Jesus.

Bultmann attempted to deal with most of the same issues, offering his own alternative interpretation. On the side of history, Bultmann reduced Jesus' mission to expectation of the impending kingdom of God, denying Jesus' teaching on his death. The redemptive significance of that death, he believed, was a later interpretation developed by the church.[144] Jesus' ethic, "eschatological" in a figurative sense, hinged on transposition of eschatology into existential terms. Bultmann's interpretation undermined the possibility of any real eschatological future. We need to raise some questions: Since Bultmann eliminated the actual future in Jesus' teachings, what justification is there for an "eschatological" ethic? The Jesus of history issued ethical commands; what remains of this after the transposition of the message into existentialist categories? In place of a real ethics, there remains a principle: "radical obedience." But that obedience is without specific content.

Amos Wilder's view, reminiscent of Dodd's, added the notion

of "community" (as did Dodd's late work *The Founder of Christianity*). Moreover, the kingdom was the active power of God, closely identified with Jesus' mission and destiny. Hence, the disciples must be prepared to suffer for their witness. Wilder, more clearly than most, saw the connections in Jesus' ministry, as well as the connection between this ministry and his death. The new order would mean suffering and death. More specifically, as part of his sense of mission, "we cannot doubt that he related his death to the fulfillment of Israel's calling."[145] Accordingly, his death and his vindication were of evident importance in the coming of the new order and related to the full manifestation of the kingdom.[146] Nevertheless, Wilder in the end fastened on the eternal nature of God, not the eschatological kingdom of God. This nature of God informed ethical response. Thus Wilder abandoned the historical Jesus in favor of another line of Christian tradition.

Elements for a New State of the Question

The question of Jesus and ethics has been modified in recent years by various reconsiderations of Jesus and his proclamation.

Renewals. First, there are renewals of older critical conversations. Thus, Richard H. Hiers has attempted to rehabilitate the position of Schweitzer. In agreement with Schweitzer, he took the position that Jesus' eschatological proclamation had been refuted by the nonoccurrence of the parousia. This does not mean the negation of Jesus' ethical teaching, for the teaching could get along without the eschatology.[147]

Hiers pointed out that Schweitzer himself attempted to express the experience of the abiding authority of Jesus by reference to his will or to his person and spirit, as well as to his ethic of love and self-devotion to others. The "will" of Jesus was understood to be the authority of the person and words (in general) of Jesus.[148] The words were authoritative because of Jesus' insight into the nature or will of God. Out of this awareness he presented the claim of God upon people. Schweitzer, however, did not fill his concept of Jesus' will with particular content.[149]

For Hiers, though Jesus was mistaken about eschatology, his eschatology can still signify that for every person time is short and the opportunity for response is limited. It can signify the experience of judgment "in, and ultimately at the end of, our individual and collective histories."[150] Hiers has spoken meaningfully of love by reference to Jesus' teaching. The teaching of Jesus is significant for ethics in setting a direction, but it provides no ethics for life in community.

In response to Hiers, we maintain that the authoritative ethical teaching of Jesus has as its correlative the kingdom of God. Hiers recognized the need for purpose and hope to support what remained of Jesus' ethics. Having abandoned the eschatology of Jesus, Hiers saw the need for the equivalent of an "eschatology." Without this, the ethics may serve to condition ethical response, but they are shorn of their original character. He did not resolve basic issues left by the work of Schweitzer, such as the relation of present to future in eschatology or the assumption that the passing of time refuted the eschatology of Jesus.

Variations. Second, there are variations on older critical conversations. As Bultmann attempted to transpose eschatology into existentialist categories, so Norman Perrin attempted to arrive at much the same goal by analyzing "the kingdom of God" not as a concept but as a "symbol" designed to evoke a "myth." Bultmann dispensed with the mythological form of Jesus' proclamation (through demythologizing) but sought to retain the inner meaning of that proclamation. This meaning he took to be the understanding of human existence present in the proclamation.

Since for Perrin the kingdom of God is a symbol meant to evoke the myth of "the activity of God," time is not a factor in the coming-to-be of the kingdom. He therefore proposed that the mythology of Jesus' kingdom-of-God proclamation "has not been discredited by the subsequent course of history."[151] The activity of God is the event which every person "experiences in his own time."[152] The keynote of Jesus' ethical teaching is the response to this experience of God: in the case of forgiveness, to forgive; in the case of love, to love.[153]

We will deal with this understanding of the kingdom more fully at another point. Suffice it to say now that this understanding of the kingdom hardly corresponds to the meaning it has in

Jesus' proclamation. Perrin has not resolved the issues posed by the interpretation of Bultmann; he raised more sharply the issue of what meaning the kingdom had for Jesus himself. He recognized a definite correlation between the experience of the kingdom and the proper response.[154] It follows that if the kingdom is circumscribed as every person's inner experience, the understanding of the ethics must be limited accordingly.

Recovery. Finally, there was an effort to recover the social or ecclesial correlative to "kingdom of God" in Jesus' proclamation and teaching, a theme potentially significant for ethics as early as 1925. In 1925 Ernst Ludwig Dietrich published a technical philological study (on how to derive, analyze, and accurately construe the Hebrew expression *šub šebut*) which draws attention to a major prophetic theme expressing the hope of Israel.[155] This theme is the promise and the corresponding hope of Israel's "eschatological restoration" (*die endzeitliche Wiederherstellung*). New Testament scholarship, however, long failed to make the connection between the primitive Christian affirmation of fulfillment and this complex of biblical motifs.

Gradually, however, there appeared sporadic signs of recognition among scholars, especially British and Scandinavian ones,[156] of the content of Old Testament themes of deliverance (e.g., Isa. 52:7-10; 61:1-3). They saw how the New Testament explicitly related such themes to New Testament celebrations of fulfillment (e.g., Acts 10:36-38; Luke 2:30; 4:18-21). These themes and celebrations expressed hope precisely for the restoration of Israel. This raised the issue of whether the early Christians understood the fulfillment in question as the claim that, in them, Israel had found eschatological restoration.

In 1953, Joseph Schmitt of Strasbourg interpreted the first five chapters of Acts as providing evidence in exactly this sense.[157] Schmitt thus recovered a basic form, perhaps *the* basic form, of the earliest Christian ecclesial self-understanding.

G. B. Caird in 1965 made the restoration of Israel a fundamental theme in his effort to show the contours of Jesus' mission historically.[158] In 1979 B. F. Meyer, exploiting the correlation between biblical themes of hope and Synoptic themes of fulfillment, defined the goal of Jesus' career as precisely the eschatological restoration of Israel.[159] E. P. Sanders in 1985 added a full-dress treatment of the theme of "temple and restoration" and "other indications of restoration eschatology."[160]

Also in 1985, Gerhard Lohfink specifically proposed "the correlation between the kingdom of God and the people of God" in his effort to understand the coherence of the proclamation and activity of Jesus.[161] He considered the converging lines of evidence in Jesus' proclamation and activity pointing to this correlation between "kingdom" and "people." In the context of Jesus' mission to Israel, he asked about the universal scope of the kingdom of God: Does the correlation between the saving sovereignty of God and a concrete people prevent or hinder the universal goal of the kingdom? Or is the contrary argument to be made, that only as the kingdom of God becomes effective and visible in at least one place in the world does its universal claim come into the light of day?

This entire line of research has reintroduced the equivalent of "the church" into the Gospel history. But the church in question is simply the sum of those who responded positively to Jesus' appeal to Israel. The gain for "ethics" represented by this act of historical retrieval is that *the subject* supposed by Jesus' ethical teaching now comes into view. This subject—contrary to Weiss, Harnack, Schweitzer, Bultmann, Perrin, and countless others—is not the isolated individual person. *Jesus called for response from restored Israel, a community of disciples.*

My purpose is to lay the foundation for recovery both of Jesus' proclamation and teaching in relation to proper response. This calls for an examination of the resources for Jesus' proclamation and teaching in the next chapter. The proclamation and teaching of Jesus will then be considered in chapters 3 and 4. In this context I will proceed to define and characterize appropriate response to Jesus. For accomplishing this task, we will seek the main clues in the teaching by which Jesus followed up his proclamation, elucidated it, and commended it anew.

2

Resources for Jesus' Proclamation and Teaching

The kingdom-of-God theme is central to the whole story in the Gospels. It connects Jesus' public proclamation and mission to Israel (Mark 1:14-15) with the last evening of Jesus with his disciples in the narrative of his suffering (Mark 14:61, 62; 15:26, 32). What is the key to the meaning of this central theme?

One key, no doubt, is the context of proclamation common to the speaker and the hearers. This context was largely inherited from biblical tradition. Eventually, the words and acts of Jesus would give decisive definition to "the kingdom of God." However, Jesus began by assuming a basic understanding of the phrase on the part of his hearers. We recognize a major source of disagreements in the study of the historicity and meaning of Gospel data: prior disagreements over pre-Gospel data on "the kingdom of God" and messianism, and on the connection of these themes with the restoration of Israel and the destiny of the nations.

It is beyond our present possibilities to resolve all these prior disagreements. Nevertheless, we can survey the relevant biblical and postbiblical data on these topics in the hope that this survey will make clear what I take to be the probable common ground for Jesus and his Jewish contemporaries. I shall accordingly survey the meaning of the *malk-* theme (king, kingship, reign, kingdom) and related themes in biblical tradition and its use in noncanonical literature and synagogue practice. It is not my purpose to trace in detail the full history and development of these great themes, but simply to survey the data constituting an inheritance available to Jesus the proclaimer and to his hearers. This will allow us to discern the thematic legacy that Jesus seized upon and reshaped. Two questions give focus to the inquiry. First, what were the biblical resources for Jesus' proclamation of the kingdom of God? Second, how were eschatology and ethics related in Jewish tradition?

It may be well to emphasize once again that neither question calls for detailed historical investigation in the manner of contemporary critical scholarship on the Hebrew Bible. We wish merely to recover the character of the theme as providing resources for Jesus' proclamation. Since modern scholarship on the Hebrew Bible was unknown to the Jews of antiquity, its relevance to the following survey is secondary, at best. Thus, modern critical questions about the origin and dating of particular biblical texts have virtually no importance in the present context. My main interest is in how Palestinian Jews of the age of Tiberius heard the scriptural theme of God's kingship. What texts nourished the synagogue and shaped its hopes?

I will treat pre-Jesus data on the kingdom of God, the Messiah (*mashiakh*, Christ, the anointed one), the restoration of Israel, the destiny of the nations, and the nexus between eschatology and ethics. These will mainly follow a thematic rather than a chronological order. I am attempting to reconstruct the common convictions of a people who lived long prior to the rise of modern historical consciousness; they did not take the trouble to date the origins of their views. First, we shall deal with the kingdom of God, the Messiah, Israel, and the nations. Second, we shall take up the ways in which the Jews of antiquity correlated eschatology and ethics.

God's Kingship for Israel and the Nations
According to the Scriptures

Biblical texts frequently depict Yahweh as King of Israel and of all the earth. Whereas biblical scholarship has found here a whole tangle of historical issues on which consensus has proved to be elusive, it is sufficient for our purposes to review the biblical data. Contemporary debates on these issues will for the most part be relegated to the notes.

God's Kingship and Israel

Our first text is the Song of the Sea, describing God's victory and deliverance of Israel from the power of Egypt at the *Yam Sup* (Red/Reed Sea; Exod. 15:1-21).[1] The theme of the song is the exercise of God's "military" power for the salvation of Israel (cf. 15:3). The victory is complete and it is completely the work of God. His action brings Israel's redemption. He continues to lead and guide them by his faithful love (15:13). Therefore, the Song of the Sea culminates in the acclamation of God's kingship: "The Lord will reign for ever and ever" (15:18). His action is creative of Israel as a people and the ground for his reign over them. Therefore, Israel acknowledges him as king (15:18 forms an *inclusio* with 15:3).[2]

In accord with the theme of this song, God is involved in Israel's history as the one who *alone* gains the victory. This experience consequently issues in the recognition of God *alone* as king.[3]

The active rule of God therefore appears from the earliest moment in the story of Israel. God's kingship was the exercise of power.[4] In his action for Israel, Israel recognized the claim of God and acknowledged it in song. Was the Sinai covenant itself conceived within this framework? Did Israel recognize God as king in the act of making the covenant?[5]

The covenant established both a new relationship with God and new community of people. The sovereign action and call of God culminated in the formation of a people. This was more than a call to service of the true God; this formed them into the people of God. It united diverse ethnic groups under the leadership of Yahweh. This relationship bound them in certain specific ways both to God and to one another. The allegiance of Israel, in contrast to dominant patterns of ancient Near Eastern kingship, was a new loyalty to Yahweh. The covenant thus signified Israel's acceptance of the lordship of Yahweh. Here, if anywhere, was the rule of God over his people.[6] God was more than a protector of Israel; he accompanied and led his people as a king (e.g., Exod. 7:4; 13:17-22; 19:6; Num. 23:21; Deut. 1:30-33; 33:5).[7] If politics had to do with the formation and the direction of the community, God's saving action and his making of the covenant were in the fullest sense "theopolitical."

It is significant that Exodus 19:3-8 and 20:1-17 both begin with an acknowledgment of Yahweh's deliverance of Israel from Egypt (the historical prologue). In the covenant relationship, God alone was recognized as sovereign Lord, and the people of Israel were his "kingdom of priests" among all the nations (Exod. 19:6).[8]

In exodus and covenant alike, then, God was acclaimed as *the king of Israel*. All human alliances were therefore regarded as a form of apostasy from him (cf. Hos. 7:10-13). Israel could not make overtures to Egypt and Assyria and maintain fidelity to God. The covenant carried with it an alternative to conventional politics. Israel's special identity demanded a radical separation from the ways of the nations.[9] This also had definite implications for Israel's internal governance. If all Israelites were vassals and fellow members in the "kingdom of priests," then, strictly understood, one Israelite could not be set over another as king. That place was reserved for God alone.[10] The emphasis in the Exodus narratives is the concern of God not for the king but for his people.[11]

At a later period, when Gideon was invited to become king, he replied in terms of the covenant tradition, "I will not rule over you, and my son will not rule over you; the Lord will rule over you" (Judg. 8:23). Samuel expressed the same opposition to human kingship; the people, however, cried, "No! but we are determined to have a king over us, so that we also may be like other nations, and that our king may govern us and go out before us and fight our battles" (1 Sam. 8:19b-20). What was this but rejection of the kingship of Yahweh?[12]

In accord with the covenant, Israel affirmed God as king (cf. Num. 23:21; Deut. 33:5). The Song of the Sea celebrated Yahweh's reign over Israel. The material in the book of Exodus became the primary means of celebrating Yahweh's victory for Israel and his rule over the whole of Israel's life. Present in this work are the narratives that describe the Passover feast in Exodus 12-15 and God's making of covenant with Israel in Exodus 19-24. In the face of Israel's rejection of Yahweh in favor of the human institution of kingship, three distinct references are made to Yahweh's deliverance of Israel from Egypt

(1 Sam. 8:8; 10:18-19; 12:8-12). Through the experience of Yahweh's victory at the sea, Israel recognized his kingship; and in the covenant made at Sinai, Israel acknowledged Yahweh as king long before adopting human kingship.[13]

In the midst of other peoples, the people of Israel became painfully conscious of the differences that affected the character of their national life and political organization. These differences defined what was at stake in danger from enemy peoples (cf. Judg. 4:14; 1 Sam. 8:10-20; 10:17-19; 1 Kings 11:26–12:16).[14]

The meaning of God's kingship was clearly defined in the effort to resolve the question of national leadership (cf. 1 Sam. 8-12). The structure of the narrative dealing with leadership as a whole alternates between narratives of meeting and narratives of action (1 Sam. 8:4-22; 9:1—10:16; 10:17-27; 11:1-13; 11:14—12:25).[15] They describe the stages in the transition to human kingship. The absolute nature of the opposition to human kingship, on the basis of Israel's covenant traditions, is not left in doubt (1 Sam. 12:16-19). The result of the intercession of Samuel is an accommodation. Even the pro-kingship texts give evidence of this. Kingship is defined within the framework of theocracy: Israel is God's people and has no other Lord but him.[16] In the accommodation the king is to be designated by God through the prophet as "prince" and not as "king" (1 Sam. 9:16, RSV), and he is to function in holy war by instruction from the prophet (cf. 1 Sam. 13:8-14; Exod. 17).[17]

The lordship of Yahweh and the limits of human kingship are indicated in the classic statement contained in Nathan's oracle (2 Sam. 7:4-7). It guards against the king taking the dominant role, according to the pattern of the Canaanites (cf. Amos 7:12-13). The covenant with David, like that with Abraham, is an eternal covenant, but instituted within the framework of the Mosaic covenant (Deut. 17:18-20; 1 Kings 9:4-5; 2 Sam. 7:14). The promise to the Davidic dynasty is given from the viewpoint of the shrine for the ark of the Sinaitic covenant (2 Sam. 7); that shows the primacy of the Sinaitic covenant over the Davidic.[18]

Since the king functioned within the framework of the Torah, the challenge and judgment of David following his sin (taking

Bathsheba, the wife of Uriah) indicates that the primacy of the law was more than a formality.[19] In Israel the king also was to be subject to judgment under the covenant made between God and his people (1 Sam. 10:25; 12:14-15). This is to affirm God's lordship for the whole of Israel's existence.

God's Kingship and the World

The kingship of God was both acknowledged and celebrated in the worship of Israel. In recognizing God, Israel came to see that his kingship properly included the world. God's sovereign power, victorious over chaos at creation and demonstrated decisively in the victory at the sea, was celebrated in the feast of Passover. But the festival most closely associated with the celebration and proclamation of Yahweh's kingship was the Feast of Ingathering, or Tabernacles, in the autumn of the year (cf. Exod. 23:16; 3:22; Deut. 16:13-15).[20]

Certain of the psalms, perhaps belonging to the liturgy of the feast, expressly celebrate the kingship of Yahweh.[21] Psalm 29 dramatizes the kingship of God by reference to his activity in thunder and his mastery over the waters of the flood (29:3-4, 10). Although the psalm presents more general views of the divine, it also reflects Israel's own traditions.[22] This is suggested by the effect of the voice of God in the wilderness of Kadesh, a reminder of God's gift of covenant and God's gift of peace to "his people" (29:8, 11).

Psalm 65 may also celebrate the autumn festival. Though the kingship of God is not expressly stated, there is the anticipation of the early rains and the consequent fruitfulness of the earth (65:9-13). The psalm opens with the appeal for restoration and forgiveness in the affirmation of God as the one who has saved and will save Israel (65:5).[23] The appeal for renewal of God's favor and the affirmation of his salvation, followed by the enumeration of his mighty works, is fitting as part of the renewal of the covenant in the autumn festival.[24] The psalm then directly proclaims God's powerful deeds, effective through the whole cosmos, in which he upholds the order of creation against the threat of chaos.[25] As Creator, God has acted to fulfill his purpose and will continue to do so. The tradition of the covenant with its historical prelude (65:5) is associated with God's kingship expressed in his sovereign power over creation (65:6-8). And God is therefore the hope of all the inhabitants of the earth (65:5).[26]

It is also evident in these psalms that "kingdom of God" (*malkut*) refers first to the reign or rule of God, "and only secondarily to the realm over which the reign is exercised."[27] This point is underscored in Psalm 145:11-13:

> They shall speak of the glory of your kingdom,
>   and tell of your power,
>   to make known to all people your mighty deeds,
>   and the glorious splendor of your kingdom.
> Your kingdom is an everlasting kingdom,
>   and your dominion endures throughout all generations.

This dynamic understanding of the kingdom of God is closely related to God as the one who *comes* to his people to accomplish his purpose in the world.

> Say among the nations, "The Lord is king!
>   The world is firmly established; it shall never be moved.
>   He will judge the peoples with equity."
> Let the heavens be glad, and let the earth rejoice;
>   let the sea roar, and all that fills it;
>   let the field exult, and everything in it.
> Then shall all the trees of the forest sing for joy
>   before the Lord; for he is coming,
>   for he is coming to judge the earth.
> He will judge the world with righteousness,
>   and the peoples with his truth. (Psalm 96:10-13)

The occasion for rejoicing is not that God sits enthroned as king in the heavens and is exalted above the earth, but that he will come to judge the peoples and so establish his reign effectively among the people "who do not now acknowledge it."[28]

This note of creation anticipating the reign of God is sounded again in Psalm 98:8-9:

> Let the floods clap their hands;
>   let the hills together sing for joy

> at the presence of the Lord, for he is coming
> to judge the earth.
> He will judge the world with righteousness,
> and the peoples with equity.

To look for salvation is to anticipate the coming of God.[29] The Lord comes to act for the salvation of his people. The history of Israel, from its beginning in the exodus to the anticipation of final redemption in the kingdom of God, is set within God's coming.[30] He showed himself to be their king in this action toward his people in the wilderness and in covenant love calling them into being as his people (Deut. 33:2, 5; Hab. 3:3, 10-13).[31] This coming is often associated with cosmic reverberations, whether God comes in response to the need of one person or the future of humanity (cf. Ps. 18:3-19). If the Creator steps forth, the whole creation resonates to his coming. However it was understood in earlier times, for the psalmist this imagery portrays the mighty power of God who comes to his aid.[32] To anticipate the kingdom is thus to anticipate God coming and acting to effect his kingship.

Psalm 67 relates the kingship of God with the harvest feast and shows its worldwide scope:

> The earth has yielded its increase;
> God, our God, has blessed us.
> May God continue to bless us;
> let all the ends of the earth revere him. (67:6-7)

The God of Israel is the Creator of heaven and earth and bestows his blessings on all the nations. Therefore, the psalm has the refrain:

> Let the peoples praise you, O God;
> let all the peoples praise you. (67:3, 5)

For the peoples thus to acknowledge God would mean the universal recognition of his sovereignty:

> Let the nations be glad and sing for joy,
> for you judge the peoples with equity
> and guide the nations upon earth. (67:4)

At the Feast of Tabernacles, therefore, Israel celebrated God's kingship not only on the basis of the revelation of this kingship in the past and experienced in the present, but also as this was destined to be revealed to and for the world on a day to come.[33]

This coming day appears to be the subject of the preaching of the prophet Amos at Bethel, perhaps during the period of the autumn celebration. As in the psalms, this day will mean God coming for judgment. Amos assured them that the day they eagerly anticipate would be a day of darkness and not of light, a day in which God would judge unrighteousness wherever it is to be found, and this would include first and foremost his people Israel (Amos 3:2; 5:18-20).[34]

Once more the prophet associates the Lord's sovereign power over all creation with the coming of God in judgment on those who are complacent in their violation of the covenant (Amos 5:6-9). The prophet also breaks through the false reliance of Israel on God's election of Israel (3:1-5). Furthermore, the fact that God judges the other peoples shows that he includes them in his concern (1:2—2:3). God's activity in the history of other peoples is expressly affirmed (9:7). The God who called Israel is the Creator of the world; his righteous purpose is as wide as the world.

The Messiah and the Restoration of Israel

What was the connection between "kingdom" and "Messiah" in Jewish expectation? It is clear that in seeking the connections that bind together the whole Gospel history, the question of the meaning of the kingdom of God entails the question about the identity of Jesus. It is evident that Jesus' mission was neither irrelevant nor incidental to his proclamation. What role was the Messiah to have in the coming kingdom of God?

So far as pre-Jesus tradition is concerned, in certain texts the Messiah figures prominently in the hope of the kingdom of God, whereas in other texts he finds no mention at all. If the messianic prophecies were only one line of thought among others on the future expectation of Israel, we might conclude that the Messiah was of secondary importance. It is true that the royal psalms celebrate the reign of God alone: "The Lord is king! Let the earth rejoice" (Ps. 97:1; cf. 99:1). The most basic conviction is simply that salvation would come from God:

> For the Lord is our judge, the Lord is our ruler,
> the Lord is our king; he will save us. (Isa. 33:22)

But one must not overlook the inner connection between the various lines of thought in the Scriptures. This connection should become evident in the strands of tradition now to be considered.

The Messiah. We begin by offering a précis of the main passages, beginning with the oracle of Nathan to David. The designation "Messiah" is most commonly applied to the king of Israel. The "messianic hope" is most closely related to kingship in Israel, especially the royal line of David. The source of the messianic tradition is the oracle of Nathan to David, as outlined from the following texts:

Second Samuel 7:4-17: David proposed that he would build a house for the Lord. Through Nathan the Lord replies that he has not dwelt in a house and has not commanded David to build a house for him. The Lord took David as a shepherd and made him prince over "my people Israel." It is the Lord who will build for David a house, that is, give him a future and descendants. One of these descendants will build a house "for my name." The house and kingdom of David "shall be made sure forever before me; your throne shall be established forever."

Psalm 89:20-37: God anointed David and his "steadfast love" will be with him. He will cry to God, "You are my Father," and God will make him the "firstborn, the highest of the kings of the earth." God's covenant with David and his descendants is reiterated.

Psalm 132:11-18: In making the covenant with David and his descendants, God has also chosen Zion for blessing and as a place to dwell.

Amos 9:11-12: God will "raise up the booth of David" that has fallen. It will again be as in days of old. Edom and "all the nations who are called by my name" will again look to Israel. The Lord will bring it about.

Hosea 3:4-5: Israel shall be without king or temple for a long period. But they will again return and seek the Lord and David their king and experience God's goodness in the "latter days."

Isaiah 9:6-7: A child is to be born who will reign and who will be called "Wonderful Counselor, Mighty God, Everlasting Father, Prince of Peace." Of his reign and of his peace there will be no end; he will reign from the "throne of David" and will establish justice and righteousness forevermore. The Lord will bring it about.

Isaiah 11:1-10: A "shoot" and a "branch" shall grow from the stump of Jesse. He will be anointed with the Spirit and show that with wisdom, understanding, power, and knowledge. His faithful work will mean the triumph of righteousness and the end of wickedness, and the establishment of peace in the earth. All shall know the Lord. In that day the one from Jesse will stand as "a signal to the peoples; the nations shall inquire of him."

Micah 5:2-4: From Bethlehem, representing one of the smaller clans of Judah, will come one who is "to rule in Israel." His origin is from the days of old. This one will be born, and then "the rest of his kindred shall return to the people of Israel." "They shall live secure" because "he shall be great to the ends of the earth."

Jeremiah 23:5-6: The days are coming when the Lord will raise up "for David a righteous Branch" who will reign as king. He will execute righteousness and justice. Then "Judah will be saved and Israel will live in safety." His name will be "The Lord is our righteousness."

Jeremiah 33:14-18: God will keep his promise and cause a "righteous Branch" to come from David. He will execute righteousness and justice. The Lord says there will never be lacking one to sit on David's throne, nor will the Levitical priests lack one to carry out the offerings and sacrifices.

Ezekiel 21:27: The Davidic king now occupying the throne will fall, but there will come one who is worthy to fill this role again (cf. Gen. 49:10).

Ezekiel 34:23-24: The Lord says that the worthy one is "my servant David," whom he will set over the people as their shepherd and a prince. Then "I, the Lord, will be their God."

Ezekiel 37:24-28: God will make David king, one shepherd over all the people. Then the people will heed the instruction of the Lord and live in his everlasting covenant of peace. The people will dwell in their land with David over them as king forever.

Zechariah 9:9-10: The people of Israel ("daughter Zion") may rejoice, for "your king comes to you; triumphant and victorious is he, humble and riding on a donkey." He will bring peace and his "dominion shall be from sea to sea, and from the River to the ends of the earth."

Although the term *Messiah* may not be used, the Davidic dynasty and the covenant-promises associated therewith were decisive in the faith and in the eschatological expectation of Israel. This is apparent first from the witness of many of the psalms and then from the echo of the promise through the prophets. The anointed one for whom Israel looked was to be one from the line of David, another David. How was this concretely understood? Whatever the opinions and ascertainments of modern biblical scholarship,[35] the promise to David was associated in the Bible itself with eschatological hope.[36]

There is no question that the promise to David was the promise of a dynasty: "Your house and your kingdom shall be made sure forever" (2 Sam. 7:16). If the Nathan oracle envisioned a "Davidic dynasty," it also paved the way for a new and more exalted understanding of God's "anointed." His unique relation to God is indicated in the special promises made: for example, David will be a son to the Lord, and the Lord will be a father to him (7:14).[37] It is to be expected that this hope would be refined in the crucible of events in which the nation was shattered and the monarchy came to an end. The kingship ideologies disappeared among the peoples surrounding Israel under the onslaught of Assyria. But in Israel "the ideal of kingship deepened and developed into that of the Messiah."[38]

Under the preaching of the prophets, the collapse of the nation was understood as God's judgment on Israel. The prophets, anticipating the action of God in new promises and against the background of a break with the past, also understood the messianic promise anew. There was an important step of transition from king to Messiah in a passage like Micah 5:2-4, as Hartmut Gese has observed. No specific family could claim the promise given to the Davidic dynasty; God himself would choose this bearer of eternal lordship from within the Davidic clan.[39]

The distinctive emphasis on the coming royal figure is even more clearly evident in the promise in Isaiah 9:6-7. The fourfold designation describing him clearly surpasses even the figure of David: "Wonderful Counselor, Mighty God, Everlasting Father, Prince of Peace." Such names are likewise a statement about God; inasmuch as these designations are a description of the function of the one to come, "they also are an expression of *God's activity* through him."[40] This transcends "the course of natural world events" to proclaim an order made possible through the initiative of God:[41] "The zeal of the Lord of hosts will do this" (9:7).

The judgment of God finally brought the destruction of the nation and the end of the relationship of God to this people as constituted hitherto. But this did not mean the destruction of God's faithfulness to himself. This "judgment therefore paves the way for something finally new."[42] Moreover, in Yahweh's judgment upon Israel, there was a decisive universalizing of God's action; and this was true also for the new order of peace and righteousness anticipated from the Messiah. As early as Amos, the threat of judgment was universal: God judges all evil wherever it is to be found. And if God made use of the nations in judging Israel, then he is clearly their Lord also. The nations were bound up with the destiny of Israel and come within the range of God's action in judgment and in blessing (cf. Isa. 2:2-5; 9:6-7; 11:1-10).[43] Ultimately, it is not a question of the victory of one people over others, but the peace of all within the victory and blessing of God. The one in whom God acts to bring both judgment and blessing is the Messiah (cf. Isa. 11:3-5, 10).

The eschatological purpose of God is defined anew with the figure of the servant in the servant songs of Isaiah (42:1-4; 49:1-6; 50:4-9; 52:13—53:12). What is the relation between these songs and messianic expectation?[44] In Isaiah 11:1 the coming one is described as a "shoot" growing from the stump of Jesse. It is clear that Isaiah has one royal person in mind (11:1-5, 10). The authority by which he acts, judging the earth by the "breath of his lips" (11:4), indicates his close relation to God. In the servant songs, the servant is introduced as a "young plant" growing up before the Lord (both texts also have the key term "root"). The work of the servant is to restore Israel and bring salvation to the nations (cf. Isa. 49:5-6), and this action is identified as God fulfilling his promise of "steadfast, sure love for David" (Isa. 55:3).

All this is fully in accord with the character of God's revelation to Israel. David, like Moses, represented the people; through him the promise of the "steadfast love" of God is anticipated. Therefore, the coming of God is not to be divorced from the coming of the one who is to represent God.[45] It is said of the historical successor to David that he sits "upon the throne of the kingdom of the Lord over Israel" (1 Chron. 28:5). That must mean that the king serves to represent the reign of God over Israel. It is God who acts to subjugate the evil powers of the world, to bring the nations into submission to himself, to establish his saving sovereignty. In effecting salvation, the Messiah is to reign in order to establish the new order.[46] Although it is true that the Messiah is not simply identified with the servant, still this is also the role of the servant in the servant songs of Isaiah.

The servant is clearly dependent on the Lord, but his role is to be the instrument in the establishment of God's reign in the world. This is the theme of the first of the songs.

> He will faithfully bring forth justice.
> He will not grow faint or be crushed
>   until he has established justice in the earth;
>   and the coastlands wait for his teaching. (42:3-4)

The second song identifies the task of the servant as that of bringing Israel back to God, but not only Israel:

> I will give you as a light to the nations,
>   that my salvation may reach to the end of the earth. (49:6)

The fourth servant song is difficult to interpret as a whole. But the basic point is clear: the servant suffers and dies on behalf of the many (kings and their peoples) to purge them from sin so that they may find a place in the coming salvation of God (Isa. 53:4-8, 11-12).[47]

In the postexilic period, the themes of Zion and the Messiah are once again affirmed together. This is expressed in the well-known messianic promise of Zechariah 9:9-10. Earlier the coming of the Lord God to Zion to judge and to save was proclaimed (Isa. 40:9-10). But now in Zechariah the one who comes in triumph to Mount Zion is the anointed of God. His rule of peace is for the world; the peoples of the world are joined with the people of Israel in acknowledging this king who comes to Zion. The manner of his coming, as the peaceful and at the same time victorious king, as well as the scope of his kingdom—both point most clearly to the eschatological establishment of God's kingdom. This "Messiah" is one who is poor and humble, and comes to represent the kingdom of God.[48]

The Restoration of Israel. We may begin with a simple observation: Jesus made his proclamation to Israel. How is the meaning of the proclamation to be perceived apart from its own context? With what purpose did Jesus make his proclamation to Israel? In the effort to communicate, we might anticipate that Jesus would move beyond set expectations, but that he would, in any case, relate to them in making his proclamation. If we begin with the fact that Jesus made his proclamation in a setting of eschatological expectation, then it is important to consider what those expectations were. It therefore is appropriate to survey and set out in abbreviated form some of the key biblical passages that expressly pertain to Israel and Jewish eschatological expectation.[49]

Amos 9:11-15: In that day to come God will raise up the fallen "booth of David" and rebuild it as it was. Then Israel will again have influence over the nations. God will restore the people in their land, their cities will be rebuilt, and it will be theirs forever.

Jeremiah 30:18-22: The Lord will "restore . . . Jacob." The city (Jerusalem) with its palace shall be rebuilt. Joy will be in their midst and they shall be great. They will have one of their own to rule over them. This is restoration of a broken people; "You shall be my people, and I will be your God."

Jeremiah 33:6-11: From destruction God will restore Jerusalem to wholeness and security. The Lord says, "I will restore . . . Judah and . . . Israel," and rebuild them. He will forgive and cleanse them from all the guilt of "their sin and rebellion against me." And Jerusalem will be a cause of joy and praise among the nations. Joy and celebration will be a part of the pattern of life as in former times. Thank offerings will be brought to the "house of the Lord."

Zephaniah 3:16-20: God will bring victory to Israel. He will renew the people in love. He will judge oppressors and restore the lame and the outcast. Israel will be exalted among the peoples of the earth. God will gather them together and bring them home.

Isaiah 49:5-6: The Lord by his servant will restore Jacob and "gather" Israel to himself. He will raise the tribes of Jacob; but more, he will be as "a light to the nations." His salvation will reach to the end of the earth.

Isaiah 56:1-8: The people are to "maintain justice, and do what is right," for salvation will soon be revealed. Therefore, they are to keep the Sabbath and hold fast "my covenant." The foreigner who does so will also be accepted: the house of God is to be "a house of prayer for all peoples." God gathers the outcasts of Israel and will also gather the others.

Isaiah 60:3-14: The nations will come to the light of Israel. The sons and daughters of Israel will be gathered from afar. "The wealth of the nations" will be brought to Israel. God will glorify his "house." Foreigners will build Jerusalem, and kings will serve her. The resources of the nations will beautify "my sanctuary" (60:13). The saving action of God remains clearly centered on Israel.

Isaiah 66:18-24: God will gather "all nations and tongues." Of those surviving his judgment, he will send some among the nations to declare his glory. From these nations the dispersed Jews shall be brought to Jerusalem, where some will serve as priests and Levites. God will create a new heaven and a new earth. And all will worship the Lord.

Micah 4:1-7: In coming days "the mountain of the Lord's house shall be established as the highest of the mountains." From it will go forth the teaching of the Lord. The Lord shall bring peace among the peoples of earth. He will make a remnant out of the afflicted and the lame, and a strong people out of the outcasts. The Lord will reign over them from Mount Zion.

The words of the prophets have a particular context. They presuppose God's deliverance of Israel from Egypt, as well as the covenant and God's actions creative of Israel as a people. If Israel would turn away from this God, it would lose the very basis for its existence.[50] The prophets' characteristic response indicated the distinctive relation between God and Israel. The role of the prophet reflected the fact of Yahweh's lordship over his people; the prophet, in his social criticism, appealed to standards based on the understanding of that lordship.

The prophets appeared because Israel threatened this covenant relationship by turning away from God. Therefore, the God who saved Israel now becomes the God who judges Israel. The judgment announced by the prophets, Westermann has observed, was the necessary *continuation* of the saving working of God. "In the face of his people's apostasy, the savior must become the judge. In a hidden sense, this judgment is aimed at the saving of Israel—through and after the judgment."[51] Out of this failure in Israel's relationship to God, and so out of judgment, emerged the hope for a new age in which God would act to restore his people. The prophecy of Israel's restoration is therefore inherent in the character of God and his relationship with the people of Israel.[52]

A question arises: how is the character of God's intervention related to the question of eschatology? The answer calls first for a definite grasp of the meaning of "restoration." Ernst Ludwig Dietrich is the one who, in his study of *šub šebut*, drew attention to this theme expressing the hope of Israel,[53] namely, the promise (and corresponding hope) of Israel's "eschatological restoration" (*die eschatologische Wiederherstellung*). He determined that the basic meaning of the Hebrew expression (*šub šebut*) was restoration (on the basis of references in Job 42:10; Ezek. 16:53; Jer. 29:14; 30:18; 33:7, 11, 26; 31:23; 48:47; 49:6, 39; Ps.

14:7; 126:1, 4; etc.).[54] Restoration means "return," but it has a more inclusive scope than that.

The meaning of restoration is fully defined only as we consider the various aspects of "restoration." It will mean that Israel will be in its own land and there "rebuild the ruined cities" (e.g., Amos 9:14). Jerusalem in particular shall be rebuilt (e.g., Jer. 30:2-3; 33:10-18; cf. Mic. 4:1-2), and the temple as well shall be rebuilt (e.g., Jer. 33:11; cf. Ezek. 40—43). The dispersed of Israel shall be restored (e.g., Isa. 49:9-13; Ezek. 34:11-16; 37:21-23). "David" shall be raised to rule (e.g., Jer. 23:5-6; Ezek. 34:23-24; 37:24-28). The Gentiles shall come to serve and to participate in the blessing of Israel (e.g., Isa. 56:6-7; Mic. 4:1-4).

The order in which items appear in a list does not necessarily indicate the order of importance. At times the order in these passages stresses the concrete or directly tangible blessings, and at other times the intangible blessings are emphasized. So then, restoration can mean "abundance" and "security," and it can also mean the "forgiveness" of sin against God and the removal of "guilt" (e.g., Isa. 40:2; 44:23; 53:8). Restoration goes before the event of nations coming to know the ways of God (e.g., Jer. 33:9; Mic. 4:2-3).

It is apparent that hope in the king from David's line and hope of restoration have a prominent place. Indeed, there exists a strong correlation between them. In the book of Amos, the hope for fulfillment of the promise to David and hope for restoration are joined (Amos 9:11, 14). All the major prophets include expressions of hope for both the messianic king and for the eschatological restoration of Israel (Isaiah, Micah, Jeremiah, Ezekiel). The correlation is clearly exemplified in Jeremiah 23:5-6. In the days to come the Lord "will raise up for David a righteous Branch" who will reign as king. He will execute justice and righteousness; then "Judah will be saved" and "Israel will live in safety" (cf. Mic. 5:2-4). Thus hopes for restoration and a king are related. As Mowinckel acknowledged with respect to the Messiah, even when only one of this pair is mentioned, the other is often tacitly assumed.[55]

How then were "restoration of Israel" and eschatology related? Some passages convey the hope that Israel will be restored to its former place and position; in some the hope is explicitly eschatological. But in any case, we would expect that Israel would understand her future from her past experiences of God's saving actions (another David, another Zion). Expectation was interpreted by analogy to the past in seeking to understand the future, which was far to exceed the past.

Because people tended to conceive of coming events simply within the frame of the past, Israel is called to new understanding: "the former things have come to pass" and "new things" are to be anticipated. Even Israel itself is promised a new identity (a "new name" from "the mouth of the Lord" (Isa. 42:9-10; 43:18-19; 62:2). In the prophets the nations are included, first in judgment, and then "all peoples" are to be taken up into "the new coming acts of God."[56]

Inasmuch as salvation has become universal, even if it is salvation via Israel, it has become eschatological. Along with the universal range of salvation, it was also intensified to the very limits of existence. The coming action of God overcomes the experience of judgment, of humiliation and offense, of war and idolatry, and finally death (e.g., Isa. 25:1-9; cf. Ezek. 37:1-14). Thus, the prophetic message in its breadth and depth reaches the ultimate bounds of reality and thereby becomes eschatological.[57] The restoration of Israel was accordingly contained within the scope of God's eschatological salvation.

God's Reign in Daniel and Postbiblical Judaism

In this section we are not so much considering the resources for Jesus' eschatological proclamation as how different groups interpreted what they had received and appropriated from their inheritance. But we must examine this material in order to understand how the contemporaries of Jesus heard the scriptural theme of the kingdom of God. This is part of the context for Jesus' proclamation and mission.

The pertinent question now is this: Are the biblical representations of God's saving action reflected in a coherent way in Jewish expectation in the period leading up to the time of Jesus? The return of the Jews from Babylonian exile encouraged great hopes. But Israel with its earlier institutions was never fully restored. Certainly the expansive visions of Isaiah, Jeremiah, or Ezekiel were not realized. Israel as a whole (the twelve tribes) was not brought together again. Although Jerusalem was restored to some extent, the nations did not bring their wealth to adorn it or the temple (cf. Hag. 2:3; Ezra 3:12). And the expectation of "the new heavens and the new earth" (Isa. 66:22) most clearly transcended actual historical experience. Consequently, these prophecies remained comprehensible only with reference to a time yet to come.

The Kingdom of God. How did the kingdom of God figure in the Jewish hope during the second temple period? The apocalyptic writings have a place of prominence in answer to this question. Even though specific mention of the kingdom of God is sparse, a direct reference to God setting up his kingdom occurs in the book of Daniel, the literary model for later apocalyptic writings (2:44-45).

The setting up of this kingdom will mean the overthrow of evil powers: "It shall crush all these [other] kingdoms and bring them to an end." Other aspects of this event are described later in the book. The coming of the kingdom is set within the framework of God acting in judgment, and the central figure is "one like a son of man" to whom is "given dominion and glory and kingdom" (Dan. 7:9-14, RSV). This is a kingdom set up in the world, the kingdom of Israel over all the peoples (7:18, 21-22, 27). The concise reference at the end of the book to a resurrection of "many . . . who sleep in the dust of the earth" (12:2) distinguishes between some who rise to everlasting life and some to everlasting shame; this presupposes a judgment. In this work there is an emphasis on the fact that the kingdom is one "that shall never be destroyed" (7:14; cf. 7:18, 27).

A similar view of judgment appears in the Psalms of Solomon (not properly described as apocalyptic). God judges the peoples and is "our king forevermore" (cf. Ps. Sol. 17). With the precedent already set in the prophets (e.g., Isa. 65—66), there is now an emphasis "on the transcendent features of the future kingdom." That led, at least in the time of 4 Ezra, to an expectation that God would exercise judgment in conjunction with "the son of man" for all people. This would introduce a kingdom of God set within a transformed creation.[58]

By contrast, the author of the book of Jubilees looks for no cataclysmic event, but for a gradual establishment of the kingdom. The human life span will gradually increase until it reaches a thousand years (Jub. 23:27). There is no reference to resurrection in the book, only that the "spirits" of the righteous will have joy forever (23:30-32). In the work known as the Assumption of Moses, the kingdom is expected to appear suddenly throughout creation (10:1). God himself will punish the Gentiles and destroy their idols, and the power of Satan shall be no more (10:7). God will bless Israel and bring its enemies low (10:8-9). There is no reference to a Messiah, to a great conflict as prelude to the end, or to the resurrection. There is only a description of the happiness of the righteous in heaven and the torment of the Gentiles in hell (10:8-10).

In 4 Ezra there is a distinction between the messianic kingdom and the final form of the kingdom. The first remains subject to the conditions of this age in which death prevails. Only after the time of the messianic kingdom is the resurrection to take place, and God will judge the nations (7:28-34). In the Apocalypse of Baruch the messianic kingdom has a more significant but apparently similar place. It is simply said that the Messiah will reign "until the world of corruption has ended" (2 Bar. 40:3).[59] The teaching of Daniel 7 is repeated in this book in the vision and interpretation of the four kingdoms that are to arise. The last of the four is "harsher and more evil than those which were before it" and is replaced by the rule of the Messiah (36-40). The coming of his kingdom is the fulfillment of prophetic "predictions" and marks "the end of that which is corruptible" (74:2-3).

At this point Qumran appears to reflect a more general understanding of the connection between future hope and the kingdom. On the one hand, the "visitation" of all who walk in the ways of truth will be "healing, great peace in a long life, and fruitfulness, together with every everlasting blessing and eternal joy in life without end" (Manual of Discipline: 1QS 4.7-9). On the other hand, for those walking in darkness and deceit, the "visitation" will mean "everlasting damnation" and the "avenging wrath" of God. Though the doctrine of the resurrection is barely suggested, in some form it is probably presupposed (Hymn Scroll: 1QH 5.34; cf. Dan. 12:1-2).

The community understands itself to be living in the last critical time before the conflict with the forces of darkness under the direction of Belial (War Scroll: 1QM 1.5, 13-15). Evidently the advent of the Messiah(s) of Aaron and Israel is expected before this final decisive conflict (cf. 1QS 9.11). In the end the kingdom appears to be set in a renewed world (1QH 3.28-36). But the hymns of the community express thanksgiving for a salvation in which they are currently participating; already they belong to the heavenly Jerusalem and share in eternal life (1QH 3.19-23; 6.24-27; 8.5-9). This is a distinctive understanding of eschatological salvation as it concerns the relation of present and future.[60]

In summary, there appears to be unity in all the strands of tradition on the kingdom with respect to the events of judgment, the establishment of God's righteousness in the world, and (not always included) the "final event" of the kingdom set within a new creation (Dan. 12:2-3). Further, a messianic figure or figures are often associated with the coming into effect of the kingdom of God (cf. Dan. 7:13-14).

The Messiah. The understanding of the kingdom of God and of the Messiah in the kingdom are closely related. Geza Vermes notes that if all the references to the Messiah in the Jewish literature of this period are compiled, as if all are of equal importance, the result is a variety of views, but no clear depiction of "the Messiah."[61]

What form did messianic expectation take in the intertestamental period? Vermes points to the converging lines of evidence derived from the Psalms of Solomon, the Jewish prayer of the Eighteen Benedictions (*shemone 'esre* or *'amida*), and the Qumran liturgical blessing, as well as rabbinic interpretation of messianic prophecies.[62] Psalms of Solomon 17 and 18 are part of a collection of poems from the first century BCE reflecting "the mainstream of Jewish religious ideology."[63] In these psalms several references to the one "anointed" of the Lord appear (e.g., Ps. Sol. 18:6, 8).

The prayer of Psalm of Solomon 18 reflects Isaiah 11: the

anointed of the Lord will use his "rod" to instill "the fear of his God" in people and direct them to "righteous acts."[64] This prayer is preceded by the supplication in Psalm 17 that God would raise up for his people "their king, the son of David." He shall gather his people; the "gentile nations" will serve him, and he will effect the righteousness of God; all will "be holy" under the reign of "the Lord Messiah" (Ps. Sol. 17:23-36).

The outline of this figure is clear enough. It is in accord with the figure already sketched in the prophets. The mission of this king as portrayed in Isaiah 11 is one of peace. The emphasis is not on a triumph wrought by the usual coercive or militant means. Therefore, he judges the poor "with righteousness" and strikes the earth "with the rod of his mouth." In the Psalms of Solomon the accent is more strongly on the exercise of power; for the ordinary Jew the portrait of the Messiah would not have "excluded the idea of a future triumphant king."[65]

In the blessing concerning David in the Eighteen Benedictions, the "righteous Messiah" is clearly a royal figure who will rebuild Jerusalem and "establish in it the throne of David."[66] And in the liturgical blessing at Qumran, it is the royal, probably Davidic, conception along the lines of Isaiah 11 that predominates. The blessing is for "the prince of the congregation that he may establish the kingdom of his people forever." In the blessing there is a call for the Lord to exalt him to "everlasting heights," that he may strike the earth with his scepter and bring death to the ungodly.[67]

Rabbinic expectation is concisely reflected in the view of the great Rabbi Akiba. He believed that the leader in the second Jewish war against Rome, Bar Kochba, was the "king Messiah" in whom was fulfilled the promise of Numbers 24:17: "A star shall come out of Jacob, and a scepter shall rise out of Israel."[68] Basic features of the messianic expectation are maintained in all the groups and stand out in clear relief. The Messiah is a figure from the line of David endowed by God with power and knowledge to enact his kingdom of righteousness.

But messianic expectation was not confined to this form. There was also a strong emphasis, for instance, on the priestly character of the Messiah. Indeed, in the Testament of Levi the full range of messianic expectation is directed to one who shall come from the tribe of Levi (18:2-5).[69] The concept of two Messiahs is present in the Testaments of the Twelve Patriarchs at a number of points. "The savior come from God" shall arise from the tribes of Levi and Judah; God will raise up "from Levi someone as high priest and from Judah someone as king" (T. Sim. 7:1-2; cf. T. Reub. 6:5-12; T. Jud. 17:5-6; 22:2-3; 24:1-6).

How are we to understand this development? We know that after the reforms of Nehemiah and Ezra, the life of Israel was centered on the temple and the high priest. Even before that the emphasis in the description of Israel restored in Ezekiel 40-48 lies on the new temple and its worship. Whatever the reasons, the Levitic Messiah came to have the primary place in some circles for a time (cf. T. Jud. 21:1-4; T. Reub. 6:10-12).

In a still more comprehensive fashion, a statement from the Qumran community refers to "the coming of a prophet and the Messiahs from Aaron and Israel" (1QS 9.10-11). This probably refers to three eschatological figures: a prophet (cf. Deut. 18:18-19), a Priest-Messiah from Aaron, and a King-Messiah of Israel. The two Messiahs apparently have a role in bringing the deliverance that issues in the kingdom; particularly the King-Messiah seems to function as commander of the army in the final conflict (cf. 1QM 5.1-2; 13.1-2). The two Messiahs are again clearly referred to in the Florilegium from Qumran Cave 4 (4QFlor 1.10-13): the offspring of David (2 Sam. 7:11-14) is interpreted to be "the branch of David who shall arise with the Interpreter of the Law [to rule] in Zion [at the end] of time."[70] The Davidic Messiah arises to "save" Israel, and alongside him is the Priest whose role is defined by his name, "The Interpreter of the Law."

The emphasis on the cult and the temple in the postexilic period may have resulted in a division between the priestly and the royal functions of the Messiah. Earlier these functions were embodied in one figure (cf. Ps. 110:1-4). Traces of a separation of function appear early. In Ezekiel's vision of restored Israel (40-48), the king has a subordinate place in a "priestly" community. In Jeremiah 33:14-18 there is "alongside the choice of David and the covenant with David the choice of the Levites and the Levitical covenant of priesthood."[71] Still later, at the beginning of the postexilic period, the priestly and the royal figure appear side by side (Zech. 4:14). Does this mean the importance of the Messiah is reduced? Not necessarily, if we recognize that both functions belong together. The priestly and the royal aspects of messiahship are both preserved in the double concept of messiahship.

The apocalyptic prophecy of the Son of man in Daniel presents a distinctly different tradition. How, if at all, is it to be related to the messianic tradition? This "one like a son of man" is associated with God and receives "dominion and glory" and a kingdom that will not be destroyed (7:9-14, RSV). In the interpretation that follows, the son of man is identified with "the saints of the Most High" (cf. Ps. 34:9). The interpretation of the one like a Son of man as a collective figure is in accord with the concept of the Messiah who represents the people of God.[72]

The prophecy in Daniel 7 is concerned "with the establishment and triumph of God's kingdom on earth through God's human representative, just as is the messianic tradition."[73] In the one case this representative is the Davidic king; in the other this representative is the exalted Son of man. This ensures that the kingdom is understood in its transcendent character as indeed the kingdom of God.

The special relation to true Israel is maintained, but his kingdom also includes "all peoples" who serve him (7:14, 27). This connection between the Messiah and the Son of man is affirmed in later Jewish literature. In the book of Enoch the Son of man is twice described as God's "anointed" or "Messiah" (1 En. 48:10; 52:4) and as one possessing the spirit of righteousness (cf. Isa. 11:1-5). In 4 Ezra there is a fusion between the two traditions of "the man" and the Messiah; the Man is addressed by God as "my son," a title for the Davidic king (13:32, 37).[74] He comes to judge on Mount Zion and to restore Israel (13:9-13, 35-40).

There is thus more than one emphasis attached to the concept of "Messiah." This figure is called to bring justice, judge between the righteous and the wicked, deliver from enemies and gather Israel, exercise judgment, and then rule over the world. But these variations give depth and scope to the concept. Furthermore, they indicate that the Messiah has a significant role in the eschatological kingdom of God.

The Restoration of Israel. Jewish expectation included the hope of a restored Israel. Already in Daniel the coming of the one "like a son of man" is for the deliverance and vindication of "the people of the saints of the Most High" (7:13-14, 25-27, RSV). As one who effects God's judgment and kingdom, he represents the afflicted people of God. There is a relation between the kingdom coming into effect and the people of God.

This hope of restoration is correlated in the Psalms of Solomon with the hope of the coming Davidic Messiah. Then God in his mercy will "bring together the dispersed of Israel" (8:28). The children of Israel will be gathered "from the east and the west" (11:2). God will raise for Israel the son of David as king (17:21), who will destroy lawless Gentile nations (17:24). He will gather a "holy people" and "judge the tribes of the people that have been made holy by the Lord their God" (17:26). The Gentiles are included among those who will serve the king of Israel; they will "come from the ends of the earth to see his glory, to bring as gifts her children who had been driven out" (17:31). Israel restored is Israel purified under judgment. And central to all is the gathering of the dispersed of Israel.[75]

The Qumran community in its own way also bears witness to the expectation of the eschatological restoration of Israel. We would expect that the interpretation of restoration would include priesthood and temple. They saw themselves as a community of the last days. This group even defined the community itself as the temple, since for them temple worship was performed through the community's observance of the Law and its own liturgy (cf. 1QS 5.2-7; 8.2-6, 9-10; 11.7-11; Cairo Damascus Document: CD 5.4-7).[76]

Because of their reinterpretation of "temple," there is some question about their expectations concerning the temple. Although "temple" was in important ways redefined, the actual temple appears still to have a place in their hopes (1QS 8.4-10). As E. P. Sanders points out, the document that most clearly depicts a new temple, including reference to the sacrifices to be made there, is the War Scroll (cf. 1QM 2.1-3). The Temple Scroll focuses on proper sacrifice and purity of officiants, confirming the importance of the temple in the expectation of this community. Thus there was a strong emphasis on the restoration of Israel, with the temple in some form in the eschatological renewal.

The traditional expectation of Israel's eschatological restoration is confirmed from Diaspora Judaism by Philo. In his treatise *On Rewards and Punishments* (94-97; 162-172),[77] he refers to the peace promised by the prophets for creation. Along with this, he defines the role of the Messianic figure who will subdue great nations with the help of God: there shall "come forth a man" (Num. 24:7, LXX). Further, he expects the gathering of Israel from all the places where they had been scattered. He counts on a restoration of the exiles, or at least of all those who accept God's chastisement and repent of sin (163-165). When the exiles return, the cities shall be rebuilt and the people will live in abundance under the blessing of God (168).

This survey of passages makes clear that the emphasis can vary between the elements of eschatological expectation. Yet at the same time there is a remarkable coherence among the different forms of this expectation. The basic question before us is whether eschatological expectation continued in this period to the time of Jesus, or what specific elements of this hope were maintained: the coming of the Davidic king or Messiah, the gathering of dispersed Israel, the building of a glorious new temple, the participation of the Gentiles, etc.

The messianic hope remained a primary part of Israel's expectation, though the eschatological agent can be presented under various forms. Prominent in this expectation was the restoration of Israel. Present, but less prominent, was the inclusion of Gentiles, most often in subordination to Israel. Depending on the account, the elements of expectation may be explicit or only implicit. The pertinent points were summed up by T. W. Manson: (1) "The restoration of the dispersed of Israel to their own land is a principal element in the description of the coming deliverance." (2) This "deliverance" is expected in conjunction with the coming of the Davidic Messiah.[78] There never was a stage in Israel's history when the kingdom was expected apart from the saving activity of God or one who acts for God (cf. Isa. 40:9; Zech. 9:9).

Eschatology and Ethics in the Scriptures and in Postbiblical Judaism

Was there a relation between the kingdom-of-God theme and ethics? What place did ethics have in Jewish eschatological thinking?

Eschatology and Ethics in the Scriptures

If God takes the initiative in purposeful action and word, he seeks human response. Human response is integral to everything in Scripture that is said about God. The Lord in his speaking or acting seeks to elicit human response.[79] The Sinai covenant expresses the meaning of God's lordship in relation to Israel. As King he provides instruction and gave command; he directs and goes out before his people[80] (cf. Num. 23:21). The content of the commands is expressive of the relationship of God to Israel: "I am the Lord your God" (Exod. 20:1-6). The Torah presupposes God's initiative toward his people: "I am the Lord your God, who brought you out of the land of Egypt, out of the house of slavery" and opens up a "life of peace in relation to God."[81] This means that the law is not to be separated from the saving action of God and absolutized apart from him.

God, who took initiative for the salvation of Israel, at the same time gives commands to Israel. To act according to his commands and laws is response.[82] Nothing can take the place of the response to God's will, and that includes response in deed (cf. 1 Sam. 15:22). God in the same exodus event reveals himself to Israel ("I am Yahweh," Exod. 3:13-15; 20:2; Hebrew tr.) and constitutes the relationship to Israel. In accord with the covenant, as reflected in the first commandment of the Decalogue, Israel was related to God in all the spheres of existence; in all life situations Israel "was dealing with this one God."[83]

Thus, integral to the revelation of God was the revelation of his will.[84] The commands reflect the character of God. To hear the commands was both to respond out of the relationship to God as his people and to be called to reflect him. The fundamental statement is presented in the formula, "You shall be holy, for I the Lord your God am holy" (Lev. 19:2). Central to this teaching is the character of God in relationship to his people:

"When an alien resides with you in your land, you shall not oppress the alien. . . . Love the alien as yourself, for you were aliens in the land of Egypt: I am the Lord your God" (Lev. 19:33-34). The prohibition against permanently holding a fellow Israelite as slave is followed by further instruction:

> When you send a male slave out from you a free person, you shall not send him out empty-handed. Provide liberally out of your flock, your threshing floor, and your wine press, thus giving to him some of the bounty with which the Lord your God has blessed you. Remember that you were a slave in the land of Egypt, and the Lord your God redeemed you. (Deut. 15:13-15)

In this relationship to God, Israel is directed not only to the past but to the future. The event of the exodus itself was the great act of hope in the Hebrew Scripture. From it arose the certitude that God would sooner or later act to bring justice and freedom into the world. This was a confidence that arose in the midst of an oppressed people who groaned and cried out. They recognized and found words to express oppression, itself the first step in hope. God heard and saw their condition (Exod. 2:23-25). Zimmerli emphasizes that knowledge of God for Israel was founded on concrete encounter.[85] It was nevertheless not the unknown God who made himself known ("I am Yahweh"), but the same God who was with the fathers (Exod. 3:15-17). This God had already given evidence of his power.

In receiving God's word, Israel anticipated coming events. Yet by reference to the earlier action of God, the hoped-for event of deliverance took its place in the history of God with his people to that point. This speaking of the new event by reference to God's past action makes the point "that God is the same God all the way from promise to fulfillment" (cf. Exod. 3:16-17; Ezek. 37:14).[86] Hence, knowing God must mean knowing God in his lordship; God is revealed where "his promises of blessing, peace and righteousness are fulfilled by him."[87] God is to be known where he shows himself to be the same, in his faithfulness.

Inasmuch as there was a correlation between Israel's faith and God's faithfulness, faith had a future content. The warning of judgment and the promise of salvation in the prophets are different ways of depicting the future of God in terms of particular circumstances. That future is anticipated in present action in one way or another. On one hand there is the pattern of correspondence between sin and judgment.[88] Fundamentally, judgment is dependent on covenant relationship and follows from it. "Because you did not serve the Lord your God joyfully and with gladness of heart for the abundance of everything, therefore you shall serve your enemies whom the Lord will send against you. . ." (Deut. 28:47-48). An Israel that does not serve the Lord God "will find as her punishment that she must serve her enemies" (cf. Exod. 20:4-6; Jer. 5:19; 6:19).[89] This correspondence pattern is true for both evil and good; the prophets call for a clear response from Israel (cf. Isa. 3:10; Hos. 10:12).

The relation between eschatology and ethics becomes explicit in the promise of the new covenant (Jer. 31:31-34; cf. Ezek. 36:25-28). Under this covenant, men and women will live fully in the relationship to God, and the alienation of sin will be overcome. This is made possible through the forgiveness of sin; everyone will "know" God, because the Torah will be written on the tablets of the heart. People will live in the power of a new spirit.[90] According to Isaiah 2:2-4 and Micah 4:1-4, there will be a new giving of the Torah from Zion in the "latter days." Then the peoples will flow of their own accord to Zion in order to learn God's ways and "walk in his paths."

This is not a simply "spiritual" reality. It is concretely anticipated as a historical, economic, and social order in this world. The eschatological revelation from Mount Zion will make possible the participation of the peoples in the Lord's ways and in his peace. Thus already for people hearing the prophet, righteousness was characteristically anticipatory or eschatological and called for definite response: "Keep justice, and do righteousness (*sedaqa*), for soon my salvation will come, and my deliverance (*sedaqa*) be revealed" (Isa. 56:1, RSV). This is to wait for, and to anticipate in actual experience, the eschatological righteousness (in salvation) as the gift from God.[91]

Eschatology and Ethics in Daniel and Postbiblical Judaism

One line of thought in current scholarship holds that an apocalyptic emphasis was primarily on the future to the neglect of life in the present. Is apocalyptic determined by a setting of crisis and deprivation, from which it springs? If apocalyptic is not simply determined by this setting, it is clearly affected by the restrictions of existence under the domination of foreign nations.

Yet the prophetic literature was in large part produced under similar circumstances. At the same time, there is a difference in outlook between the prophets and the apocalyptists. But is it correct to say that the prophets saw the future in relation to the present, whereas the apocalyptists saw no causal connection between present and future?[92] If apocalyptic had its rise in the radical dichotomy between the present and the coming age, in a situation of despair about any good arising in the present, then apocalyptic can be distinguished as one theological current among others. This view is stated succinctly by J. A. T. Robinson:

> With the apocalyptists, eschatology developed into a subject in itself, a science of the end. . . . One could produce treatises on the last things and treatises on ethics, the one dealing with the future, the other the present. And for late Judaism the two were distinct, the apocalyptic writers giving schematic arrangements to the divine promises, the scribal tradition providing precise codification of the divine demands.[93]

This depiction of apocalyptic has been generalized to the point of distortion. First, it cannot be assumed that there is in apocalyptic a unified eschatological scheme which varies only in minor details. Against the idea that apocalyptic is simply to be identified as a particular form of eschatology, Christopher Rowland shows that apocalyptic has a variety of interests and concerns: for example, in the first section of 1 Enoch, cosmology instead of eschatology occupies the key role.[94] Apocalyptic does not sever the connection between God and the creation, but maintains faith in God the Creator even in the face of evil in this world. Apocalyptic therefore expresses hope for creation and not merely for the salvation of individuals from the world.

Second, there was in Judaism a definite connection between

eschatology and ethics. This is shown not only in apocalyptic but also in a nonapocalyptic work like the Psalms of Solomon, containing both eschatological and ethical teaching.

Further, we cannot assume that the role of eschatology and ethics will be uniform in the Jewish literature. In general, the contrast in apocalyptic between the present evil age and the future blessed age is sharpened. In 1 Enoch 6, the evil character of this age is described with reference to the work of fallen angels. Ultimately, however, God remains sovereign (2:1; 5:1-2; 9:5). He is Lord of the ages (12:3; 22:14; 25:7). He is aware of evil and permits it without acting to restrain evil on earth (9:11). In the face of overwhelming evil, God had no word for his people in their terrible plight, "except the promise of final deliverance."[95]

Again, the view is that God guided Israel's historical pilgrimage until the Babylonian captivity. Then God withdrew his protection and leadership, giving up his people to the wild beasts to be destroyed and devoured. The Lord "remained quiet and happy because they were being devoured, swallowed, and snatched; so he abandoned them into the hands of all the wild beasts for food" (89:58). Next God handed over the people to seventy shepherds with instructions on the number of Jews who could be slain. Upon receiving the reports of the cruel and heedless conduct of the shepherds, God set aside the reports without taking any action (89:71, 75). On one hand it is apparent that the writer believed God had ultimate control over history; on the other hand, during this whole period the Lord was inactive and no "deliverance could be expected before the messianic era."[96]

The circumstances out of which this apocalyptic work arose severely tested human response; the assurance of the ultimate triumph of God provides the antidote to unrelieved despair. From this perspective the issue is only whether people will align "themselves with God's way or the way of the world." The present is open to opportunity for people to decide for or against the will of God (1 Enoch 81:5ff.).[97] The emphasis is on God's action only in the future, to provide ultimate salvation. This resulted in a restricted view of ethical response in the present because the present is largely without God. Ethical concern is limited to the preservation of personal righteousness by avoiding violations of the law.

To bring to clear focus the relation between eschatology and ethics, we may examine the teaching of Daniel and 4 Ezra. In this setting of Daniel, the oppressive political power makes absolute claims. Nebuchadnezzar wants the people to concede the absolute authority of the imperial system over their lives. The story of the refusal of the young men to eat at the king's table emphasizes that they will not simply be accommodated by the system. They thrive on simple food. The clear implication: conduct in accord with the will of God is the way of ultimate wellbeing (1:8-20).

The actions of others flow out of trust and hope in God: the three who refuse to bow down in worship to the image, and Daniel facing the lions because of his devotion in prayer. They do this recognizing that God is wholly set against evil and is himself the power to bring the new order. In the present this means great moral struggle—life itself is at stake. They do not submit even if this should mean death (3:1-26; 6:6-23). They count on a future from God not under the control of the king. And they count on God in the present amid the most difficult circumstances: God has not abandoned his people. The triumph of the Son of man is also the triumph of the saints of God in the face of the kings of the earth (7:11-27).

The character of God himself is the basis for assurance of God's forgiveness and action for his people (9:17-19). This same character of God has significance for ethical conduct that extends even to the heathen. Daniel calls upon the king, "Atone for your sins with righteousness, and your iniquities with mercy to the oppressed, so that your prosperity may be prolonged" (4:27). Turning to God calls for conduct in accord with God's will (cf. 9:7, 14).

Fourth Ezra, like 1 Enoch, maintains a formal doctrine of God's activity in history (e.g., 3:27, 30; 5:28). The key to this author's understanding of the present in relation to the future is the "two ages" concept (cf. 7:50). From this standpoint the historical period beginning with Adam is understood to be under the control of sin and fate (cf. 4:26-32; 7:5; 8:1-3). Because God decreed the two ages, the few righteous can only resign themselves to the situation with the hope of a solution in the age to come.[98] The future age of salvation is for the few, those who persevere amid the many difficulties of this world (7:11-14) and have perfectly kept the law (7:20-25, 45-61). Since this age is completely dominated by evil, the response can only be patient resignation.

Central to the book of Daniel is the future kingdom of God, but not in contrast to God's activity in the present. He works through and will act for his people in history (2:21; 5:25-28). God "is the living God. . . . He delivers and rescues, he works signs and wonders in heaven and on earth" (6:26-27). And his righteousness will be finally and fully vindicated in the establishment of his kingdom (7:14). This provides a basis for hopeful participation in life.

Both Daniel and 4 Ezra are in agreement that the promise of the coming kingdom of God is a basis for hope and perseverance in the present. But in 4 Ezra, the law circumscribes the action of God and the relation of God to his people. Expectation means the exaltation of the few righteous and the condemnation of the sinful, as determined by the law. Absent from this work, for example, are the "new things" to come (e.g., Isa. 42:1-9) and the expected new giving of the Torah from Mount Zion, that would bring the nations to participate in the eschatological peace of God (cf. Isa. 2:1-5). But in the circumstances of oppression after the exile, the emphasis was on the keeping of the law.

Was Qumran exceptional or only the most rigorous at this point? The War Scroll gathers together a number of components of the kingdom theme. A future divine action will bring a realm of justice and blessing. This involves the conquest and the humiliation of enemies (1QM 12.7-15). It is therefore coercive in means and national rather than universal in its concerns. There is a marked dualism of Belial and the people of his domain on the one hand, and the realm of the saints on the other (1QM 14.9-10; 18.1-11). The anticipation of God's constructive action in history is apparently restricted to what he will do in the end for "the few righteous" who have kept the Law.

This community interpreted and meditated on the Law as it waited for the future age. Entrance into the community is in fact equated with making a "return to the Law of Moses with a whole heart and soul" (Cairo Damascus Document: CD 15.7-11). This means learning and obeying the interpretation of the Mosaic Law as determined by the priestly leaders of the community (Manual of Discipline: 1QS 5.8-10). The heart of their program, as they awaited the future, was meditation on and observance of the Law. They glimpsed the possibility of participation in the future age on the basis of their obedience in the present.[99]

Conclusion

To interpret Jesus' proclamation and teaching, we need to understand the nature of Jewish eschatological expectations. What an interpreter assumes about these hopes will therefore be crucial for understanding the kingdom of God in Jesus' proclamation. The recovery of eschatology by Weiss and Schweitzer continues to be important. To the extent that they assumed Jesus reproduced Jewish eschatological and apocalyptic expectations, certain aspects of their view need to be reconsidered.

For instance, is apocalyptic expectation simply to be equated with the destruction of this world, the resurrection, and the judgment, followed by the creation of a new heaven and earth?[100] Schweitzer proposed that "the eschatology of Jesus" could only be "interpreted by the aid of the . . . Jewish apocalyptic literature."[101] In this category he included the works of Daniel, 1 Enoch, the Psalms of Solomon, 2 Baruch, and 4 Ezra (2 Esdras).[102] On the basis of "Jewish apocalyptic expectation," Schweitzer contrasted "Messianic ideal" (including the restoration of Israel) with end-of-the-world eschatology. He affirmed that by the time of Jesus, the latter had displaced the earlier "political" messianic conception.[103]

In contradiction to Schweitzer, Daniel 7 *is* concerned with the triumph of the kingdom in this world (Dan. 2:44; 7:17, 27). Second, even in Daniel the coming of the kingdom means the restoration of God's holy people (Israel), who are vindicated in the coming of the kingdom. The Psalms of Solomon affirm that God will raise from the line of David a king to "rule over . . . Israel." In God's strength he will "destroy the unrighteous rulers" and godless nations "with the word of his mouth" (17:21-24). Here is the traditional figure of the Messiah with an emphasis on particular aspects of his work.

Similarly, 4 Ezra and 2 Baruch, though late, probably reflect earlier Jewish eschatological expectation; they depict a Messiah who reigns for a limited period on the earth. In 4 Ezra this period lasts for 400 years (7:28-33), followed by the judgment, resurrection, and new creation. The central figure is "a man" who arises from the sea, symbolizing the emergence of one who has been concealed, like the Messiah (cf. 13:52). This is not a descent from heaven nor is this an end-of-the-world eschatology.

Furthermore, in 2 Baruch the Messiah reigns as long as the earth endures, until "the world of corruption has ended" (40:3). Among the apocalyptic works following Daniel, the Similitudes of Enoch (1 Enoch 37-71) present a transcendent figure, "the Son of man," who comes to judge and rule in the kingdom of God (62:2-5). It is almost certainly later than the period of Jesus and in certain respects stands alone in its eschatology. In any case, it does not reflect all the elements required to establish Schweitzer's "late Jewish view" of apocalyptic eschatology as the sole context for Jesus' proclamation.[104]

So, contrary to the view of Schweitzer, in Jewish apocalyptic the kingdom *is* put into effect in this world. Indeed, in three authorities the Messiah is clearly a figure of this world as the king of a victorious people; only at the close of this reign does the new creation take place. This is in direct opposition to what Schweitzer held to be the "late Jewish" expectation. What we have is the expectation of a messianic kingdom of God in and for this world, which is then followed by the judgment and the kingdom of God in the setting of a new creation.

These works present different eschatological views, but by no means do they present what Schweitzer described as "the late Jewish view." Some do not mention a messianic figure at all; when he is mentioned, his reign is usually closely related to the eschatological restoration of Israel. Sometimes a period of tribulation is said to occur, sometimes not. According to some sources, the tribulation precedes the coming of the Messiah (cf.

4 Ezra 5:4-12); in others it follows his coming. There was not a monolithic eschatological expectation in Judaism. This means that the indications derived in particular by Schweitzer from Jewish apocalyptic for Jesus' eschatological proclamation do not hold true. The announcement of an impending end of time as the sole and sufficient definition of eschatology derived from Weiss and Schweitzer cannot be the starting point for the interpretation of Jesus' eschatological proclamation.

At every stage in Jewish tradition, there is a connection between the kingdom, the restoration of Israel, and the coming Messiah. There is reason to think that the most immediate but not the only source for Jesus' eschatological proclamation is the kingdom to be set up by God as described in Daniel. In particular, two key passages, Daniel 2 and 7, appear as a basis for understanding Jesus. In the first we have the vision of "a stone . . . cut from a mountain by no human hand," which itself becomes a great mountain filling the whole earth (2:35, 45, RSV). The stone signifies the kingdom set up by God, which shall never be destroyed (2:44). The vision of Daniel 7 is evidently parallel to the one in chapter 2. Now "one like a son of man" represents the "saints of the Most High," to whom is given dominion and a kingdom never to be destroyed (7:13-14, 27, RSV).

These references from Daniel are crucial for understanding Jesus. First, there is no precise distinction between "spiritual" and poitical redemption. The alignment of Daniel with Jesus' proclamation is clear as this relates to God's kingdom to be set up in the future. Significantly, the two Daniel passages are in Aramaic, the language probably most widely spoken in first-century Galilee. These passages would therefore have been more directly accessible to people than the rest of the Hebrew Bible.[105]

Second, it is clear that the kingdom in Daniel 2 and 7 is properly understood as God's kingdom. God will set it up, and the saints, now suffering (7:21), are apparently to be given a share in his reign (cf. 7:14, 27).

Third, the language of Daniel provides the framework for understanding Jesus' proclamation of the kingdom of God "in the context of the Jewish eschatological hope for a new age and for

God's restoration of his people Israel."[106] The relation between "kingdom of God" and "people" in Jesus' proclamation remains to be investigated, but the correlation is clear in Daniel.

Further reasons for thinking that Daniel serves as the most immediate resource for Jesus' kingdom proclamation are the other important points of contact with Jesus' proclamation and teaching. In particular, the Son of man concept, the idea of the desolating sacrilege, and the concept of the saints participating in the reign of God—these have their origins in Daniel (cf. Mark 13:14; 14:62; Luke 12:32).[107]

At the same time it is clear that Jesus drew upon a range of resources in making his proclamation and carrying out his mission. To identify the meaning of his healing and preaching, he connects his work to the expectations of God's eschatological salvation in Isaiah (Isa. 29:18-19; 35:5-6; 61:1-2; Matt. 11:5-6; Luke 4:16-21; 7:22-23). The vision is of the kingdom as social in character, as universal in ultimate scope, and to be initiated for and within this creation. In particular, the connection between Jesus' proclamation of the kingdom of God and Isaiah is clear: note the mention of messenger, kingdom, and the eschatological restoration of Israel (cf. Mark 1:15; Isa. 52:7-10).

This is sufficient to indicate the resources as well as the context for understanding Jesus' proclamation and mission. For the kingdom of God, whether described in prophecy or apocalyptic, Israel waited upon the coming of the Lord. God was expected to send his Messiah, restore his people Israel, and establish his righteousness in the world.

3

The Kingdom of God and the Proper Response

The question of Jesus' purpose is related to the response he expects (cf. Mark 1:38; 4:9; Luke 4:43). Jesus makes his proclamation with the expectation of response. The question to which this chapter is meant to provide an answer is this: What response does Jesus seek to elicit to his proclamation of the kingdom of God?

New State of the Question

Appropriate response to Jesus exhibits more than one dimension or facet. Jesus addresses people in different ways, in accord with their different relations to him, and in accord with the unfolding of his mission in stages. Initially, he calls all Israel to repent and be baptized (John 3:22—4:3). Once he initiates his own independent career, he calls some to travel with him in his entourage. He calls upon all to refashion their lives in accord with the coming of the kingdom of God. At a certain point as the climax of his career looms before him (Mark 8:34//Matt. 16:24), he calls his disciples to a commitment without reserve, to be prepared for extreme self-denial.

My particular interest centers on the specifically moral component of the appropriate response to Jesus' public proclamation and teaching. Since I want to highlight the ethical aspect as much as possible, I will fill out and clarify the contours of the issue.

First, the question presupposes four things: Jesus does, in fact, have a public proclamation to make, and he makes it. Like the

Baptist, he addresses his proclamation to Israel at large. The object of the proclamation is the kingdom of God and the meaning of its coming. Finally, "the kingdom of God" signifies God's climactic and definitive saving act.

Second, I intend to build on these presuppositions: Both Jesus and his audience understand that at the heart of God's saving act stands the eschatological restoration of Israel. Inattention to this "ecclesial" dimension of Jesus' proclamation has been a grave defect in historical-Jesus research from the nineteenth century to the present. Liberal theology was blind to the specifically ecclesial significance of Jesus' word, and the kerygma theology that supplanted it deliberately reduced all aspects of the proclamation to the demand for personal decision. The result was a curiously de-Judaized and unhistorical retrieval of Jesus' word.

Third, I also will build on the contemporary recovery of this "restoration eschatology" at the heart of Jesus' proclamation. My purpose is to reconstruct the context and thus make the ethical component of the response sought by Jesus to be concrete, and concretely intelligible.

"The kingdom of God" is a central term, doubtless *the* central term, in the words of Jesus. The alternative expression, "the kingdom of heaven," occurs mainly in Matthew and therefore in a Jewish setting, where "of heaven" was an indirect way to speak of God (cf. Matt. 5:3//Luke 6:20; Matt. 8:11//Luke 13:29). "The kingdom" appears in many of the forms of oral discourse differentiated by modern analysis: in proclamation (Matt. 4:17; Mark 1:15), parable (Mark 4:26; Matt. 13:31; Mark 4:30; Luke 13:18, etc.), prophetic saying (Matt. 5:19), esoteric instruction (Mark 4:11; Matt. 13:11), vow or prophecy (Matt. 26:29; Mark 14:25), and so on.

Furthermore, in key instances "kingdom" appears in a saying of Jesus in the explication of something else. That is, the kingdom is not directly at issue, but it is referred to in order to identify or explain something else, such as the "mystery" of the kingdom (Mark 4:11; cf. 13:11; Luke 8:10), the "word" of the kingdom (Matt. 13:19), the "sons" of the kingdom (Matt. 8:12; 13:38), the "keys" of the kingdom (Matt. 16:19), and the "gospel" of the kingdom (Matt. 4:23; 9:35; 24:14). The kingdom itself is not the concern in these cases. Instead, it is assumed that the hearer or reader knows enough about the kingdom that reference to it will shed light on the subjects actually at issue. The situation is similar in the teaching on anxiety (Matt. 6:33//Luke 12:31); people are simply told to seek the kingdom.

In all of these instances, the impression is confirmed that Jesus speaks of the kingdom consistently, and that it is central in his proclamation and in his teaching.[1] The Synoptic tradition makes Jesus' proclamation of the kingdom of God foundational with respect to all the other uses (Matt. 4:17; Mark 1:15; Luke 16:16). In view of the natural and inevitable relationship between public proclamation and the many forms of public teaching, scholarship has affirmed this relationship as reflecting the history of Jesus.

Like the Baptist's proclamation of imminent judgment, Jesus' proclamation exhibits a key trait of apocalyptic eschatology: it bears on the consummation of history. Still, Jesus' proclamation stands apart from that of the Baptist. As several scholars (e.g., David Flusser and Joachim Jeremias) recently urge, Jesus alone proclaims the divine act of salvation as already inaugurated and in process of realization. He evidently understands his own mission to be related to the mission of John as its distinct complement and crown.

Flusser notes that Jesus is "the only Jew known to us from ancient times" who proclaims "that the new age of salvation had already begun." Jeremias agrees that Jesus' proclamation is accordingly "without analogy."[2] This, to be sure, does not yet yield a historically secure recovery of exactly how Jesus understands God's saving act—its agents, beneficiaries, scope, and character. But this basic ascertainment sets this inquiry on track, and I presuppose it but propose to develop and confirm it.

Does anyone today seriously deny that Jesus addressed to Israel at large a public proclamation of the kingdom of God? Direct denial is all but nonexistent. Indirect denial, however, is occasionally to be encountered. In Morton Smith's *Jesus the Magician*, proclamation is downplayed to the point of virtual disappearance. Again, in Marcus Borg's *Jesus: A New Vision*, the kingdom of God is reduced to a metaphor for a "new and improved social-historical situation."[3] These are two among a number of recent studies which, whatever their merit in other respects, are similarly eccentric in this particular: they so depict Jesus' public career as to make proclamation marginal or nonexistent.

A full-blown refutation of such studies necessarily falls outside the purview of the present investigation. For our purposes it will have to suffice to make a statement in common with the vast majority of scholars: there is no basis, either in the sources or in a sober analysis of the distinctive tendencies of the sources, for removing Jesus' proclamation of the kingdom of God from its foundational position.

As for the imminence of the kingdom of God, the critical discussion was launched, toward the end of the last century, by the discovery of the eschatology of Jesus and of the synoptic Gospels; it continues today almost without diminution. This topic, then, cannot be relegated entirely to the present brief category of presuppositions. I will deal with it below in greater detail.

I have said above that I take the expression "the kingdom of God," as used by Jesus, to refer to God's climactic and definitive saving act. As long ago as 1898, Gustaf Dalman correlated Jesus' use of the expression "the kingdom of God" with fundamental prayer texts in use in the time of Jesus, the early forms of the Eighteen Benedictions (*shemone 'esre* or *'amida*) and of the Kaddish (*qaddish*). Both look to the full earthly realization of the sovereignty of God.[4] Though this, too, is among our presuppositions, I intend in the course of this chapter to spell out more fully what it entails.

In his work (mentioned above) Ernst Ludwig Dietrich in 1925 offered a technical philological study which drew attention to a major prophetic theme expressing the hope of Israel.[5] This theme is the promise and the corresponding hope of Israel's "eschatological restoration" (*die endzeitliche Wiederherstellung*). Though New Testament scholarship failed to make the connection between this complex of biblical motifs and the public proclamation of Jesus, there did appear sporadic signs of recognition that somehow the restoration of Israel was tied in with Jesus' career.

In chapter 1 (above), I mentioned the work of Joseph Schmitt, G. B. Caird, B. F. Meyer, and E. P. Sanders. My present purpose is to recover Jesus' proclamation and teaching with a view to defining the appropriate response to both. The main clues to this task will be sought in the teaching by which Jesus followed up, elucidated, and commended anew his proclamation.

What did Jesus mean by "the kingdom of God"? In seeking an answer, we shall do well to start where Jesus' own contemporaries must have started. Jesus came into an environment in which the question about what it means to be God's holy people is a live one. The distinctive contribution of Jesus to this question is the proclamation that the kingdom of God is at hand. In this environment there can be no understanding of "kingdom of God" apart from its relation to Israel.[6] Jesus himself comes representing the Lord God of Abraham, Isaac, and Jacob (cf. Matt. 8:11; 22:31-32). That is to say, Jesus represents not God in general but the one true God as revealed in the history of his people Israel.

This insistence, however, is in direct contrast to liberal theology as reflected, for instance, in the work of Adolf von Harnack.[7] He assumes that the effort to understand Jesus in the context of Judaism was fundamentally wrong. Instead, the essence of Christianity has to do with "something common to us all," and he is accordingly persuaded that "Jesus Christ's teaching will at once bring us by steps which, if few, will be great, to a height where its connection with Judaism is seen to be only a loose one, and most of the threads leading from it into 'contemporary history' become of no importance at all."[8]

The same perspective is inherent in the negative application of the criterion of dissimilarity; this holds that sayings attributed to Jesus that are not dissimilar to Judaism and to the early Christian community cannot be regarded as authentic. Application of this criterion is a prominent feature of scholarship in the tradition of Bultmann. Bultmann states the significance of the negative application of the criterion: "Where opposition to the morality and piety of Judaism . . . are expressed, and where on the other hand there are no specifically Christian features, it is easiest to conclude there is an authentic parable of Jesus."[9] The negative application of the criterion leads Ernst Käsemann to conclude that, with regard to both Torah and eschatological expectation, Jesus makes "a break with Judaism." This means that differences between Jesus and Judaism are methodically requisite and alone determinative for understanding Jesus.[10]

The relation between Jesus' kingdom-of-God proclamation and Israel is difficult to comprehend in this line of criticism. In the work of Norman Perrin, we find perhaps the most thorough effort to understand Jesus' proclamation of the kingdom of God through the application of the principle of dissimilarity.[11] He accepts Jewish apocalyptic as the background for Jesus' understanding of "the kingdom of God." But he proposes that Jesus uses it in his own way as a symbol to evoke a human experience of God as king, "which every man experiences in his own time."[12] He therefore argues that instruction on the kingdom and the parousia in Luke 17 and Mark 13 is a transformation of Jesus' use of the symbol of the kingdom of God, and a distortion of Jesus' message.[13] In these passages apocalyptic language about the kingdom of God is related to divine intervention that would bring judgment and redemption.

However, in Perrin's view the significance of Jesus' proclamation of the kingdom is a challenge to "explore the manifold ways in which the experience of God can become a reality to man." He therefore maintains that it is not "legitimate to think of Jesus' use of kingdom of God in terms of 'present' and 'future' at all."[14] The reason for the "illegitimacy" of this distinction is that in Jesus' usage, kingdom of God is not a conception but a symbol. The kingdom is not to be identified with the historic and concrete action unfolding in Jesus' ministry or with ultimate salvation and judgment. It is something "which every man experiences in his own time."[15] This is to present a clear alternative as the context for understanding Jesus' kingdom-of-God proclamation: historical Israel, with its long history of promise and eschatological hope, is dropped in favor of "every man and his experience." Despite the new idiom on myth and symbol, this is a return to liberal theology.

Whatever degree of religious validity there be in the approach represented by Perrin, the historical question of how Jesus used the term "the kingdom of God" cannot be answered apart from its own original context. Since Jesus makes his proclamation within and to Israel, the question of context and purpose perforce involves the relation between this proclamation and this people.

John the Baptist and Jesus

The Gospel accounts are united in their witness to the beginning and the outcome of Jesus' career. The beginning of Jesus' public work is closely associated with John the Baptist. At the end, after his death and resurrection, there is a community that recognizes Jesus as the Messiah. These two facts, the connection of John to Jesus and the community that results, both set Jesus' mission in an eschatological framework.[16]

What does the connection at the beginning to John the Baptist tell us about Jesus? The answer to this question depends on the meaning of John's work. He "appeared" in the wilderness north of the Dead Sea "in the fifteenth year of the reign of Tiberius Caesar" (Mark 1:4//Matt. 3:1; Luke 3:1ff.). The proclamation of judgment and a summons to repentance identifies John as a prophet of the end-time: "Repent, for the kingdom of heaven has come near" (Matt. 3:2). John's preaching is rooted in a recognition that the supremely critical moment has come for Israel. That is evident in the strong images of judgment that fill his preaching: Spirit and fire, wheat and chaff, winnowing fork and threshing floor, ax and root. And it is equally evident that the standing resources of Israel, such as the cultic means of expiation, are not sufficient to meet the new situation.

Furthermore, this call is decisive not simply for individuals within Israel but especially *for Israel as a people*.[17] First, this call excludes no one but is addressed to all.

> Do not presume to say to yourselves, "We have Abraham as our ancestor"; for I tell you, God is able from these stones to raise up children to Abraham. (Matt. 3:9//Luke 3:8)

God is now summoning Israel in view of the arrival of the end-time. The message of John presents a scheme of salvation in two stages: the repentance John proclaims and baptism by him; and then the baptism in "the Holy Spirit and fire" by the "more powerful" one coming after John (Matt. 3:11-12). The two stages are related as prelude to judgment and judgment itself.[18]

Second, with a view to John's background, it is impossible to think that he conceives of judgment merely along individual lines. Instead, he understands judgment in "ecclesial" terms, in terms of "God's people, Israel." To miss this is to miss the context out of which come his words and acts.

> In Torah and prophets alike the drama of history is the covenantal dialogue of God and people. Judgment is turned against *Israel* and *Israel* is the object of salvation. John's summons was accordingly directed to all Israel as the people of God. Diversity of response could not cancel the ecclesial character of the encounter.[19]

On the contrary, the diversity of response will concretely determine the destiny of Israel as such: its division (the coming separation of wheat and chaff) and restoration (the wheat gathered into the granary).[20] The object of the judgment will be the salvation of Israel. Since judgment means the sifting of the wheat from the chaff, saved Israel will be a remnant.[21]

In the synoptic Gospels, the event that marks the move of Jesus from Judea to Galilee and the beginning of his public ministry is the arrest of John (Mark 1:14//Matt. 4:12//Luke 3:19). The beginning of Jesus' ministry has been closely bound up with the work of John. From the circle around John, Jesus calls his first disciples. With them he works in alliance with John, though apparently not alongside him (John 3:26).[22] Jesus acknowledges the mission of the Baptist in clear terms: his baptism is "from heaven" (Mark 11:30), and he came representing "the way of righteousness" (Matt. 21:32). In the desert John called Israel to a new beginning, to be sealed by a rite of baptism. Jesus not only responds positively to the Baptist's call to Israel but actively shares in it; this underscores the eschatological character of his ministry. The close association of Jesus with the Baptist suggests participation in the Baptist's aim: the reconstitution of Israel in view of the coming kingdom of God.[23]

The statement of John about the coming "mightier" one

(Matt. 3:11, RSV) bears on the relation between John and Jesus. To speak of it as a "Christian accretion"[24] overlooks important evidence for authenticity. John can hardly have referred to God coming to judge humankind in such terms. Moreover, the question later put to Jesus by those sent from John, "Are you the one who is to come?" (Matt. 11:3//Luke 7:19) is most likely an echo of John's speech. Furthermore, that John is a prophet of repentance is implied in the account of Josephus.[25] His depiction of John and his message confirms the account of the Gospels: the preaching in the desert, the dress that recalled Elijah, and the message of repentance in view of coming judgment. There are thus many common elements between John and Jesus; there are also important differences.

It is important, in seeking to understand the purpose of Jesus, to discover how he sees his work vis-à-vis that of John. The Gospels highlight several mutually reinforcing factors. John's role as the precursor and as Elijah (Matt. 3:1-6; 11:7-15//Luke 7:24-27; Matt. 17:10-13//Mark 9:11-13) means that "the law and the prophets were in effect until John came; since then the good news of the kingdom of God is proclaimed . . ." (Luke 16:16//Matt. 11:12-13). That is, John marks the watershed between the period of the law and the time of the kingdom.

The language in Matthew is similar, but the emphasis is different: "From the days of John the Baptist until now the kingdom of heaven has suffered violence."[26] In Matthew there is some rearrangement of terms so that John's ministry is included within the time of the kingdom. But Matthew and Luke agree on the main point: the period of the law and the prophets climaxed in John's ministry, and that ministry served to introduce the eschatological era (Matt. 11:10, 14). John's ministry represents the link between the old order and the new, not so as to belong to neither, but so as to belong to both.[27]

This saying affirms the presence of the kingdom of God in the period following the appearance of John the Baptist. Obscurities of interpretation should not divert attention from the central point: the kingdom of God is powerfully operative among people in the labors of Jesus, a stage prepared for and introduced by the ministry of John the Baptist.[28] The work of Jesus is closely identified with that of John; at the same time, there is a significant distinction between them (a matter to which I shall return).

John's word of warning and of judgment (the sifting of wheat from chaff) divulges a singular hope: to assemble, by the call to repentance and to baptism, the Israel destined for restoration.[29] The mission of John the Baptist fastens on eschatological fulfillment. He appears in the wilderness calling the people to repentance in view of the imminent coming of the kingdom of God. John issues this call to the people of Israel, descendants of Abraham (Luke 3:8).[30] The people come to him and recognize the prophetic authority of his message: "All regarded John as truly a prophet" (Mark 11:32). He announces the judgment to be accomplished by the "coming one" for whom he himself was preparing the way.

Jesus, in coming to John, identifies fully with the mission of John, as confirmed and reinforced in Jesus' teaching about John (cf. Matt. 11:7-15//Luke 7:24-28). Because of John's unique service in relation to the coming kingdom, he is a prophet and "more than a prophet" (Matt. 11:9-10). Jesus not only identifies with John's mission but himself participates in it. Jesus' conscious contrast with John in the character of his ministry serves to underscore their unity in basic purpose. This prepares the ground for a preliminary observation on the purpose of Jesus' mission: Jesus understands his mission as the enactment of the age-old scriptural promise of *the restoration of Israel*. This he sees not as something exclusively reserved for some future, but to be effected now and already begun—indeed, already prepared for and begun in the work of John. Thus Jesus begins to move into the eschatological task that he takes to be his.

Jesus' Proclamation, Acts, and Teaching

What is the significance of the transition from "the days of John the Baptist" (Matt. 11:12) to Jesus' own independent ministry? John and Jesus alike understand the culmination of history in terms of judgment and salvation: in biblical thinking one entails the other. But this leaves room for them to be quite different in emphasis. John, through his strong images of judgment, emphasizes "the wrath to come" (Matt. 3:7//Luke 3:7). In Jesus' proclamation the term of decisive significance is "the kingdom of God."[31] With Jesus, the focal point is no longer warning or exposition of promise, but announcement of the coming kingdom of God. This language of the kingdom resonates with the promise that God will vindicate his name and his people. The emphasis is on God's initiative; Jesus therefore preaches the gospel of the kingdom of God (cf. Matt. 4:23; Mark 1:15).

According to Jesus the coming of the kingdom does not validate exclusion of the sinners from Israel, but reverses that situation. Jesus restores men and women to their place with God's people as he welcomes the sinners (e.g., Luke 19:1-10) and heals the sick (e.g., Mark 1:40-44; 2:5-12). This helps to define the kingdom of God in relation to the restoration of Israel. Already in Deutero-Isaiah, the announcement "Your God reigns!" is a proclamation of Israel's imminent redemption. Features of Isaiah 52:7-9 are often reflected in Jesus' ministry: the herald of salvation, the kingship of God, and the peace and restoration of Israel. These appear in the several facets of preaching, teaching, and healing (cf. Matt. 4:23; 9:35; 11:5).

But Jesus' kingdom-of-God proclamation carries the meaning not only of vindication but also of judgment for Israel.[32] What Jesus has to say about the kingdom challenges and disturbs current expectations. This feature stands out sharply in the profile of Jesus' mission. Jesus sees Israel passing into a crisis: this generation will see the end of the present situation of the people of God.[33] A number of the parables are designed to make this point: this is how the kingdom of God comes—like a harvest, or a distribution of wages, or a settlement of accounts.[34] All these are images of judgment. As harvest (judgment) brings the separation of the weeds from the wheat (Matt. 13:24-30), so the kingdom of God brings the separation of the evil from the good (Matt. 13:24-30). As with the great catch of fish of every kind that are sorted into the good and the bad, so it is with the kingdom of God (Matt. 13:47-50).

Indeed, the danger of condemnation is so acute that only resolute action will avoid it. The call is to recognize the judgment ahead, to take steps to avoid it, and to gain the entrance to the kingdom instead (Luke 16:1-8). The warning of coming judgment is no less evident in the parable of the Great Feast (Matt. 22:1-10//Luke 14:15-24). Everything is at stake in the response to Jesus' proclamation of the kingdom. According to the parable, "everything is ready," the preparations are complete, the guests have only to come in and eat. But some people are not prepared to recognize the fact that the time has come, and they would not accept the summons to the feast. The situation is one of present grace and imminent judgment.

Explicit warnings in the synoptic Gospels fit into this framework. Israel is confronted in the situation: this generation may participate in the climactic fulfillment that Jesus brings, but to repudiate the opportunity is to face judgment and to answer for it (Luke 11:49-51; Matt. 23:34-35).[35] The little parable of the fig tree expresses the urgency of response: the tree is to be tended with care and has one more year to bear fruit, and "if not, you can cut it down" (Luke 13:6-9). There is the warning that those who perished in one of Pilate's brutal suppressions of Jewish aspirations will set the pattern for all, unless they repent (Luke 13:1-5).[36] Further, without probing for the full meaning of Jesus' action in the temple, one thing clearly symbolized in this action is judgment. This is in accord with the predictions of the temple's destruction (e.g., Mark 13:1-31).[37] Indeed, these warnings of the destruction of the temple draw to a climax this theme of judgment upon unrepentant Israel.

The purpose of Jesus is to "gather" the children of Israel, but because Israel fails to recognize the hour of divine visitation, Jesus warns of judgment on Israel and its temple (Luke 13:34-35; 19:41-44). The Jewish hope includes the central conviction that God, out of faithfulness to the covenant, will act to save his people from the power of Rome. Jesus, however, turns this around. Hope is based not on a large-scale "military" deliverance from the enemy without, but on repentance in light of the kingdom of God already present in their midst (cf. Luke 17:20-21).[38]

The bond between the kingdom of God and the restoration of Israel is apparent. Why does Jesus proclaim the kingdom of God to Israel as such unless it bears on the destiny of Israel as such? This relation between the proclamation of the kingdom of God and the salvation of Israel belongs to the pattern of biblical eschatology. The announcement "Your God reigns" had become a proclamation of God acting for Israel's redemption (e.g., Isa. 52:8-9). This reappears in Jesus' proclamation, and from the start he couples the kingdom of God with a call to conversion. The proclamation is made with a view to appropriate response and attains its end in such response. The nature of the kingdom includes response. Israel can not be the passive beneficiary of eschatological salvation; there must be a "willed act of acceptance."[39]

If "kingdom of God" in Jesus' proclamation entails restoration of Israel," one expects to find evidence for this in his public actions. Here Jesus' choosing of the twelve becomes an important issue (cf. Mark 3:13-19//Matt. 10:1-4).[40] There is strong support for the view that Jesus chooses the twelve. It is significant that the record of Jesus choosing the disciples is in all four Gospels, in the Acts, and in 1 Corinthians, with variations in the order and in the presentation of the names, but always adding up to twelve. A key fact concerns Judas. How does Judas come to be included in this elect group? Suppose one holds that the church originated the account of the twelve and included Judas. Then that calls for an explanation of the tradition that replaces Judas with Matthias. The choosing and sending out of the twelve is intended to embody the concept of the people of God.

I have recalled above that Jewish hopes for the future included restoration of the twelve tribes of Israel; the motif of "the twelve" is maintained even by the Qumran community. In the milieu of this vital expectation, for Jesus to appoint the twelve is to make of them a "sign" of the eschatological restoration of Israel. This is why Jesus speaks of his followers as a "little flock" (Luke 12:32), reminiscent of prophetic texts on the Israel of the messianic age (Mic. 5:4; Isa. 40:11; Ezek. 34:12-14). The very existence of the twelve is an appeal to the whole people of Israel.

The relation between the choosing of the twelve disciples and Israel is confirmed by Jesus saying to them that they will be "judging the twelve tribes of Israel" (Matt. 19:28//Luke 22:28, 30).[41] The twelve are described both as those who participate in the kingdom and those who will exercise judgment. The people of God will participate in God's rule, and judgment is a function of that rule. Thus, Jesus makes the twelve a sign of the future. Furthermore, he calls them to participate in its coming-to-be, by sending them out in groups of two (Mark 6:7//Luke 10:1). This mission to Israel, set under the announcement of the coming of the kingdom of God, confronts Israel with a decision of faith or of unfaith.[42] The action of choosing the twelve points to Jesus as one who brings the eschatological restoration of Israel. As the one anointed by God, Jesus calls "the twelve": they are to be the beginnings of renewed Israel.

To sum up, the character of Jesus' mission is epitomized in his word on the feast of the kingdom of God (Matt. 8:11-12//Luke 13:28-29).[43] This may be understood against the background in prophecy of the pilgrimage of the nations to the mountain of God, Jerusalem. The people would come bringing gifts, and along with them would come the dispersed of Israel to participate in the feast of the Lord (cf. Isa. 2:40, 51; 25:6-9; 45:14, 23-24; 52:10; 56:7).

This, however, is more than Jesus states; none of the supporting elements of the pilgrimage of the nations is present in the Gospel passage. There is no mention of the defeat of the Gentiles or their subjection to Israel within the kingdom of God. Instead, the Gentiles are described as coming from every quarter of the world to participate in the feast of the kingdom of God with the patriarchs of Israel, whereas the Jews will be excluded from the kingdom. This is a shocking declaration of judgment on Israel. It stands in coherence with other utterances of Jesus dealing with judgment on Israel (e.g., Matt. 23:34-36//Luke 11:49-51). Prophetic declarations of judgment are given with the aim of encouraging the hearers to repent, and even this saying is to be understood as a warning rather than as a pronouncement of sentence.

Negatively, this note of judgment confirms that the eschatological salvation of Israel will not be realized apart from "a willed act of acceptance." Positively, Jesus anticipates that multitudes of the nations will share with Abraham, Isaac, and Jacob in the kingdom of God, while those who properly are expected to share in the kingdom will be cast out because of unbelief: "heirs of the kingdom" are those who would inherit the kingdom but lack faith (cf. Matt. 8:12//Luke 13:28; War Scroll: 1QM 17.2).[44]

Thus the kingdom of God in Jesus' proclamation concretely entails the people of God or restored Israel, together with saved Gentiles, as the new eschatological community. How Jesus represents both the present and future of the kingdom of God—that I will develop more fully in the following sections and in the following chapter. It is enough now to note that Jesus heals, he welcomes outcasts and sinners, he calls and sends out the twelve, he embodies and teaches a way of life that in the power of God creates a transformed people. The kingdom coming into effect in the word and work of Jesus enables the response that is appropriate to the kingdom of God.

Response to Proclamation, Action, and Teaching

What is the relation between Jesus' kingdom-of-God proclamation and the response he expected? A relationship between them has often been presupposed, but ideas about what that relationship is have varied greatly. Insofar as the pattern of the expected response can be discovered, it might well shed light on the nature of the kingdom of God. I will deal with proclamation and response in correlation.

The accent in Jesus' proclamation falls on God's initiative; the accent in his teaching falls on the human response. The proclamation and the teaching cannot be separated, nor can they simply be equated with each other. It is apparent that proclamation is coupled from the first with the expectation of response (e.g., Mark 1:15). When Jesus proclaims the kingdom of God, his purpose is to call "the children of the kingdom" (Matt. 8:12, KJV) into it; their entrance into the kingdom would be an event anticipating the inclusion of humankind (Matt. 8:11). Thus, the teaching clarifies and specifies the appropriate response. It presents concrete examples of how life is renewed in response to the kingdom of God. Our task is to correlate proclamation with response and, within the response, to correlate general perspective with specific instances of "right response."

The Beatitudes

The form itself of the Beatitudes (Matt. 5:3-12//Luke 6:20-23) calls attention to the primary meaning of Jesus' teaching and action. The focus of Jesus is the activity of God, to bring blessing. Jesus is concerned not with the refinement of law but with the enactment of new reality. The macarism or beatitude is a declaration. It declares (1) good fortune for some particular beneficiaries (2) accruing to them in some particular and appropriate forms. The literal meaning of the opening word "blessed" (*makarioi*) is: "Happy (destined for good fortune) are they/you!" The second part of each beatitude says why these particular beneficiaries are happy or blessed. The pattern is this: Happy the poor and oppressed, for they are to be blessed.[45] This describes people who benefit from something not determined by them.

Jesus accents the imminence of the kingdom. Despite the present tense of "theirs is the kingdom of heaven/God," the original reference is to the future. The kingdom is about to be theirs (cf. Matt. 19:14).[46] When the kingdom comes—and it can be announced and already is becoming effective—it is the poor who will receive it. No greater gift could be given to anyone. People to whom the kingdom belongs, people who shall be satisfied (in the face of hunger and oppression), people who shall be comforted (in the face of humiliation and destruction)—these are blessed people now. To those who make no claims for themselves, everything is given. If the kingdom belongs to the poor, they have new dignity; this breaks through the system of values in which it is only the rich who have the status of "real persons." The kingdom of God will bring a complete "reversal of human conditions and values."[47]

In this case, however, what significance do the Beatitudes have for describing the human response to Jesus' proclamation? To see in the Beatitudes simply a list of virtues or deeds of good people—this is hardly apt to bring their full or proper meaning into focus. The Beatitudes reflect a divine initiative. As for the beneficiaries, one can not simply decide to mourn or to hunger and thirst for righteousness. Again, the actions of showing mercy and of making peace presuppose a resource beyond that of a demand requiring these actions. Accordingly, there are no direct imperatives save in Matthew 5:11-12, and the eschatological content in the second part of each beatitude is evident. The Beatitudes, then, are not in the wisdom pattern, presenting the correlation between wise action and its corresponding reward. They are in the apocalyptic pattern, presenting God as sovereign and merciful and about to vindicate his righteousness for those who are poor, who mourn, who hunger (cf. Luke 7:21).

These declarations also challenge those who hear them to realign their values in accord with the coming kingdom of God. If the kingdom comes with the power to renew life, this cannot leave the pattern of human attachment and concern as it is: thus the connection between poverty of spirit and participation in the kingdom, between mourning and comfort, between hunger and thirst and fulfillment. The proclamation of the kingdom of God makes this renewal possible. If hearers trust this message and the one who proclaims it, they will reshape their life in harmony with the kingdom of God. Against the background of Isaiah 61:1-2, the Beatitudes point clearly, if only indirectly, to the one who enacts the salvation of the coming kingdom. Therefore, response to the kingdom is response to Jesus (5:11).

What this response means is made concrete in the motif of persecution of the disciples. The coming of the kingdom of God calls for a reversal of values. In contrast to life as a struggle for success and power, the Beatitudes proclaim God's initiative in favor of those who are poor, who mourn, who are meek, who seek righteousness above all, who are merciful, who are pure in heart, and who make peace. The kingdom of God will come to them. They are the ones formed by the kingdom and who will be at home in the kingdom.

In the Beatitudes, accordingly, Jesus proclaims the kingdom as God's initiative and as his gift. Response in this field of God's active force becomes a live option. It involves a single-hearted (Matt. 5:4, 8) desire for God's vindication (Matt. 5:3, 6). The proper response to God's goodness is wonder and praise. It is the opening of one's heart to God's way. It is the inclination to celebrate God's revelation of salvation. It is to align oneself with the poor, the mourners, the hungry, the peacemakers, the seekers after righteousness.

The disciples participate by anticipation in the future announced by Jesus; they participate immediately in what is becoming effective in Jesus. This explains why the Beatitudes are declarations rather than exhortations. As declarations they have a striking character in announcing the coming of the kingdom as effective in the present.[48] The Beatitudes themselves proclaim and presuppose the kingdom of God (cf. Matt. 4:23-25): the gracious initiative of God was already becoming effective in Jesus.

Joachim Jeremias emphasizes that for the whole of Jesus' teaching, the proclamation of the kingdom is presupposed. In support of his point, he cites several examples. One is Jesus' statement, "You are the light of the world" (Matt. 5:14). In his view, this makes no sense taken by itself; in their weaknesses and failures, the disciples are not all that illuminating. The statement presupposes their relation to Jesus himself, "the light of the world" (cf. John 8:12; 1:9).

Another example of God's prior action is Jesus' word, "If you do not forgive others, neither will your Father forgive your trespasses" (Matt. 6:15).[49] This is only properly understood when God's "great debt cancellation" is presupposed as expressed in the parable (Matt. 18:35) and indicated in the Lord's Prayer (Matt. 6:12). Again, Jesus' call to love one's enemies presupposes the message of God's grace and unbounded goodness. The Beatitudes, then, are not an anxious expression of demands in the face of catastrophe (e.g., Weiss). Instead, what was decisive for Jesus was something quite different: knowledge of the time of salvation.[50]

How then are present and future related in Jesus' announcement of blessing? Does the significance of the announcement depend on the one who makes it? On one hand, if salvation in the full or final sense is not yet, on the other hand the anointed one has appeared and brings good news to the poor and comforts those who mourn. These are themselves eschatological events (Isa. 61:1-2). Further, the prophet pointed to the coming salvation when the people would "neither hunger nor thirst." Instead, there would be joy because the Lord would show compassion for the afflicted (Isa. 49:8, 10, 13).

Inasmuch as Jesus, in his mission, brings consolation to the poor, the hungry, and the grieving, the salvation he promised already becomes effective in the present (cf. Luke 4:21; 7:22). If the Beatitudes have their significance as announcement of eschatological salvation, the disciples are "blessed" precisely because they accepted this salvation. They did not take offense, but received Jesus as the one sent from God (cf. Matt. 11:6, 25-27). They therefore can be said to have eyes that see and ears that hear what the prophets and the righteous in past ages desired but were not privileged to see and hear (Matt. 13:16-17).

The Proclamation

Proclamation emphasizes announcement of what was awaited and is now coming into effect. In Mark's summary, Jesus' gospel proclamation is presented in two parallelisms:

- The time is fulfilled,
  and the kingdom of God is at hand;
- repent,
  and believe in the gospel. (Mark 1:15, RSV)

In this announcement, of first importance is God's action in bringing the kingdom; of first importance is response of the hearers to it. In Jesus' proclamation, it is clear that the coming of the kingdom of God does not depend on prior human repentance.[51] The coming is simply proclaimed. The proclamation links announcement and command; two parallel announcements are followed by two parallel commands.[52] The relation of announcement to command is not defined, but the sequence suggests dependence. The imperatives "repent" and "believe" make sense in relation to Jesus' announcement. The whole sequence indicates dependence on God's initiative and action. The grasp of any one part depends on the grasp of the coherent whole.[53]

On the supposition that the proclamation is simply the announcement of an event to be fulfilled in the immediate future, some limit response to accepting this announcement and expecting its fulfillment (e.g., Weiss). A variation on this view is that since God fulfills his purpose and acts on behalf of his people, there can be no expectation of active human response.

This view, however, represents an oversight because it leaves the relation of the proclamation to the messenger undefined. It will not suffice to say that in Jesus' proclamation of the kingdom of God, we are confronted only with the proclamation and not with the one proclaiming it. The proclamation of the kingdom combined with his calling of the twelve surely means that Jesus is also assuming a role in it. The commands have validity only if Jesus' proclamation is grounded in true knowledge of the coming of the kingdom of God. The response presupposes that claim to prophetic knowledge.[54] The sequence is decisive: the call to repentance corresponds to the dawning of the new time.

Second, this quietist view of appropriate response fails to observe that repentance and faith were coordinates. Repentance is defined by faith in the good news. Would repentance be possible without the trust implied in "believe"? Conversely, would trust in Jesus' good news be possible without repentance? Is not repentance here the turning of one's life toward a new point of the compass? The hearers, it seems, are being invited to reorder their perceptions and commitments. A change of direction (*metanoeite:* repent) takes place in conjunction with the emergence of trust in Jesus and his message.[55] The call to repentance depends on the prior announcement of the kingdom of God. We understand this by observing the intrinsic connection between repentance and faith in the good news: *metanoeite kai pisteuete en tō euaggeliō*: "repent, and believe the gospel." Response to the good news of the imminence and presence of the kingdom of God is to stake one's life on this good news.

The Issue of Repentance

The realignment of perception and trust is indeed a response, not an initiative. Appropriate response is an answer to the initiative of God. This is expressed in Jesus' proclamation of the coming of God's kingdom. The ethical dimension of the response is situated in this context.

What is the meaning of repentance in Jesus' teaching? The answer turns in part on how to resolve the conflict between two current views. The first view is that repentance is fundamental in Jesus' teaching; the second and opposite view is that the motif of repentance is conspicuous by its absence from Jesus' preaching.

This issue ties in with another: Jesus' association with sinners, and the offense that this creates. Jesus' initiative toward sinners and the teaching on repentance are variously construed by interpreters as well as by his audience: (1) Controversy arises because Jesus offers people forgiveness and thus admission to the kingdom before requiring repentance. In Judaism, however, forgiveness is offered to the righteous, that is, only after proper repentance.[56] (2) Controversy arises because the call to repentance is directed not only to the wicked but to all. Jesus' call puts all on the same level; all need repentance.[57] (3) Controversy arises because Jesus does not call for repentance according to the standing requirements of Jewish law and ritual; therefore, Jesus is accused of being the friend of tax collectors and sinners[58].

What place does Jesus in fact give to repentance in his proclamation and teaching? To answer, we must begin with the sense of repentance *in Judaism*. Because sin is understood as a turning away from God, repentance is the action of turning back from sin to God. Thus, repentance derives its meaning from the relation between God and his people.[59] It belongs to the sphere of covenant and Torah. Turning to the law comes to be identified with turning to God. The covenantal theme of repentance is the axis on which the book of Jeremiah turns. There is, on one hand, the lament that Israel has forsaken God for idols (Jer. 1:16; 2:13, 17, 19; 5:7, 19; etc.). On the other hand, there is the call to repent or turn to the Lord (Jer. 3:12-14, 19-22; 36:3, 7; etc.).

In postexilic Judaism, repentance has its content and meaning with reference to the law. Indeed, repentance is specified with reference to particular sins understood on the basis of individual commandments, as in the Testaments of the Twelve Patriarchs (T. Reu. 1:9; T. Jud. 15:4; T. Jos. 6:6). The Psalms of Solomon refer to God's chastening for the purpose of leading the righteous to repentance: "If I sin, discipline (me) that (I may) return" (16:11). The repentant righteous are those who walk in God's commandments (14:1-2). They are careful to avoid even the sin of ignorance (3:8). If they do sin, they repent and make atonement (3:7-8; 9:6-8).

Ben Sira identifies the law with the eternal wisdom of God "that Moses commanded" (Sirach 24:22-23). The exhortations to repentance are given in general terms: "Return to the Most High and turn away from iniquity, and hate intensely what he abhors." Yet what it means to "turn back to the Lord and forsake your sins" is clearly determined by the law (cf. 5:5-7; 17:24-26). In Jubilees, repentance is identified as turning away from "defilement" to "keep the commands of God Most High" (21:23). The author of the work looks forward to a time when "the children will begin to search the law, and to search the commandments, and to return to the way of righteousness" (23:26).

Repentance as return to the law also finds emphatic expression in the Qumran community. To become members of this community is to enter a "covenant of repentance" (Cairo Damascus Document: CD 19.16; or ms. B, 1.16). Accordingly, "every man who repents of his corrupted way . . . return(s) to the Law of Moses" (CD 15.5-7; 16.1-3). The Eighteen Benedictions also presented repentance as return to the law. "Cause us to return, O our Father, unto thy Law; draw us near, O our King, unto thy service and bring us back in perfect repentance unto thy presence. Blessed art thou, O Lord, who delightest in repentance."[60]

Repentance, then, has its meaning with reference to the law. The Lord is expected to be "gracious to those who turn in repentance to his law" (4 Ezra 7:63). In the Isaiah Targum, repentance is precisely defined as "return to the law." Bruce Chilton examines the view of repentance in this Targum.[61] It regularly and explicitly defines repentance as adherence to the law. The call of God in Isaiah (1:16-18) to "wash yourselves" was interpreted as a call to "return to the law." As a parallel to the prophet's statement, "My people do not understand" (1:3), the Targum has "my people have not considered repenting to my law" (cf. Targ. Isa. 17:11; 42:14; 57:19).[62] Corresponding to this emphasis on repentance is the emphatic declaration that God's action was responsive (cf. Targ. Isa. 8:18). This raises the question of how God might be expected to show his initiative in restoring his people.

Jesus, however, does not make his proclamation a refinement of the law (cf. Mark 1:21-22; Matt. 7:28). He spoke and acted with an authority distinctly his own. In taking the initiative of table fellowship with sinners, he breaks through the social form that defines identity within Judaism. Both his proclamation and his action thus leads us to anticipate that Jesus in some way goes beyond the standard call to repentance within Jewish law and ritual. But if there is a difference in the meaning of repentance, the difference is not simply a matter of contrast. What in Judaism and what in Jesus accounts for their collision? Since in Judaism the victory of God's righteousness appears to mean no more or less than the exaltation of the righteous and the putting to shame of the unrighteous in accord with the Torah, this leaves only one relevant word to sinners: Repent! One thing is quite clear: Jesus does something other than simply reiterate the standard call for repentance.

In Matthew, Jesus' proclamation is epitomized in one concise statement, "Repent, for the kingdom of heaven is at hand" (4:17, RSV). As in Mark, there is a sequence in which announcement and response are interdependent. In the immediate context, Jesus' proclamation is precisely identified as "the gospel of the kingdom" (4:23, RSV; cf. 24:14; 26:13). Matthew uses the same words to summarize the proclamation of Jesus and that of John the Baptist: "Repent, for the kingdom of heaven is at hand" (3:2, RSV). By itself this leaves the way open to the interpretation that they were the same in their proclamation: the proclamation of an imminent eschatological event.[63] It is true that both proclaimed the same coming event. Nevertheless, the differences between John and Jesus are important.

Let us compare John and Jesus. John is an ascetic (Mark 1:6; Matt. 11:18//Luke 7:33), and his mission is to serve as the precursor for the coming Lord (Matt. 3:3). John and his disciples fast, while Jesus and his disciples celebrate (Mark 2:18-20). Jesus is known as a "glutton and a drunkard" (Matt. 11:19), and his mission includes the extension of forgiveness to sinners (Mark 2:5-12; cf. Luke 4:16-21). John's call is essentially associated with ascetic, penitential practices. The call of Jesus is associated with fellowship, eating and drinking together in joy of God's gracious initiative. These differences are expressed in terms of how John and Jesus have different relationships to the event proclaimed by both of them (Mark 2:18-20): Jesus is already engaged in the ultimate event of which John is the precursor.[64]

Jesus' consciousness of participating already in the coming event finds explicit expression in his saying, "The law and the prophets were in effect until John came; since then the good news of the kingdom of God is proclaimed (Luke 16:16//Matt. 11:12-13). Again, the advance beyond John in the eschatological drama present in and through Jesus is highlighted by the note of fulfillment, particularly the emphasis that the "time is fulfilled" (Mark 1:15). The time of waiting for the kingdom is completed; the time of the kingdom has begun.[65] This coordination of Jesus' time with the time of fulfillment highlights the beginning of Jesus' proclamation in all three Synoptic accounts (Matt. 4:14-17a; Mark 1:14-15; Luke 4:19, 21).[66]

The emphasis on fulfillment in Jesus' proclamation distinguishes him from John. John announces the imminence of the eschaton; this is surpassed by the note of fulfillment that marks the proclamation of Jesus. Therefore, that proclamation is aptly described as "the good news of the kingdom" (Matt. 4:23; cf. Mark 1:14b, 15b). This correlates the herald of salvation—"Your God reigns"—with the restoration of Israel (Isa. 52:7). The appropriate response is a new orientation in the face of fulfillment. Repentance or conversion takes its character from this new situation.[67]

Accepters Versus Rejecters

Of the two sons called by the father to work in the vineyard, one refuses but then changes his mind and goes, while the other son says he will go but does not (Matt. 21:28-32). The parable turns on the change of thought and action. But repentance with reference to what? Interpreters have been inclined to think that the issue is hypocrisy, the discrepancy on the part of leaders of the community (21:23) between profession and practice, between word and deed.

Two possible understandings emerge: (1) The leaders' response was a verbal yes to Jesus and a repudiation of that yes in their conduct. But there is no indication that the opponents of Jesus agreed in word with Jesus. (2) Their response was a yes to God's commands as they understood them, but nonobservance in actual practice. This second understanding, however, is excluded on two counts:

First, there is clear evidence that the Pharisees do take practice seriously, in accord with their own understanding. And this, in part at least, is confirmed even by the criticism directed toward them (cf. Matt. 23:23-24).

Second, the parable makes clear that their nonobservance does not consist of failure in living up to the understanding of their obligation. Their nonperformance is set in contrast to the way sinners are accepting what Jesus initiates. They give their yes by word to God, but in being confronted by the eschatological fulfillment of God's will as initiated in Jesus, their response in fact becomes a no. Their yes really "amounted to a nonperformance of the will of God—not because they failed to perform that to which they had committed themselves, but because that to which they had committed themselves was not the will of God."[68] Specifically, Jesus exposes his critics' failure to discern and to follow up the eschatological call of John the Baptist, and he equates that with their refusal to repent (Matt. 21:31-32).

This provides a well-focused confirmation of the ascertainment reached above: Jesus' call for repentance gains its meaning with reference to the kingdom of God. It also raises a new question. Does Jesus accept that basic premise of Jewish moral judgment which distinguishes the righteous from the sinners? We may begin by asserting, first of all, that Jesus' mission is directed to all Israel. Jesus' preaching focuses on the kingdom of God (Mark 1:14-15), offered to all Israel. Henceforward repentance receives its meaning from proclamation of the kingdom (e.g., Mark 1:15; Matt. 21:21-32), which precedes and invites a new response. Second, Jesus' table fellowship with sinners converts God's gracious initiative into action. Often Jesus defends this initiative with parabolic teaching (Luke 15:1-32).

This policy of "defense of mercy" is an effort to win the "righteous" over to God's way. Yet Jesus also warns the righteous that their refusals are blocking their entry into the kingdom of God (e.g., Matt. 21:31). This is an extraordinary turnabout. The crucial division is no longer drawn with reference to law, "the righteous" versus "the sinners"; instead, it is drawn with reference to Jesus, accepters versus rejecters. Everything hinges on the response to Jesus.

Let us explore several facets of this new situation. First, the call of repentance is directed not only to the "sinners," meaning the lawless or wicked; it is directed to all without distinction. Yet Jesus does distinguish between the righteous and the sinners. This is apparent in his response to criticism of his association with sinners. "Those who are well have no need of a physician, but those who are sick. . . . I have come to call not the righteous but sinners" (Matt. 9:12-13//Luke 5:31). This distinction is the basis of the parable of the two sons (Matt. 21:28-32). From the righteous, informed by law and promise, a positive answer is expected. In reality it happens otherwise. The parabolic statements, therefore, also indicate the crisis of this righteousness. The concern of the righteous with traditional regulations is now revealed as a closed system in which the sense of God's mercy is stifled (e.g., Matt. 9:12-13; Mark 7:8-13). Jesus' word and action can not be appropriated within the limits of that system.

We glimpse a second facet of this new situation in seeking an explanation for Jesus' break with standard Judaism. The Gospels claim that his transcending of the system has its immediate source in his relation to God as Father (e.g., Matt. 11:25-27//Luke 10:21-22; cf. John 1:18; 3:34-35). Jesus bases his table fellowship with sinners on the need of sinners, the sick who need a physician (Mark 2:17//Matt. 9:12//Luke 5:31). Yet even more fundamentally and emphatically, he bases it on the goodness of God (Luke 15) and his "joy" over the converted sinner.[69]

A third facet of the new situation created by Jesus' prophetic career consists in a new view of the nearness of the kingdom. As the Baptist makes clear, the ordinary economy of Mosaic religion no longer suffices (cf. Matt. 3:7-10//Luke 3:7-9). All Israel is called to repent—righteous as well as sinners (Matt. 21:32). John requires repentance as readiness for the judgment; Jesus in his proclamation and action summons people to repent as a response to the kingdom of God. Jesus' proclamation of the kingdom takes its point of departure from the future rather than simply from the past. Thus, a new pattern of living comes into view: disconcerting, upsetting, unpredictable. Its foundation is the "repentance" that consists in the birth of trust in the good news which Jesus brings.[70] The proclaimer makes it possible for those who believe to participate proleptically in the kingdom.

A fourth facet immediately presents itself: one and the same act is both "repentance" and "faith." Repentance is associated with Jesus' proclamation (e.g., Matt. 4:17//Mark 1:15; Matt. 11:21-24//Luke 10:13-15; Matt. 12:38-42//Luke 11:29-32). It is likewise associated with the proclamation of the disciples sharing in the mission of Jesus (Mark 6:12).[71] Repentance is present in varied forms of teaching, such as parables, warnings, historical analogies, editorial summaries; this fact lends support to the authenticity of the teaching on repentance. Jesus specifically relates the gift of forgiveness to those coming in faith (Matt. 9:2//Mark 2:5//Luke 5:20). The authority to forgive sins is confirmed by the word that conveys healing (Mark 2:11).

The "mighty acts" of Jesus constitute part of his mission to Israel. In this way it is evident that he is the one who concretely brings God's help and salvation. Where this design is not recognized, the mission of Jesus is misinterpreted,[72] as in the response of the Nazarenes to Jesus (Mark 6:2-6). The people can and do accept the fact of Jesus' power to do mighty works. But they want him to do the kind of "irresistible" works that would spare them the challenge of a decision (cf. Mark 8:11-13).

The decisive issue is faith in Jesus as one empowered by God to heal and to save (e.g., Mark 5:36; 9:18-24; 10:46-52). In the case of the Gentile who comes to Jesus seeking his help for her daughter, the meaning of faith in relation to Jesus stands out. In her persistence, she expresses faith in God whose salvation is first for Israel but then also for the Gentiles. As the one-sent-to-Israel, Jesus acknowledges this faith (Mark 7:25-30//Matt. 15:22-28).[73] The woman responds with the faith that should come from Israel (cf. Matt. 15:28).

Thus Jesus looks to Israel for the response of faith in him as the one sent by God to restore the people of Israel. Forgiveness and healing are part of Jesus' eschatological mission to Israel.

This also means, therefore, that Jesus' mission to Israel is a summons to faith, and lack of faith represents a condition that keeps Jesus from doing his healing works (Matt. 13:58//Mark 6:5-6).[74]

Proper Response to Jesus' Initiative Toward Sinners

We have already suggested that the public action of Jesus which most calls for an appropriate religious response is Jesus' table fellowship with sinners. He is accused of being "a friend of tax collectors and sinners" (Matt. 11:19//Luke 7:34). Numerous Gospel texts register the impact this makes on contemporary Israel and the intense reactions it sets in motion (Mark 2:16-17//Matt. 9:11-13//Luke 5:30-32; Matt. 11:19; 20:1-16; 21:28-32; Luke 7:41-43; 15:1-32; 19:8).[75]

Dining together expresses a special bond; its violation represents rank betrayal (Ps. 41:9). Exclusion from table fellowship signifies the repudiation of social ties generally.[76] By means of table fellowship, the distinctions between clean and unclean and between good and evil find concrete social expression.[77] These distinctions define one's identity within Judaism. To contravene them challenges the social order. This is just what Jesus does. The act of initiating table fellowship with sinners is not an incidental development but the vivid translation of Jesus' proclamation into action. Jesus' table fellowship with sinners highlights God's free initiative. Thus it dramatizes the gracious character of the restoration of Israel as Jesus envisages it.

The parables of the lost sheep and the lost coin dramatize the real contours of the event of the conversion of sinners. One parable is taken from men's experience, the other from what is familiar to women. The recovery of the lost means joy on earth and in heaven (Luke 15:5, 9-10). Jesus' critics are thus invited to see the meaning of the event. It is a cause for rejoicing. They are themselves urged to share in that celebration.

This theme of communal rejoicing is particularly evident in the parable of the prodigal son. As Jeremias puts it: "His hearers were in the position of the elder son who had to decide whether he would accept his father's invitation. . . ." The father says to the elder son, "We had to celebrate and rejoice, because this brother of yours was dead and has come to life; he was lost and has been found" (Luke 15:32). In response, the hearers, the righteous people shocked by Jesus' policy, have to make their own decision. There is no doubt about what Jesus thinks is the appropriate response. It is a change of heart, a change of view, and a change of relation. The sour critic is being invited into joy.

Eschatological and Social Dimensions of Jesus' Ethics

Since the twentieth-century effort to retrieve the eschatological ethics of the historical Jesus has often failed for want of concreteness, can we specify exactly what has been missing and move to supply those missing elements?

In this quest, there is a lack of adequate concreteness in dealing with historical-Jesus questions and notably with those questions that most directly and immediately bear on his purposes and on the quite concrete terms in which he conceived them. This bedevils the work of even the most notable scholars. Bultmann, Manson, Jeremias, Kümmel, Schnackenburg, Schürmann, and others concur—whatever their disagreements in other areas—in overlooking or underestimating the interaction of aims and responses.

The common tendency of these writers is to exclude the prospect that Jesus might have taken fully into account negative responses to his proclamation on the part of individuals, groups, whole villages, and so forth. To be sure, all of them take notice of the prominent and varied Synoptic data on negative response to Jesus. Jeremias gathers together materials on Jesus' warnings against the lack of appropriate response.[78] Schürmann proposes that, as the situation of indifference in the face of approaching judgment grew more desperate, Jesus dispatched seventy disciples to launch a last appeal to every sector of the country.[79] Still, these scholars as well as the others listed above take Jesus' intention to be the winning of the allegiance of all Israel. Yet they do not ask how Jesus might have adjusted and achieved his purpose despite the failure of all Israel to respond positively to him.

This prospect, however, is fully conscious on the part of Jesus, as witnessed by the parable of the sower. Though much of the seed does not take root and grow, the harvest comes in its fullness! Jesus is acutely aware of the diversity of response to him.

He attends to those who reject his summons by urgently announcing, again and again, that they stand in dreadful danger. He attends to those who accept his summons by spelling out the new mode of life into which they are entering. Though he occasionally confronts his critics with specifics of his ethical teaching (e.g., Mark 10:1-12//Matt. 19:1-12), he generally reserves this teaching for his followers. In the end it could only be intelligible to them and could only be meant for them.

Jesus' discerning choice in relating to people meets the diversity of response to his call in the most realistic fashion. It does not signify the retraction or contraction of the summons to all Israel. But inattention to the realism of Jesus has confused the issue of "audience" for his ethical teaching. Contrary to Manson, Bultmann, and Perrin,[80] neither Jesus' proclamation nor his teaching is addressed to the isolated individual in Israel. Contrary to the suppositions of Oepke, Schnackenburg, and others,[81] Jesus' ethical teaching is not addressed to all Israel regardless of their response to Jesus' proclamation. His ethics is indeed an ethics for society, but the society in question is the Israel that is coming into being in and through positive responses to the eschatological call of God. Jesus' ethics is a pattern of discipleship for restored Israel.

A second concrete factor is the correlation of messianic ethics with Jesus' eschatological perspective. Irrelevant here are extremist views on the eschatology of Jesus, such as the wholly unrealized and exclusively futurist eschatology hypothesized by Schweitzer, and the wholly realized and nonfuturist eschatology proposed by Dodd in his writings of the 1930s. Most efforts to retrieve Jesus' eschatological perspective occupy the middle ground between these extremes, affirming two factors in tension: the "already" or realized factor and the "not yet" or future factor. Some (e.g., W. G. Kümmel) tend to overstress the "not yet,"[82] and others (e.g., T. W. Manson and John W. Bowman)[83] to overstress the "already."

The truly centrist position of Schnackenburg, Jeremias, Beasley-Murray, and many others defines itself by acknowledging the following: (1) The kingdom of God in the full sense of the term has yet to come. (2) The reign of God has nevertheless already become operative and effective in the career of Jesus. (3) The second is intrinsically based on and ordered to fulfill the promise of the first, and the first is possible only through the happening of the second.

Since the kingdom of God becomes effective in history through Jesus, this makes possible in the midst of history the anticipation of the kingdom of God. But this anticipation is not yet identical with the complete reign of God. Because Jesus in his mission and destiny represents the coming kingdom of God, the abstract alternatives of present and future are transcended. In his solidarity with sinners, Jesus brings forgiveness and thus reconciliation in new community.

In the same way, the ethics corresponding to the kingdom transcends the conventional pattern of life but has its place within the conditions of history. The coming of the kingdom signifies the resurrection of the dead and the judgment, and "when they rise from the dead, they neither marry nor are given in marriage, but are like angels in heaven" (Mark 12:25//Matt. 22:30//Luke 20:35). Yet there is also an essential unity between the kingdom and the response by which a person participates in it (cf. Luke 6:35-36). Life in the consummated kingdom, for instance, will not simply leave behind the action or attitude required by the love command. Therefore, the person who will participate ultimately in the kingdom will do so as one who has already reflected the life and power of the kingdom.[84]

The place of the ethics of Jesus is not the situation prior to John and Jesus, nor is it the situation of final consummation. It is the interim between the inauguration of Jesus' independent mission and the coming in fullness of the kingdom he proclaims. With respect to the past of historical Israel, this interim supposes the election, covenant, and law of Israel, and it is new and climactic. With respect to the future, it is a beginning founded on the proclamation of Jesus and ordered to, anticipating, and tending toward the longed-for consummation of time.

Jesus, then, prescribes an ethics for the life of a community living in expectation of the eschatological future. Indeed, the ethics is the anticipation in the life of the community of that eschatological future in the present. The ethics has its meaning only if this future is initiated and anticipated in the present. All Israel is summoned to constitute this community, but only the accepters of Jesus actually do so. His ethics corresponds to the structure of his eschatology; and it takes fully into account the opposition of rejecters. Let a parable make this twofold point:

The parable of the wheat and the weeds accents the presence of the kingdom beginning with Jesus (Matt. 13:24-30). This happens in the face of a reality regularly understood as a negation of the presence of the kingdom; the weeds signify the presence of evil. In this parable, as in other parables of growth, the sowing corresponds to the initiation of the saving reign of God in the word and deed of Jesus.[85] Sowing and harvest call attention to the present and the future of the kingdom of God.[86] Response does not take the form of waiting simply for the coming of a future event. Instead, positive response is participation in the kingdom of God beginning in the ministry of Jesus and to be revealed at the end in glory.

To understand the kingdom only as an end-of-the-world event is to miss completely the point of Jesus' teaching on the kingdom in this parable. For present along with the kingdom of God are also other powers: "An enemy has done this" (13:28). The kingdom becoming effective in the face of evil means that appropriate response has to be based on critical discernment. Jesus in his mission reckons with the power of evil. Appropriate response today will also reckon with the reality of evil. The statement on the opposition of evil is in accord with the saying that the kingdom of God is the object of violent attack (Matt. 11:12).

Jesus understands his work in terms of conflict with evil powers (cf. Matt. 12:28; 13:28). The parable spotlights this problem of evil, "weeds among the wheat" (13:25).[87] The question of the presence of evil becomes critical precisely with the understanding that the kingdom of God is already effective in the present. It is the ground of John the Baptist's question to Jesus: if Jesus is indeed the Coming One, then why is Herod allowed to carry on his evil work (11:2-3)? The purpose of the parable is to point to the fact that, along with the incursion of God's kingdom in Jesus' activity, an enemy opposing the work of God is also at work.

The Kingdom of God and the Proper Response 125

To this problem Jesus presents a distinctive solution: the Master commands, "Let both of them grow together until the harvest" (13:30). This approach is different from that offered by any of Jesus' contemporaries because it is based on a different understanding of the kingdom and of the time in which they stand. It presupposes that the gracious initiative of God is indeed operative in Jesus and that his mission is not to mediate the judgment of God but the redemptive powers of the kingdom. Hence Jesus appeals for the opposite of separation from sinners: he extends to them divine compassion and opportunity to participate in the kingdom.[88] Nevertheless, this is not the final stage. To participate in the kingdom is to anticipate the end of evil and the vindication of God's righteousness.

This response must reckon with the power of evil in the present. But there is a strong sense of assurance that supports response. As the kingdom of God has begun, despite the powers of evil, just so the end will bring the triumph of the kingdom. Response therefore corresponds to a reality begun. To participate in it is at the same time to anticipate the future fulfillment that is to come. The kingdom is enacted in the grace and patience of God. Conduct that corresponds to the kingdom, participates in this spirit of grace and patience to others. Such patience gives opportunity for the hitherto unresponsive to open themselves to the initiative of God. The parable calls for faith and patience in confronting evil: God has initiated his kingdom and will bring the problem of evil to full resolution in judgment at the end.

The basic structure of the proper response is clear. It gains its distinctive character from the reality of the kingdom. It is shaped by the fact that the kingdom "has come" (12:28) into effect in the ministry of Jesus in anticipation of the fullness of God's righteousness to be revealed at the end. The parables are designed to create the anticipation of the new; they aim to take people beyond the understandings and expectations of the past. The heart of parable is metaphor, and the purpose of metaphor is to challenge the hearer to a new apprehension of reality.[89] It is the nature of the parable to provoke active thought so that the listener may become a participant in the parable's sphere of meaning.[90] That is, the parable has one purpose: to lead people to actively participate in the "secrets of the kingdom" of God (13:11). Thus the parables open up new possibilities for appropriate response and set out the contours of the same.

We conclude with a brief outline of the kind of community that Jesus envisaged and sought to shape by his teaching. This community would be most fundamentally defined by its living in acknowledgment of the goodness and power of God revealed in Jesus and by living in anticipation of God's kingdom, coming ultimately in the fullness of glory.

A Community Intent on God

To think of the kingdom is necessarily to think of God and the righteousness by which he establishes his kingdom. This receives explicit emphasis in Jesus' teaching on the giving of alms, praying, and fasting (Matt. 6:1-6, 16-18).[91] The threefold teaching makes one basic point with great force: desires for human and divine acclaim are mutually exclusive. This is clearly important for the whole of conduct, as shown by the pronouns alternating between the plural and singular (Matt. 6:1-6, 17-18). The integrity of the community depends on the personal response of each disciple. Against the subtle and pervasive danger of hypocrisy, Jesus directs people to God. Even the most exalted activities may become elements in a system of "righteousness" springing from within the framework of human social approval or disapproval. This teaching is a call to repentance, integrity of action, and purpose intent on God (cf. Matt. 5:8).

Another teaching directly in support of this is the double love command, to love God and neighbor: this means the whole person in all of life is to be directed by love toward God (Matt. 22:37-40//Mark 12:29-34//Luke 10:27-28). Here is ethics within the response of love toward God, and it reveals the fulfillment of his eschatological purpose.

This orientation toward God is also exemplified in the question to Jesus about paying taxes to Caesar, the emperor (Matt. 22:15-22//Mark 12:13-17//Luke 20:20-26). Taking the coin with the image of the emperor on it, Jesus replies: "Give therefore to the emperor the things that are the emperor's, and to God the things that are God's." The question is about duty to the human ruler. But this cannot be determined apart from the question of what belongs to God. The proper response can only be discerned from the standpoint of life intent on God. Therefore, this community intent on God invokes the name of God in prayer with the recognition that God enacts the kingdom and is the source of all good things.

Servant of All

Jesus presents the coming new order in simple but sharp alternatives: "The last will be first, and the first will be last" (Matt. 20:16//Luke 13:30). The thrust of this saying can vary, depending on context. Within the proclamation of the kingdom, it is a challenge to the self-sufficient and to the proud. For the disciple thinking of position in the coming kingdom, it is a challenge to conversion, from the center to the circumference of life (Mark 9:35). The self-sufficiency of the righteous stifles response to Jesus, whereas the open receptivity of the simple people positively conditions it. Therefore, response to Jesus means to break from a confining self-preoccupation and to become "like children" (Matt. 18:3-4).[92]

The topic of last and first has its full meaning in anticipation of the judgment to come. Jesus therefore portrays the coming reversal in a similar saying: "All who exalt themselves will be humbled, and all who humble themselves will be exalted" (Matt. 23:12; Luke 14:11; 18:14). This has its ultimate significance with reference to the judgment, as is made clear by the divine passives pointing to God's action: "will be humbled/exalted." The precedent in Ezekiel 21:26 also correlates reversal with God's judgment.[93]

Accordingly, Jesus warns that in view of their respective responses, "sinners" were headed for participation in the kingdom and the "righteous" for exclusion (Matt. 21:31; Luke 14:24; 18:14). Thus, participation in the kingdom calls for a revolution in the standard of values. Jesus' words are in contrast to the conventional view of becoming "great" and identifying "first" with position, power, and privilege. He identifies becoming "great" or being "first" with the servant: "Whoever wants to be first must be last of all and servant of all" (Mark 9:35). Such teaching is itself creative of community in anticipation of the new order of the kingdom of God.

The Way of Liberation

Jesus' proclamation of the kingdom cannot remain abstract; it comes to be filled out in different ways. Certainly his acts accompany and serve to interpret this proclamation (cf. Luke 7:18-23//Matt. 11:3-6). But the central proclamation also finds expansion through the explication of promise in fulfillment.[94] In the synagogue at Nazareth, Jesus read from the Isaiah scroll and applied the words to his own ministry:

> He has anointed me to bring good news to the poor. He has sent me to proclaim release to the captives and recovery of sight to the blind, to let the oppressed go free, to proclaim the year of the Lord's favor. (Luke 4:18-19; cf. 4:43)

The allusion in this announcement from Isaiah 61:1-2 is to the year of Jubilee commanded in Leviticus 25. It illuminates Jesus' mission in word and deed to the poor. His proclamation directed to them is itself a mark of the eschatological good news, and they are no longer "invisible." The Jubilee was designed to provide release from indebtedness, the end of enslavement among the people, and less exploitation of the land. This year for Israel represents a time of concrete renewal (Jer. 34:8-17). Jesus does not simply reiterate the historical meaning of this institution; he announces the eschatological fulfillment in terms of this event. What it means is clear: a concrete reordering of community and economic life.

Elements from the Jubilee are central to the teaching of Jesus. He deals with the impoverishment of people through a system of debt and interest, and enslavement because of debt (cf. Matt. 5:42; 18:23-25). The Lord's Prayer refers to "debts" (6:12), and the primary meaning of "forgive" (*aphiēmi*) is the cancellation of debt and, by extension, of sin. (The related noun *aphesis* appears in the key text of Deut. 15:2, LXX.) The meaning of "debts" is so definite that the comment following the prayer makes clear that the word here also includes offenses in general (*paraptōma*, Matt. 6:14-15). Thus the prayer, in accord with the prophetic vision of the Jubilee, recognizes that the time has come to forgive all debts binding the poor of Israel; God's initiative has come and makes possible the time of renewal.

The identity of this community involves the issue of possessions. This community would be formed in the "leaving" of certain things and the "receiving" of other things (Mark 10:29-30). As a reconciling community, it is required to deal with the issue of rich and poor. Jesus recognizes the anxieties created by the sense of need and the awareness of dependence (Matt. 6:25-33). Yet he points out the alternative as worse: the anxieties and blindness generated by the pursuit of wealth (Matt. 6:19-24). The realignment of trust is related to liberation from the anxious attempt to find identity and dignity in the accumulation of possessions (Luke 12:15-21). Response to the kingdom calls people into a community of sharing (Mark 10:29-31). In the light of the coming kingdom of God, remission of debts, setting free the bound, and respect and care for the earth—these become the appropriate and possible response.

The End of Domination

Response to the kingdom meant a reordering of relationships within community. This is evident in Jesus' comment when some of his own family attempt to intervene in his ministry.

> They said to him, "Your mother and your brothers and sisters are outside, asking for you." And he replied, "Who are my mother and my brothers?" And looking at those who sat around him, he said, "Here are my mother and my brothers! Whoever does the will of God is my brother and sister and mother." (Mark 3:32-35)

Jesus identified himself with this family; indeed, he is the center of this new family. To those around him, he says: "Here are my mother and my brothers!" Who is included in this new family? Around Jesus at the time are not only the disciples but the "crowd" (Mark 3:32). Jesus himself sets forth the basic criterion: "Whoever does the will of God is my brother and sister and mother." In this setting, what does it mean "to do the will of God"? In the Jewish context, this normally means to fulfill the Torah. That cannot be the meaning here, for the members of Jesus' family are surely fulfilling the law, and yet they are clearly not included in this reference to God's will.[95] The will of God must refer to the eschatological purpose of God becoming effective in Jesus. Participation in the kingdom means the transformation of relationships.

This is further illuminated from another standpoint in Mark 10:29-30. The radical significance of Jesus' words comes to the fore in the contrast between what the disciples "left" and what they will "receive." On one hand Jesus relativizes all these ties and relationships. It is possible, and even necessary, to leave all this behind. But the horizon within which this becomes intelligible is the coming kingdom of God. How does renewed community correlate with relationships in that community? To those with him, Jesus promises that they will receive houses, brothers, sisters, mothers, children, and fields.

Fathers, however, are not included. Fathers are also left out of the first saying that identifies the renewed community as new family (Mark 3:31-35). In the new family there is apparently no place for "fathers." This means that patriarchal autocratic authority has no place in the renewed community. There is only one father in the community, God himself (Matt. 23:9).[96] In Matthew this saying is incorporated in a section against the scribes and Pharisees and their love for titles of honor and authority (i.e., "rabbi," "father," "instructor": 23:8-11). In the eschatological community, God is to be received as the Father in a new, more intimate sense (Matt. 6:8, 32; Mark 11:25; Luke 10:22-24; 12:32; cf. Rom. 8:15-16). Within the community of disciples, there are no longer any relations of domination (cf. Mark 10:42-43).

This model extends to the way persons are included with dignity in the community. It is characteristic of the mission of Jesus that he constantly establishes community precisely for those who for one reason or another were excluded. Jesus turns to the healthy and the sick, to the poor and the outcast. The coming of the kingdom means a break with convention in the way women are included.[97] Both men and women are included in Jesus' circle of disciples, and both are brought into the service of the coming kingdom of God (Luke 8:1-3; Mark 15:40-41).

Of the women who associate with Jesus, two who stand out are Mary and Martha (Luke 10:38-42; John 11:1-44; 12:1-8). Mary, in taking the place of a disciple, and Jesus in teaching her, challenge conventions about the place of first-century Jewish women. Jesus commends women (e.g., Mark 12:41-44) and defends women (e.g., Luke 7:39-40; Mark 14:3-9). His inclusion of women is attested by all the Gospel traditions. Jesus breaks down ethnic and sexual barriers in conversing with the Samaritan woman (John 4:7-27).

We also read of the increasing insight of Martha into the meaning of Jesus' mission (John 11:17-27) and the act of Mary in anointing Jesus. These persons are held up as authentic attestations to the mission of Jesus (John 12:3-8; Mark 14:6-9). Some of the women disciples are the first to be entrusted with the announcement of the resurrection (Matt. 28:5-10; Mark 14:6-8; Luke 24:4-12; John 20:11-18). The coming of the kingdom means the full inclusion of women, and this "will not be taken away from her" (Luke 10:42). In this fellowship men and women find their destiny in the kingdom of God.

A Community of Reconciliation

The community anticipated in and beyond Jesus' circle of disciples is more than an ideal. What makes for community and holds it together? If the kingdom becomes effective in Jesus' initiative toward sinners, this is a community of forgiveness.

The eschatological community is founded on the mercy of God and thus participates in his gift of forgiveness. This is recognized in the Lord's Prayer—"Forgive us our debts, as we also have forgiven our debtors"—and in Jesus' comment that follows the prayer (Matt. 6:12, 14-15). Forgiveness is a unity: to receive it is also to extend it. Forgiveness is a whole that includes God and the sister and brother. As Jesus says, "If you remember that your brother or sister has something against you," go and seek reconciliation (Matt. 5:23).

Jesus brings the commandment "You shall not murder" to its full eschatological measure by moving it to the level of personal intention: "If you are angry with a brother or sister, you will be liable to judgment; and if you insult a brother or sister, you will be liable to the council; and if you say, 'You fool,' you will be liable to the hell of fire" (Matt. 5:21-26). Jesus directs the most serious attention not to the act but to the inner attitude toward the other. Yet intention is not independently evaluated. The criterion for the evaluation of intention is the other person. Without being reconciled to the brother or sister, one cannot even worship God. Jesus presupposes the community of forgiveness. This teaching is expressive of the essential bond between love of God and love of neighbor.

Disciples are to allow nothing to stand in the way of reconciliation. In Luke 17:3 the focus of concern is simply a fellow disciple who sins. The motivation is not to meet the need of the offended to confront the offender, but rather to seek reconciliation and to meet the need of the guilty person for correction and forgiveness. Every community is compelled to deal with offense in some fashion. The eschatological community depends on Jesus' reconciling initiative toward sinners. It receives from him the command to "forgive" (Luke 17:4). The command "You shall not kill" (Matt. 5:21, RSV) finds eschatological completion, not on the basis of some concept of the absolute value of the person, but by relating it to the fellowship between person and person as the reflection of fellowship with God.[98]

The Community and the Ethic of Love

The twofold love commandment (Matt. 22:34-40//Mark 12:28-34//Luke 10:25-28) is handed down as a controversy saying in which Jesus sets forth his own summary of the law. The form it takes is limited by the issue to which it is a response: "Which commandment in the law is the greatest?" "Love God with your whole being, and your neighbor as yourself," Jesus replies (summarized; cf. Deut. 6:5; Lev. 19:18). Jesus reveals the indissoluble unity between love of God and neighbor. He thus emphasizes the profound accord between the religious and the ethical response. Proper response to the neighbor takes place within response to God.

In extending love, Jesus breaks through conventional patterns of reciprocity (Matt. 5:46; Luke 6:32). In the place of holiness, Jesus speaks of mercy as the paradigm for the eschatological community. Jesus makes mercy the content of the imitation of God. The meaning of mercy is epitomized in the statement immediately preceding the call to be like God: "He makes his sun rise on the evil and on the good, and sends rain on the righteous and on the unrighteous" (Matt. 5:45). Jesus calls the disciples to a correspondingly inclusive mercy. "The practice of mercy was not to be limited by the expectation of reciprocity: do good even to those who abuse you, lend without expectation of return."[99]

Out of the mercy paradigm flows a new stance toward the enemy. Holiness, as then understood, reinforces violent resistance (cf. 1 Macc. 2:23ff.); mercy calls for love of enemies and for blessing on the peacemakers. Three of the six examples Jesus gives in this connection involve the issue of enmity, violence, and vengeance (cf. Matt. 5:43-48). The concrete expression of love is revealed as the central concern of Jesus. So to love others is to do good to them, to pray for them, to bless them (Luke 6:27-28, 31-36). Disciples are called to be like God just at this point, not in his power, or his sinless character, but simply in the completeness of his love (Matt. 5:45//Luke 6:35).[100] Participation in this kind of love is integral to being children of God (Matt. 5:45; Luke 6:35).

Jesus accordingly envisages a community formed and informed by response to the kingdom of God. This, and not simply some directive, grounds the love of the neighbor and the enemy, because that is the way God is revealed in Jesus. This, and no dreamer's confidence in the natural goodness of people or refinement of society, enables the perseverance and confidence of the disciple.

Jesus provides an orientation that puts aside as trivial or irrelevant the quarrels and grudges that hitherto have dogged everyday life (Luke 12:57-59//Matt. 5:24-26; Matt. 5:39-42//Luke 6:29-30). Here is the basis for a society that in faith and repentance finds the resources through forgiveness to deal with offenses that might otherwise generate hatred and erupt in vengeance and murder (Matt. 5:22, 39-42//Luke 6:29-30). Jesus brings a community that abolishes the artificially created and shabbily treated depressed classes of the "little" (*mikroi, elachistoi*) and instead includes women (Mark 10:1-12//Matt.

19:1-12) and children (Matt. 10:42; Mark 9:42//Matt. 18:6; Matt. 19:10, 14).

The enabling condition of a community so dealing with its conflicts is allegiance to Jesus himself (Matt. 10:37-39//Luke 14:26-27) and to the God who—now above all, in the face of approaching judgment—shows himself to be "Father." Yet the piety of this community is to be secret, not ostentatious (Matt. 6:3-6, 17-18). This is a community that learns the great secret of reconciliation: forgiveness. A community that makes mutual forgiveness its watchword and, moreover, cherishes the ideal of forgiving even enemies—this indeed will be a beacon to the world (Matt. 5:14). A community shaped by these commands and prescriptions expressive of the kingdom of God will, like a city on a hill (Matt. 5:14), orient the traveler. Even more, it will be messianic Zion, drawing the whole world to itself.[101]

The empirical society that is the Israel of Jesus' time presents a viable but somewhat crass everyday world of injustice and widespread resentment, of dispute and litigation, of economic disorder routinely sanctioned by those in positions of wealth and power. This society is divided by the phenomenon of Jesus himself. Before the resolution of the looming eschatological "test" or "ordeal," the division over Jesus and his followers will disrupt families, setting a man against his father and daughter against mother (Matt. 10:35//Luke 12:53).

As his career carries Jesus forward to a confrontation with religious authority in Jerusalem, he clearly sees that the community formed and informed by him is headed for a future like his own. In accord with the prospect of his own destiny, he foresees hatred and persecution for them. These appear most emphatically in the esoteric instruction, but they are also directed to the larger circle of Jesus' following (e.g., Mark 8:34–9:1//Matt. 16:24-28//Luke 9:23-27). Nevertheless, this "little flock" (Luke 12:32) is not to fear, for God is preparing a future of splendor for them: in this remnant of Israel he will bring to fulfillment the restoration promised in the prophets.

4

Jesus' Messianic Mission

We have established that the purpose of Jesus is the eschatological restoration of Israel, and with that the salvation of people from the nations. How, then, is his mission and his destiny related to that purpose? The proclamation and the activity of Jesus creates certain definite expectations (e.g., Matt. 20:20-24//Mark 10:35-41; John 6:15). But this proclamation and this activity of Jesus does not yet reveal the inner connection between purpose and destiny. The course of his destiny as he envisages it remains in important respects a puzzle even to his disciples. At this point the esoteric teaching takes up its pivotal place. By means of this teaching Jesus invites his disciples to grasp his words and acts as a whole and, in particular, the deep and far-ranging significance that he attaches to his personal destiny.

Each of the synoptic Gospels has its own distinctive structure, but all three present Jesus' word on his destiny at the beginning of a distinct and final phase in his teaching and in his career. The event that opens this final stage is at Caesarea Philippi: Simon Peter's confession of Jesus as "the Messiah." The confession has as its own proper follow-up the word on Jesus' destiny; this in turn is closely related to the call to discipleship (Matt. 16:13-28//Mark 8:27-38//Luke 9:18-27).

This complex of messiahship, destiny, and discipleship suggests a definite strategy of inquiry. It calls first for an examination of the distinction between Jesus' public proclamation and teaching on one hand, and his more intimate teaching within the circle of his disciples on the other hand. Both the purpose and the authenticity of the esoteric teaching are at issue in the modern study of the Gospels. Second, if Jesus himself makes the disciples' acknowledgment of his messiahship a condition of the esoteric teaching that follows, what is the rationale of this strategy? Third, there is the critical issue of the relation between the good news of the kingdom of God and—at the heart of the esoteric teaching—the suffering and expiatory death of Jesus.

The public teaching concentrates on the kingdom of God, the esoteric teaching on the destiny of Jesus. The public teaching presents the gracious forgiveness of sin to all who turn to God, the esoteric teaching presents Jesus' death of atonement for sin. How shall we account for this difference? Is there a contradiction in meaning between the kingdom-of-God proclamation and the teaching on the destiny of Jesus? Or is there an intelligible coherence between them? And finally, if "kingdom of God" is now taken up and defined anew in Jesus' destiny, what does this mean for discipleship, for the ethical dimension of response?

Authenticity and Purpose of Jesus' Esoteric Teaching

We have noted that Jesus offered his disciples private explication of public teaching from the beginning of his ministry (e.g., Mark 4:10-20, 34; 7:17-23). Nevertheless, according to all four Gospels, there is a particular context for the core of Jesus' esoteric teaching. This is the explication of messiahship as issuing in repudiation, suffering, death, and resurrection (Mark 8:27-33; Matt. 16:13-23; Luke 9:18-22; John 6:61-65; 12:23-24; 14:1-7). The aim in this section is to deal with the setting for the esoteric traditions (Gospel texts depicting Jesus alone or Jesus alone with the disciples) and with Jesus' esoteric teaching, reserved for his disciples.

In the field of Gospel study and the effort to give account of Jesus' teaching as a whole, one regularly meets with a void, a failure to distinguish between the public and esoteric teaching of Jesus. What accounts for the oversight or the rejection of the idea that Jesus made a distinction between public teaching and esoteric teaching?

First, concentration on Jesus as teacher, apart from the context of his life and death, will itself inevitably result in generalizing the teaching. Apart from the context of his mission and destiny, the teaching will be presented within the framework of some formula or concept: the assumption is that, to be consistent, Jesus must have the same message in much the same terms for everyone.[1]

Second, if the difference between Jesus' public teaching and the esoteric teaching is converted into a lack of coherence between the two forms of teaching, this inevitably leads to a discounting of one or the other.

Third, Jesus' more intimate teaching to the disciples as we have it in the Gospels is regularly ascribed to the post-Easter community. The guiding assumption for this move is that Jesus' self-understanding was nonmessianic, that the messianic view in the Gospels' portrait of Jesus was derived from the post-Easter faith of the church, and that the Gospels were cast to reflect this faith (this will be examined in the next section).[2] If the key elements of the esoteric teaching are transposed into the context of the Christian community, this eliminates it as a category in Jesus' teaching. Although form critics expend effort to locate the various elements of Gospel tradition in terms of occasion and function in the life of the church (*Sitz im Leben*), this does not necessarily entail the denial that Jesus is the ultimate source for these traditions. Therefore, the elements of esoteric tradition are properly judged in the light of their coherence with what we know of the life and destiny of Jesus.

But what in Jesus' life and destiny supplies the rationale for the esoteric teaching? The public activity of Jesus involved proclamation, teaching, healing, and reconciling of notorious sinners. This inevitably prompted the question, "Who then is this?" (e.g., Mark 2:7-12; 4:41//Luke 8:25). What place does this man have, or claim to have, in the scripturally attested eschatological purpose of God (Mark 8:27-29)? The synoptic Gospels represent Jesus as offering these disciples private explanation of public teaching at key moments in his ministry.

On one hand, the Gospels furnish abundant evidence that Jesus had a clear awareness of the kinds and degrees of responsiveness to him on the part of his hearers (e.g., Mark 8:18; Matt. 13:15-16//Luke 10:23-24). A striking example of this occurs in the saying which the Synoptic redactions connected with Jesus' use of parables (Mark 4:11-12//Matt. 13:11-13//Luke 9:10). Here the tradition differentiates between "you" (the twelve disciples and those about him with the twelve) and those outside (*hoi exō*: Mark 4:11). Essentially, the distinction is between two groups: those around Jesus who receive "the secret of the kingdom of God" and "those outside" to whom everything is enigma, or who, at any rate, do not get any further than the parables (4:11).[3]

To "you," the first group of hearers, Jesus both speaks and explains his parables. This accords with their understanding "the secret of the reign of God."[4] If the intention of Jesus is to reveal fully the secret of the kingdom of God, the esoteric teaching serves this intention. Ultimately, meaning is related to response. The proper response to this full revelation is a total and totally positive response. The raison d'être of the esoteric teaching is precisely this response.

Furthermore, Jesus' choosing of the twelve disciples itself is a condition that provides strong warrant for the expectation of an esoteric teaching. To choose these men to be "with him" puts them in a special position to learn from Jesus (cf. Mark 3:13-19). The fact that they are sent out to participate in Jesus' own mission to preach, heal, and teach presupposes that Jesus will seek to lead them into the fullest possible measure of understanding of that mission, given their readiness and the stage of his ministry.[5] The twelve disciples have a special place in Jesus' purpose; and inclusive of this purpose is mission that relates disciples to the crowd (*ochlos*). In the Gospels this "crowd" refers, for the most part, to people who are much more than an amorphous group of bystanders. The disciples receive the special training and preparation in order to extend this mission to the crowd (Matt. 9:35–10:16).

This "crowd" (*ochlos*) itself has a very significant role in the events of the Gospels. Of course, the word can also be used to refer to a hostile company (e.g., Mark 15:11, 15), and on occasion to a group of casual onlookers (Mark 5:24, 27, 30-31; 12:41). But in the majority of cases, these "crowds" demonstrate strong interest and even a measure of commitment to Jesus.[6] They are often described as following him (Matt. 4:25; 8:1; 12:15; 14:13; Mark 2:13; 3:8-9; 4:1; 5:21; 6:34-45; 7:14, 17, 33; 8:1-2; 10:1-2, 46). They recognize Jesus' authority and hear his teaching (Matt. 7:28; 8:18-22; 9:8, 33; 15:31; Mark 2:12; 3:32-34; 4:1; 7:14; 10:1; 11:18, 32; 12:12, 37). They glorify God for the redemption of Israel (Matt. 9:8; Matt. 15:31//Mark 7:37). They accept Jesus as a prophet (Matt. 21:11, 26, 46). They hail him as Son of David (Matt. 12:23; Matt. 21:9//Mark 11:9). The rulers fear this crowd (Mark 11:18, 32; 12:12), because of their numbers, certainly, but also because of the measure of acceptance they are giving to Jesus' teaching (Mark 11:18, 32; 12:35-37).

The significance of this "crowd" should not be overlooked. These people are attached to Jesus and ready to hear him as the authorized proclaimer of God's kingdom. The crowd's measure of acceptance of Jesus is clearly an important factor in making intelligible the hostile response of these leaders to Jesus. For our purposes, if we define the character of the crowd, this helps to make sense of Jesus' call, teaching, and sending out of the disciples.[7] The disciples and the crowd often stand in close relation as hearers of Jesus' teaching (e.g., Mark 4:1-2, 10; 8:34).

Interpretation has always taken some account of "audience" in Jesus' teaching, but the scholar who first clearly relates diversity in Jesus' teaching and vocabulary to diverse audiences is T. W. Manson. In "matter and method the teaching of Jesus is conditioned by the nature of the audience."[8] He identifies three different groups of hearers to be distinguished in Jesus' teaching: the opponents (e.g., scribes and Pharisees), the disciples, and the general public. The most important result is the differentiation that points to and makes intelligible an esoteric tradition in the synoptic Gospels. This esoteric tradition has as its main themes the identity and destiny of Jesus and the events of the eschatological crisis and its resolution.[9]

Others, such as Paul Minear, build on the work of Manson and further refine the process of audience criticism. In this investigation, a primary concern is the context of Jesus' sayings. Once the assumption is made in form criticism that much of the material is created for "typical situations" as a function of some need in the church, the context for sayings of Jesus is generally assumed to be secondary, or simply editorial. Yet, it is one thing to recognize that sayings or events are sometimes included with little or no reference to context and therefore receive their placement within the account as determined by the author (e.g., Mark 1:40-45; 2:23-28). It is another thing to say that the context is in general a midrashic creation out of nothing.

At this point form criticism is simply inadequate. To start with, it fails to account for the inherent relation of setting, action, and speech within the Gospel narratives (e.g., a saying depends on an action to make the point: Mark 2:5-12; 9:35-37; 14:22-24). At issue is the formation and character of the Gospel records. As a whole the question is not yet settled, but certain points are clarified and established. A basic point of form criticism appears valid: the early followers of Jesus emphasize and retain traditions as they serve the needs of life and faith. But this does not set the early church in contrast with Jesus, as if Jesus simply becomes a subject of church formation. There is a crucial distinction between events as the originating cause for a tradition and the conditions in which a tradition is enacted and passed on. The church from the beginning holds itself accountable to Jesus. Indeed, one of the concerns inherent in the faith and life of the church is just this: to remember faithfully certain things about and from Jesus (e.g., Matt. 23:8-10).

Clearly the Gospel authors do not separate interest in who Jesus was from who he now is as the risen Lord. Yet they are required to refer to Jesus' past history to understand at all why and how he came to be crucified and in order for them to comprehend the significance of his resurrection. This presupposes a strong continuity in the relation of his followers to Jesus before his cross and resurrection and their relation to him after these events. The fact is that the study of the Gospels is compelled to confront an abundance of pre-Easter traditions remembered and taken up in them.[10] What we have in the Gospels, in accord with ancient biographical writing, is a portrayal of Jesus by the indirect method of allowing the words and actions of Jesus to speak for themselves.[11]

Accordingly, it appears that the synoptic Gospels are not intended to be a direct full-scale proclamation of the Christian gospel. Instead, they are to provide explanation and to support the proclamation of the full gospel culminating in the death and resurrection of Jesus. The Gospel accounts, then, are not to be understood simply as "Easter interpretations" of the gospel. This is evidenced for Mark (1:1, RSV) by the abrupt way in which he sets out "the beginning of the gospel" as the fulfillment of prophecy, and by his concentration on the death of Jesus, concluding abruptly with the resurrection.

Also, there is the further fact that within the body of the Gospel of Mark the reference is to "Jesus" and not to the "Lord." The writer apparently assumes that his readers know something, that they have heard the basic proclamation about Jesus. In the case of Luke, this difference in Christology is concretely attested in a comparison of Luke 1—23 with Luke 24 and Acts, where Jesus is proclaimed as Christ and acknowledged as Lord after the resurrection.[12] What is true of Luke at this point holds in general for the Synoptics: the early church in the post-Easter period boldly proclaims Jesus as Christ and Lord. But the synoptic Gospel traditions portray Jesus as one who carries out his mission of teaching and healing, and they let that speak for him without regularly making direct claims.

We see the church responding to various situations, but substantial narrative traditions are not fabricated in making response. The main principle of form criticism is that the forms making up the Gospels correspond to and arise out of typical activities or needs of the church; this principle fails. It fails to account for the Gospels as they are, and more particularly it fails in its own terms. The Gospels are aimed to present concrete narratives about Jesus. But if we turn to the other writings of the New Testament, we can say with equal certainty that the contrary holds: their aim is clearly not to present concrete narrative traditions about Jesus. Outside the Gospels we do not find substantial narrative traditions about Jesus; inside the Gospels we have complete texts, not just essential points.[13]

As Sanders observes, in combination these two points serve to undermine the basic form-critical position that much of the Gospel material had its origin in "typical situations" in response to diverse needs in the church. What we have on one hand is ethical instruction without narrative about Jesus, as in James. On the other hand, we have in the Gospels much narrative about Jesus which serves the purpose of ethical instruction (especially in Matthew), but no evidence that the need for ethical instruction led to the creation of narrative about Jesus.[14] For activities such as exhortation and apologetic, the church develops primarily points and does not necessarily need the reading of complete narratives.[15]

This assessment breaks through in certain essential respects the view developed in form criticism on the origin of the Gospel material. Particularly, it means that audience identification in a narrative is information present for serious consideration as part of the narrative. The work of Minear reveals that there is a large measure of agreement in the Gospels with respect to audience identification within the framework of Jesus' teaching.[16]

This tradition of audience identification does not stand by itself. Often the content gives a clear indication about the audience to whom a particular saying or teaching is addressed. From the content it is evident, for example, that controversies are carried on with opponents and that the instructions for messengers are given to the disciples.[17] Indeed, the distinction between public teaching and private explanation is intrinsic to certain teachings. Jesus' teaching about clean and unclean in Mark 7 reflects this in corresponding to an early rabbinic pattern of teaching. This is a pattern that involves (1) a question put by an outsider, (2) a reply sufficient for him but not revealing the deeper truth, (3) the request of the disciples, and (4) the full explanation to the circle of disciples.[18]

Similarly, Jesus' question designed to highlight and to identify for the disciples the meaning of his own mission is first appropriately asked in the circle of the disciples (Mark 8:27-30). Jesus now engages in a full-fledged interchange with his disciples. Jesus' questions invite reflection with the intent of more complete understanding (Mark 8:27, 29; 9:11; 10:38). More important, to link messianic mission with repudiation, suffering, and death involves a revolution in popular Jewish thought. This change is so great that Jesus can meaningfully and properly disclose it only to those with a large measure of loyalty and understanding—the disciples (cf. Mark 9:31). Thus the esoteric teaching is decisively conditioned by Jesus' anticipation and disclosure of messianic destiny in suffering rejection and death, and the anticipation of vindication from God (e.g., Mark 8:30-31; 10:38-39//Luke 12:49-50). But this is already to speak of the matter at the heart of the esoteric teaching: the messiahship and mission of Jesus.

The Content of the Esoteric Teaching

We cannot expect to understand the esoteric teaching without examining what is explicitly presupposed in this teaching, namely, the recognition and acknowledgment of Jesus as the Messiah.

Since the appearance of William Wrede's work on the messianic secret in 1901, the hypothesis that messiahship was first attributed to Jesus only after his death has had a wide following.[19] Certain data respecting the death of Jesus, however, seem to call for the articulation of messiahship at the time of Jesus' trial. These make explicit what was implicit at certain points earlier (e.g., Mark 2:19-20, 25-28; 3:22-27; etc.). These data include, first, the messianic connotations of the riddle on the destruction of the sanctuary and the building of a new temple in three days (Mark 14:58//Matt. 26:61; John 2:19; cf. Mark 15:29//Matt. 27:40; cf. Acts 6:14). The building of the sanctuary was a kingly prerogative and, as a Qumran text (Florilegium: 4QFlor 1-13) suggests, a messianic prerogative.[20]

There are other crucial data which support messiahship: the symbolic entry into Jerusalem and cleansing of the temple;[21] the symbolic mockeries in the passion story, such as with the purple cloak and crown of thorns; and, above all, the inscription on the cross, "The King of the Jews." Thus, N. A. Dahl urges that Jesus must have been accused of pretension to messiahship to explain the details of his suffering and death.[22]

More recently, several scholars are opening up a new position favorable to the attribution of messiahship to Jesus during his public career: Marinus de Jonge has his own set of reasons relating to Mark 1—8,[23] and R. A. Horsley and J. S. Hanson establish their position largely on the basis of distinct data related to the messianic issue in Josephus.[24] This view is already being urged by many scholars. Many aspects of the esoteric teaching of Jesus are intelligible without resolving the issue of Jesus' messiahship or messianic consciousness. Yet Dahl, Hengel, de Jonge, and others underscore the convergence of probabilities that point toward a positive resolution of the issue. Therefore, I shall proceed on the basis of the view that Jesus, in fact, understood himself to be the messianic Son of God (2 Sam. 7:14 in the light of 4QFlor 1-13; Ps. 2:7; 89:27; 110:3; cf. Mark 14:61-62a//Matt. 26:63-64a; Luke 22:70-71).

Peter's Confession at Caesarea Philippi

To elucidate the relations between Jesus' messiahship and his mission, we will examine several texts in the esoteric teaching. Notable among these are Peter's messianic confession (Matt. 16:16-20//Mark 8:27-30//Luke 9:18-21) and the following tie between messiahship and a destiny of repudiation and violent death (Matt. 16:21-23//Mark 8:31-33//Luke 9:22).

Crucial to the whole pericope is the initiative of Jesus in putting the opening question: "Who do people say that I am?" (Mark 8:27). The significance of this question is to relate Jesus in a specific way to Israel's history of promise and fulfillment. Jesus' question is asked in pursuit of one crucial point: an answer to the question of the sense and significance of Jesus' work. "Identification by reference to Israel's eschatology was meant to illuminate the final meaning of words and actions already interpreted as signs of the eschaton."[25] Thus in putting his question to the disciples, Jesus is at the same time raising a question about his eschatological mission: "Who do you say that I am?" (8:29). The answer will supply the key to his purpose: the messianic task of building the house of God (2 Sam. 7:13-14; 1 Chron. 17:12-13; Hag. 1:1-2; 2:20-23; Zech. 6:12-13; cf. Mark 14:58//Matt. 26:61; cf. Acts 7:46-50; 15:15-16).

To build the house of God was, in effect, to bring about the restoration of Israel. Messiahship, in other words, merely makes explicit what we have already taken to be the purpose of Jesus. Yet to link "Messiah" and the "temple made without hands," and to link "Messiah" and destiny in death—this was to go much beyond the popular messianism of the time.

A study of the rise of popular messianic movements before and after the time of Jesus has confirmed the plausibility of a statement like that in John 6:15, in which the Galilean crowd determines "to make him king."[26] Indeed, in that period groups of Jewish peasants informed by popular memory of distant ancestors like David and other anointed figures, would form around leaders and acclaim them king. Their aim was to gain independence and the reestablishment of a just order in society.[27] Still more significant is the reflection of Marinus de Jonge on the use of "anointed" in contemporary Jewish sources, and its relation to the acts leading up to Caesarea Philippi and the confession of Peter.[28]

The first and foundational element to be ranged under the heading "the content of the esoteric teaching" is the role of Jesus as long-awaited Messiah. We call this not only first but foundational because—to use the language of Bonhoeffer—Jesus the Messiah is the "form" on the basis of which the "formation" of the disciples will proceed.

> Whenever [the Scriptures] speak of forming they are concerned only with the one form which has overcome the world, the form of Jesus Christ. Formation can only come from this form.[29]

Bonhoeffer's view exactly reflects the esoteric teaching of Jesus. It was the revelation of Jesus' messianic destiny that

> the Son of Man must undergo great suffering, and be rejected by the elders, the chief priests, and the scribes, and be killed. . . . (Mark 8:31; cf. Matt. 16:21//Luke 9:22)

This disclosure gives shape to the final and most distinctive teaching of Jesus. Messiahship is a destiny; fulfillment of that destiny will be death and resurrection. Thus the confession of Jesus as the Christ (Mark 8:27-30) is followed by the prediction of destiny (Mark 8:31-33). As distinct but related texts, they make the connection between Jesus' destiny and the coming kingdom of God. Messiahship as the theme of the first text is the basis for the second text's explication of messiahship as a destiny accomplished in suffering. The prediction of destiny serves as esoteric instruction on the meaning of messiahship.[30]

Since destiny is rooted in mission, can the relation be more closely identified? Jesus' answer to the sons of Zebedee in their request for positions of honor next to him, confirms the relation between messiahship and destiny. In doing so it points more directly to the meaning of his suffering. In a vision of the future, he anticipates his suffering (Matt. 23:29-39). By means of the double metaphor, Jesus sets out the destiny awaiting him: his death is the "cup" he must drink and the "baptism" he must endure (Mark 10:35-40//Matt. 20:20-23). In Luke 12:49-50 Jesus envisions his mission as initiation of judgment (to "kindle fire") and as suffering judgment (to endure a "baptism").[31] All these images make one point: Jesus' suffering is bound up with his destiny. These scriptural images have a long history in depicting the judgment of God or the infliction of suffering (e.g., Ps. 18:4; 32:6; 42:7; 66:12; Isa. 30:27-28; Mark 9:43-49).

Jesus, however, does not simply proclaim judgment against Israel: he identifies himself with Israel. Furthermore, he welcomes sinners, heals the afflicted, and goes to those on the margins of Israel. Therefore, more pointedly, Jesus identifies with sinful Israel. The two sets of sayings cohere as they envision Jesus enduring suffering: Jesus is the one who will drink the "cup" and endure the "baptism."

In addition, the parallelism in the second half of the two statements in Luke 12:49-50 indicates that Jesus is himself to be involved in the fire and the flood of water and that Jesus is thinking of suffering as achievement:

> I came to bring fire to the earth, and how I wish it were *already kindled!* I have a baptism with which to be baptized, and what stress I am under until it is *completed!* (italics added)

Jesus desires not simply that it be over but that its end be accomplished. It is enough to recognize at this point that Jesus envisages suffering in identification with sinful Israel and integrates it into his mission in relation to the kingdom of God.

Many scholars have attempted to relate the kingdom of God

and the destiny of Jesus. According to Schweitzer, Jesus believes, on the basis of Jewish apocalyptic, that the ordeal of the end-time must precede the coming of the kingdom of God. Jesus accordingly determines to bear the weight of the ordeal himself, and thus usher in the kingdom of God. "He must suffer for others . . . that the kingdom might come."[32] Dodd, who finds the view of Schweitzer unacceptable, offers an alternative: the proclamation of Jesus is an announcement of the presence of the kingdom and the works of Christ are, in effect, this presence itself. It follows that the death and resurrection of Jesus falls within the kingdom, representing God's ultimate triumph over all opposing powers.

Bultmann is simply negative on the relation between kingdom of God and Jesus' destiny, and he has been influential on this point. He finds no evidence in the Gospel texts of Jesus' death as the fulfillment of his work. One of his last contributions states his view concisely: "This execution can hardly be understood as the necessary consequence of his work. . . . Whether or how Jesus found a meaning in it we cannot know."[33]

More recently, the question of the relation between Jesus' eschatological proclamation and his destiny finds clear focus in the debate between Anton Vögtle and Rudolf Pesch. For some years Pesch has been dealing with Jesus' understanding of his death. Vögtle, emphasizing Jesus' public proclamation of the kingdom of God, has always questioned the coherence between the good news of the kingdom of God and the teaching on Jesus' destiny.[34] In general, Vögtle's argument is that Jesus proclaims the good news of forgiveness or salvation in the kingdom of God for all who repent. If the atoning death of the Messiah were the basis on which God would bestow these gracious gifts, this would necessarily be a key feature of the proclamation. Further, if Jesus began to hold the concept at some point in his ministry, he would have modified his message to incorporate this important change. But, Vögtle argues, there is no indication of any such modification of his teaching.[35]

This argument has been taken up and refined by Vögtle's student Peter Fiedler. He finds it impossible to accept the idea that Jesus, after preaching the triumphant love of God and his sovereign will to forgive, would in the face of his death come to the conviction that God wills his death as expiatory sacrifice. According to Fiedler, the clear implication would be that God was not so generous or so sovereign in his grace as Jesus had earlier taught, that now God required an atonement. Thus Jesus' proclamation of the kingdom of God and his atoning death are held to be incompatible.

More illuminating is the response of Pesch in seeking to understand Jesus' death of atonement and God's unconditional mercy expressed in the proclamation of the kingdom of God. He begins with John the Baptist and with Jesus' new proclamation, following the Baptist's arrest, of the good news of salvation even for notorious sinners. Jesus' offer is free, but this free gift calls for response; it is not merely optional for Israel. On the contrary, the gracious proclamation is simultaneously a radical demand. On it hinges the status of Israel. A key question must be in Jesus' awareness: what would be the result, should Israel reject him as the representative of God's eschatological salvation? The good news risks turning into condemnation. Is the mediator of eschatological salvation to become, in effect, the mediator of eschatological ruin for Israel?[36]

Pesch sees Jesus' understanding of this conflict epitomized in the parable of the wicked tenants (Mark 12:1-9). What is to be the fate of those who reject the last messenger of God? What can be done for the refuser in this situation of refusal? Pesch locates the resolution of this issue in the perseverance of Jesus in his ministry as a saving mission into death itself, intending his death as expiatory for Israel.[37]

Thus, far from competing with the good news of the kingdom of God, this intention of perseverance unto death maintains that good news against the grave consequences otherwise entailed by Israel's refusal. Conceived biblically, expiation is not a "demand" incompatible with "grace"; it is pure grace. Jesus' kingdom-of-God proclamation and the meaning of his death are not only compatible but interdependent. Moreover, the intention of Jesus respecting his death generates a new consequence of its own: the institution of the new covenant.[38]

Pesch quite clearly has the better of the argument with Vögtle on the major issue of whether Jesus' death of atonement is incompatible with his kingdom-of-God proclamation. Vögtle's reconstructs the conditions that he thinks would have had to obtain if Jesus' esoteric instruction on his death were historical. But Vögtle's reconstruction has an almost fanciful character: For example, it overlooks the inherent reason for the distinction between the public and the esoteric teaching of Jesus. Thus also it ignores the fact that Jesus not only proclaims the kingdom at the beginning but also at the end, relating his death to it (Mark 14:25, 61-62).

On the other hand, Pesch's argument has a concreteness of observation that is convincing. This is a swift review of the much-debated question of how the esoteric teaching of Jesus on his destined death relates to his public proclamation of the kingdom. My purpose is to make intelligible the stand taken here on (1) the historicity of the esoteric teaching, (2) its radical coherence with Jesus' proclamation, and (3) its importance in the whole universe of Jesus' ethical teaching.

Messiahship and the Ethics of Discipleship

If the kingdom of God is set into effect and defined through the repudiation, suffering, and death of Jesus, this in turn shapes the appropriate response of the disciple. The meaning of discipleship is thus correlated with the way in which Jesus fulfills his destiny. This relationship between Jesus' destiny and the meaning of discipleship finds repeated expression in esoteric instruction given to the disciples (e.g., Mark 8:34-38//Matt. 16:24-27//Luke 9:23-26; Mark 9:30-32; Matt. 17:22-23//Luke 9:43-45; Mark 10:32-34//Matt. 20:17-19//Luke 18:31-34; Mark 10:35-45//Matt. 20:20-28; cf. Luke 22:24-27; John 12:23-26).

Consequently, what follows the explication of messiahship almost amounts to a new call to discipleship: "If any want to become my followers, let them deny themselves and take up their cross and follow me" (Mark 8:34//Matt. 16:24//Luke 9:23). In the disciples' incomplete understanding, association with the Messiah means glory (cf. Mark 10:35-44); for Jesus, messiahship means suffering.[39]

Jesus' call to discipleship is made under the sign of the kingdom already coming into effect through Jesus. Therefore, disciples are called to relation with Jesus himself. To "follow" Jesus is to be willing to suffer with him. How difficult it is to understand this! We hear the uncomprehending response of Peter, who speaks for the disciples: "This must never happen" (Matt. 16:22//Mark 8:32). Therefore, at this juncture especially, the disciples are challenged to reorder their whole scheme of values—their perception and trust and hope. Discipleship is to be understood only in relation to Jesus and his destiny.

What then does it concretely mean to "follow" (*akolouthein*) Jesus? Is it to "imitate him"? To join with him and do as he does, to participate in his ministry (cf. Mark 3:14-15)? Surely there is some connection between following, imitation, and discipleship; but the scope of "following" is not immediately obvious. Martin Hengel[40] and Hans-Dieter Betz[41] attempt to clarify the matter in ways that are flatly incompatible. At this point, Betz refers to the pagan mystery religions for models because he assumes that this word of Jesus is not historical (Mark 8:34//Matt. 16:24//Luke 9:23). My own effort to understand the call to "follow" Jesus is more closely aligned with Hengel.

The two notions of "following" and "imitation" are reciprocally defining. We may begin with a simple recognition. "Following" is in the Gospels most often correlated with discipleship (e.g., Matt. 8:19//Luke 9:57; Matt. 8:21-22//Luke 9:59-60; Matt. 10:38//Luke 9:61; Mark 1:18; 2:14; 6:1; 10:28, 32).[42] To be a disciple is to follow and to become like Jesus, who carries out his mission, and thus the Father's will, in the face of opposition. This culminates in suffering and death oriented toward vindication (as yet unseen). Since Jesus represents a "new eschatological teaching," discipleship to him becomes possible only in association with him and taking up his way. Jesus gives discipleship his own stamp.

There already existed in Judaism a close relationship between teachers and pupils. But beyond that, there are at least three characteristics of discipleship to Jesus that mark it off from Jewish forms: (1) Disciples do not decide to follow on the basis of personal initiative. They are called or chosen by the sovereign word of Jesus. (2) The Old Testament is no longer the central focus of Jesus' message and of disciples' learning. When Jesus does make use of Scripture and the forms of his age (e.g., parable, wisdom sayings), they are used to express a new eschatological content. (3) The association with the master is permanent and not provisional (i.e., until such a time as the students themselves become masters).[43] This gives a particular character to "following" Jesus.

Concretely, the following of Jesus entails the disregarding or "denial" of self. The core of self-denial is the disowning of any claim urged by the self. Self-denial is not merely the denial of things to the self, as in asceticism or self-discipline. As a preliminary definition, self-denial is the maintenance of loyalty to God, even if as a result life would be threatened by the persecutor. This is the ultimate expression of self-denial.[44]

The link of "following" and self-denial is caught in the image of the cross. The reference to the cross would be clear and vivid since crucifixion was then a common Roman form of punishment. The command to take up the cross is, however, ambiguous. Is the point of the command to cultivate a readiness for martyrdom? Perhaps. At the same time, in the light of early Christian experience, at least a partly metaphorical meaning is indicated if disciples are to "take up their cross daily" (Luke 9:23). The metaphorical dimension of the command is suggested by its parallel with self-denial and confirmed by the concluding imperative to "follow me." This recapitulates the action in which denial of self and cross-bearing express themselves.[45]

Thus, to follow Jesus (as his disciple) means to deny self and take up the cross. Jeremias persuasively focuses on the most frightful aspect of the cross imagery. It is the moment when the condemned man, given his crossbar to carry to the place of execution, turns to face the howling mob, isolated, no longer a part of society.[46]

What stands behind the stunning tie between messiahship (Mark 8:29//Matt. 16:16//Luke 9:20) and "cross" (Mark 8:34//Matt. 16:24//Luke 9:23)? The connection becomes intelligible only if we take account of Jesus' path to the cross in historical and political context. The death of Jesus is at once integral to his eschatological mission and embedded in the social context of his ministry. In his mission Jesus is inseparable from the political concerns involved in the hopes of his people. This is shown in all the crucial moments of his career: (1) the public proclamation of the kingdom of God as now at hand, (2) the programmatic claim connected with his appearance in the synagogue at Nazareth, (3) the calling and sending of the twelve disciples, and (4) the character of his entry into Jerusalem and action in the temple at the end of his ministry.

Jesus comes into this setting talking of "kingdom," "justice," "liberation," God's blessing for the poor, and his alternative to Mammon (Matt. 6:24). He can not do this without relation to the existing network of power and authority.[47] Yet Jesus does not seize worldly power as king in order to be the Messiah. That kind of campaign would receive wide acclaim (Mark 10:35-40; John 6:15). Jesus resolutely turns from this way; he will not be this kind of Messiah. Against any such beckoning acclamation, the cross appears as a stark alternative. As his career unfolds, estrangement more and more begins to mark not only Jesus' relation to the Jewish leaders, but also to many in the crowds (cf. John 6:60, 66). Yet what Jesus chooses is not withdrawal. He moves forward in his ministry and sets out for Jerusalem.

Jesus has a conscious purpose: "I came [*ēlthon*, it is my intention, my task][48] to kindle a fire on earth" (Luke 12:49, summarized). His message becomes a source of division even within the family (Mark 10:35-36//Luke 12:51-53). Thus, the perspective and prospect of strife and suffering are not limited to Jesus himself. The terse warning "not peace but a sword" is expanded into an extended word on discipleship (Matt. 10:34-39). Just when "great crowds" are accompanying him, Jesus speaks his severe word of warning:

> Whoever comes to me and does not hate father and mother, wife and children, brothers and sisters, yes, and even life itself, cannot be my disciple. (Luke 14:26)

Here are two pertinent points: (1) Jesus calls all Israel, but (2) it is clear that not all will accept the call. Furthermore, he affirms that both the offer and the appropriate response inherent in the "kingdom of God" are divinely authoritative. The gift is free, but the gift entails acceptance. Jesus presses upon Israel a decision, thus engendering a crisis and setting up a division. The secret of Jesus' pressing the decision has to lie in its positive aspect: the reconstitution by anticipation of Israel.[49] This is shown not only by the calling of disciples into fellowship around himself, but also by the symbolism of the "twelve." In a society characterized by stable, religiously sanctioned family ties, Jesus is calling into being a community on the basis of voluntary response.

Jesus' community is to be willing for the sake of its calling to take upon itself the hostility of the surrounding society. The two parables of the builder and the king underscore the need for counting the cost of following Jesus (Luke 14:28-33). This is specified as a call to take up the cross and so to follow Jesus (Luke 14:27//Matt. 10:38).

It is disputed whether "taking up the cross" carries an explicit reference to the death of Jesus. If it does, then since cross-bearing refers to a precise event in the life of Jesus, the element of "imitation" comes into play. But this would be no individualist effort to copy the pattern of Jesus simply in an external manner. Disciples are called into relation with him and so into his community. "Taking up the cross" has to be the hallmark of a community of disciples in its relation to the larger society. But the focus remains on the quality of life to which the disciple is called. To be a disciple is to participate in that way of life which for Jesus culminated in the cross.[50] This conclusion would hold even if "taking up the cross" does not originally include an explicit reference to the coming death of Jesus.

The significance of imitation is further clarified if we begin with Israel rather than with Jesus. In accord with the Hebrew Scriptures, a series of events in Israel's history was decisive for God's relation to his people. It is essential for Israel as the people of God to maintain an intimate relation to this vital, formative period of its history (e.g., through recital, "remembering," and "meditation"). In this history the shape of life is clearly indicated by God himself. God shows that he is always prevenient: he freed his people and went before them as guide. God demonstrates that he is always provident: he accompanied them and gave commands that pointed the way to the promised inheritance and to the destiny of his people.[51]

What makes Israel to be Israel is to walk in the way of the Lord. To walk in this way calls them to obey the Lord's commands (Deut. 8:6), fear the Lord (Deut. 10:12), and love the Lord (Deut. 11:22). But all this presupposes and expresses a unique relation to God; Israel is nothing less than God's "firstborn son" (Exod. 4:22). Since God revealed himself as a just and compassionate God, Israel is called to act justly and with compassion (Deut. 10:15-19; Jer. 22:16). Israel as a people is therefore called to reflect the character uniquely expressed in God's deliverance of his people.[52]

The structural similarity to this pattern in Jesus' call is unmistakable. He is bringing restored Israel into being. Jesus as Son of man represents the kingdom of God, not by being served, but by serving (Mark 10:45//Matt. 20:28; cf. Luke 22:27). The servant model gives new definition to both "kingdom of God" and to participation in it. Son of man refers not only to Jesus but to those who participate with him in God's design with confidence in ultimate vindication from God.[53] Jesus' statement underlines this: "Those who lose their life for my sake will find it" (Matt. 16:25//Mark 8:35//Luke 9:24). Likewise, this further explains the word on self-denial and cross-bearing.[54] The persons who deny themselves are also the ones who lose themselves for the sake of Christ; thus they "save" and "find" their life. Those who refuse to deny self and wish to preserve their life, "lose" it.[55]

What is the ethical significance of this correspondence between discipleship and Jesus as the Christ? The answer requires that we examine several strands of tradition reflecting the correspondence between Christology and discipleship. We do not understand what it means for Jesus to be Christ apart from his destiny. Neither can we understand discipleship apart from relation to this destiny. The esoteric teaching has its point in bringing this relation into light.

Self-Giving Service

> You know that among the Gentiles those whom they recognize as their rulers lord it over them, and their great ones are tyrants over

them. But it is not so among you; but whoever wishes to become great among you must be your servant. . . . For the Son of Man came not to be served but to serve, and to give his life a ransom for many. (Mark 10:42-45//Matt. 20:25-28)

This word, according to the accounts of Matthew and Mark, is provoked by the request of two of Jesus' disciples for a place of privilege in the coming kingdom. Again, the issue is to be resolved on the basis of imitation: as one who came to serve, Jesus is the criterion for the reordering of the disciples' values. It is also clear that Jesus is more than an exemplar. The possibility of imitation by the disciple of Jesus is grounded in Jesus' willingness to go to his death in carrying out his saving mission. His will is at once an act of obedience to God and a creative novelty.

Is his death the serving which Jesus claims as his purpose? Does the serving consist in "self-sacrifice"? One way to understand the paradoxical connection between serving and self-sacrifice is to note the continuity between the service that is Jesus' life (Mark 10:45a) and the service that is to be his death (10:45b). The second is "service" of another and higher order. On the other hand, if Jesus conceives the coming of the kingdom of God to be mediated by the whole single event of his life and death, then his death becomes the ultimate measure of service. Jesus is like the figure in the songs of Deutero-Isaiah (Isa. 42:1-4; 49:1-6; 50:4-9; 52:13—53:12). He goes innocently to his death for the life of the world (John 6:51c; cf. Isa. 53:11-12; Mark 14:24//Matt. 26:28), and thereby he is the "servant" par excellence. His whole ministry has its climax as, in obedience to God, he gives himself up to death in the service of his mission.

The natural instinct of the disciples, on the contrary, is to anticipate honor and position in the kingdom of God. They ask a favor which assumes that Jesus is a king, soon to enter upon his royal dignity. There is no quarrel on Jesus' part with their basic assumption that he is a king. However, the expected or hoped-for answer to their request presupposes that Jesus would follow the way worldly rulers behave toward their subjects. But Jesus represents an entirely different conception of reign and kingdom. It is to be defined by his self-giving service. This *revolution*—no lesser word will do—has revolutionary significance for ethics. In their response to Jesus, the disciples are called to a new understanding of the good. It lies not in domination over others but in service of others. Indeed, it includes laying down one's life for others. The Gospel of John offers a symbolic illustration: Jesus takes the towel and the basin and washes his disciples' feet (John 13:1-13).

In its own way the statement in Mark 10:42-45 expresses what it means to "take up the cross." With that saying Jesus is creating a new kind of community. It calls for a clear decision in which the costs of commitment are consciously accepted, and it signifies a way of life distinct from that of the crowd.[56] This way of life is different, not because of arbitrary rules separating the disciple's behavior from that of others, but because of the high quality of humanness that Jesus reveals and in which the disciples are to participate. Its distinctiveness is not a matter of cultic or ritual separation, but a way of life conformed to the self-giving pattern of Jesus, not conformed to the world. This model is generating a new way of being in community, and thereby it inevitably constitutes a challenge to the powers that be.[57]

The Primacy of Love

> I give you a new commandment, that you love one another. Just as I have loved you, you also should love one another. (John 13:34)

This statement represents an instruction that Jesus gives his disciples as part of his "farewell discourse." It epitomizes in typically Johannine fashion a fundamental trait of the life as well as of the teaching of Jesus (Mark 12:28-34//Matt. 22:34-40; cf. Luke 10:25-28; 22:27). Indeed, the washing of the disciples' feet in John 13:1-17 dramatizes the saying in Luke 22:27. This is summed up in John in the "new commandment" of mutual love (13:34-35).[58] In all the Gospel traditions love is associated with the concrete self-giving in service to or for another.

It is not beside the point to see the definition of love in service; both love and service involve the unselfish giving of self for the sake of another. The imperative in both cases is based on the stance of Jesus: "I am among you as one who serves" (Luke 22:27), and again, "Love . . . as I have loved you" (John 13:34).

Both serve to define the new social order in contrast to existing society: It shall "not [be] so with you" (Luke 22:26). "By this everyone will know that you are my disciples, if you have love for one another" (John 13:35).

Facing the hostility of the "world" exemplified in the cross, how are the disciples as a community to continue to represent Jesus in the world? Jesus shows how by giving both the example and the command of love. The command is grounded in his own self-giving acceptance of death.

The Practice of Love: Forgiveness

> If another disciple sins, you must rebuke the offender, and if there is repentance, you must forgive. And if the same person sins against you seven times a day, and turns back to you seven times and says, "I repent," you must forgive. (Luke 17:3-4)[59]

The field of moral action supposes conflict; Jesus' primary response, both by the story of his life and throughout his teaching, is forgiveness. Just as God's forgiveness of disciples is boundless, in the same way the disciples are to be boundless in forgiving others. It is to include even one's enemies: to pray for them presupposes that one is prepared to forgive (Matt. 5:44//Luke 6:28). On the cross Jesus himself unites prayer and a forgiving spirit (Luke 23:34).[60] Furthermore, the covenant Jesus initiates by his death is a covenant defined by forgiveness, explicitly (Matt. 26:28) and implicitly (Mark 14:23; Luke 22:19-20).

In this matter we are told very precisely that forgiving is part of being forgiven: forgiveness is a unity. Above all, this was dramatized by its inclusion in the prayer Jesus taught his disciples: "Cancel our debts as we (hereby) cancel those of our debtors" (Matt. 6:12//Luke 11:4, my tr.). It is significant that Jesus thereby includes a performative act of forgiving in the text of the prayer—a meaning that emerges mainly from the Aramaic substratum.[61]

The imperative character of living in accord with the gift of forgiveness is expressed by Jesus' parable of the unmerciful servant (Matt. 18:23-35). The fulfillment of this teaching presupposes the powers of the kingdom; since the kingdom is already present with Jesus, new response is possible in the present. The issue is not who is offended or whether the sin is great or small. For Jesus the focus is pardon: if the person listens and repents, forgive (Luke 17:3; cf. Matt. 18:15-18). Instead of dealing with offense, people may seek to ignore or to make light of offense. This undermines relationships and withholds good news. The gift of forgiveness is creative of community; the community lives from and extends this gift.

The Willingness to Bear Suffering

> Whoever does not carry the cross and follow me cannot be my disciple. (Luke 14:27)[62]
>
> "Servants are not greater than their master." If they persecuted me, they will persecute you. (John 15:20)

The statement in Luke is preceded by the call to forsake family and is followed by the call to prior deliberation about the costs of following Jesus. Each statement in its own way emphasizes the social suffering of rejection. This is not teaching reserved for a spiritual elite. It is for all of Jesus' followers. To follow him is to share in both his mission and his destiny.[63]

The reasons for the persecution that Jesus envisages are not defined in detail. It is clear, however, that the persecution is not related to "religious" reasons independent of the ethical stance that Jesus and his disciples are to share. The "cross," whether of Jesus or of his followers, represents the world's response to that stance. It is a political punishment.[64] The dichotomy between the political and religious significance is foreign to the Gospel texts. The consequence of discipleship as part of this new communitarian way of being is to unmask the ruler's claim to be "benefactor" (cf. Luke 22:25).[65]

Death as Victory

> For those who want to save their life will lose it, and those who lose their life for my sake will find it. For what will it profit them if they gain the whole world but forfeit their life? (Matt. 16:25-26)

> Very truly, I tell you, unless a grain of wheat falls into the earth and dies, it remains just a single grain; but if it dies, it bears much fruit. Those who love their life lose it, and those who hate their life in this world will keep it for eternal life. (John 12:24-25)[66]

These statements presuppose a particular horizon. The paradox of losing life by saving it and vice versa takes both of the opposed perspectives seriously. The hearers are reminded of their deep instinctive concern to preserve their lives and of the fear that any threat to their lives instantly awakens. Such fear is founded on firm convictions about saving and losing one's life. This entirely understandable perception of the human situation is, however, just what Jesus challenges and repudiates by a sharply antithetical saying. The impact of this new perspective is to compel attention to a new possibility. Jesus tells the hearers to fear what they always want and to face what they always fear.

In the concrete experiences and sufferings of life, people come upon a critical crossroad: to withdraw or to give themselves. The temptation is to overlook suffering or aim to overcome every form of suffering. Since this is unattainable, indifference or withdrawal may be the path chosen. But life without self-giving in love is superficial.[67] If people wish to possess their life instead of receiving it and giving it in daily trust, they will lose their life. This saying of Jesus hardly fits within the conventional or established vision of life; it calls for a new beginning, challenging the rules by which conventional life is governed. The called-for response has to be radical.

The phrase "for my sake" (Matt. 16:25) makes the saving of one's life through losing it a matter of discipleship. John's Gospel expresses this by an analogy (John 12:24). The ancients held that, in order to bear fruit, a seed must "die." If it does not die, it remains alone. The dying of the seed corresponds to "hating"[68] one's life in this world. The harvest corresponds to the gift of eternal life. The analogy first has reference to Jesus (12:23-24), but then it moves to include the followers of Jesus (12:25-26).[69] These words have their decisive meaning because they are spoken by one who follows the path that leads to death. Thus the basic saying about losing and saving depends on and takes up the meaning of Jesus' self-giving, even to the point of death.[70]

The above treatment of Jesus' esoteric teaching on human values, decision, and comportment is not comprehensive in the sense of attending to every text in the esoteric tradition. Nevertheless, it does survey the core of the tradition. What remains is to integrate this core of esoteric teachings in a synthesis of the ethical responses called for by Jesus as proclaimer of the kingdom of God and as the Messiah going to a destiny of repudiation and death. This synthesis, furthermore, will aim to highlight the distinctive character of the ethics of Jesus central to the concern of this work.

Ethics for the Messianic Community

Perhaps the reader has been struck by the seemingly "individualist" character of the values commended by Jesus' esoteric instruction: a way of life marked by a bold and generous "following" of Jesus, a taking up of one's "cross," un-self-regarding love and service, and the will both to forgive and to suffer. Now it is our task to accent how the themes of all these traditions are already placed in their proper social and ecclesial context. Jesus does not offer an individualist perspective but a communitarian perspective. In the modern era, this all-pervasive trait of Jesus' purposes, actions, and words has been not only underplayed but consciously or unconsciously rejected. Many moderns are blind to this indispensable context.

Essentially, our case is already made by recovering the controlling theme of the eschatological restoration of Israel (chapter 2, above). But now we shall take up the beginning and the end of the esoteric teaching in an effort to concretize the matter. Jesus' "teaching" relates to the community of faith made up of all who welcome his proclamation and commit themselves to the messianic proclaimer himself. The communitarian or ecclesial dimension is concentrated in Jesus' statement of intention and is epitomized in the name that Jesus conferred on the disciple Simon at some point during his public career: *Kepha'*, *Petros*, Rock (in Aramaic, Greek, and English; Matt. 16:18; Mark 3:16; Luke 6:14; John 1:42).

Only the Gospel of Matthew describes the giving of the name and spells out its meaning. Once Simon Peter says, near

Caesarea Philippi, "You are the Messiah, the Son of the living God," Jesus responds:

> Blessed are you, Simon son of Jonah!
>   For flesh and blood has not revealed this to you,
>   but my Father in heaven.
> And I tell you, you are Peter [*Kepha'*],
>   and on this rock [*kepha'*] I will build my church,
>   and the powers of death will not prevail against it.
> I will give you the keys of the kingdom of heaven,
>   and whatever you bind on earth will be bound in heaven,
>   and whatever you loose on earth will be loosed in heaven.
>   (Matt. 16:17-19, with "powers of death" from RSV)

What is the significance of this text for the understanding of Jesus' eschatological mission? In Jesus' statement of intention (16:18), the image of the foundation rock has a central place. There is a larger background for this image in the ancient Near East. We are concerned with it as it relates to Israel in particular. The image refers to the temple founded on rock and thus signifies Israel's secure place in covenant relation to God.[71] Thus it is natural for Isaiah (28:16) to speak prospectively of God laying in Zion a prized foundation stone. Significantly, this word is amplified in a prayer from Qumran (Hymn Scroll: 1QH 6.23-28; cf. 7.8-9). The waves threaten, the sea roars, but the worshiper finds security by being brought within a fortified city (the community of the just) founded by God upon rock. Moreover, the Qumran text has a marked eschatological quality and context.[72]

Although the image of the foundation rock is central to Jesus' word, the oracle of Nathan also underlies the various elements of the Matthean text as a whole (God's promise to David in 2 Sam. 7:12-14a). This oracle serves as a source for biblical tradition identifying the Davidic king as God's son (cf. Ps. 2:7; 89:27; 110:3), defining the building of the temple as his task (cf. Zech. 6:12-13), and promising the perpetuity of the Davidic dynasty (cf. 2 Sam. 23:5; Isa. 9:5-11; Ps. 89:3-5, 20-29).[73]

Transposed to an eschatological key, Nathan's oracle is made to refer to the community created by God's action in the endtime (cf. Florilegium: 4QFlor 1-13). The eschatological interpretation of the oracle issues in a significant conclusion: the building of God's house is a messianic task (cf. Acts 15:16-17).[74] The themes linked and established for biblical tradition by this oracle provide the unarticulated relation between confession and commission in Matthew 16:16-19. As "the Messiah, Son of the living God," Jesus' task is to build the eschatological temple, "my church," the messianic community (cf. 1 Cor. 3:16; 1 Pet. 2:4-10).[75]

I said above that I wished to make the ecclesial aspect of Jesus' career and teaching explicit by reference to the beginning and the end of his esoteric teaching. The "beginning" (of its most important phase) is the confession near Caesarea Philippi. The "end" is the Last Supper and the trial before the Sanhedrin.

The conjunction of Jesus' messiahship and eschatological mission in Matthew 16:16-19 is strikingly paralleled and confirmed by key moments in the trial before the Sanhedrin (Mark 14:55-64// Matt. 26:59-66).[76] Once more the sequence in the Markan trial scene is illuminated by reference to the Nathan oracle. The relevant features occur as follows: Destruction and construction of the temple (Mark 14:58; 2 Sam. 7:13); the Messiah, the Son of the Blessed one (Mark 4:61; 2 Sam. 7:14); ultimate enthronement (Mark 14:62; 2 Sam. 7:13, 16).

Further, these features provide the intelligible ground for the charge of blasphemy and the sentence of death that follows. In all probability the blasphemy (Mark 14:64) is linked to the dishonoring of "the Blessed One" by the claim to be his Son—a claim ostensibly false inasmuch as Jesus stands before his judges powerless.[77] The saying about the building of the temple has a messianic significance; the direct question by the high priest to Jesus follows this up. For our purposes the most significant word is the one that marks the turning point of the entire scene: "We heard him say, 'I will destroy this temple that is made with hands, and in three days I will build another, not made with hands' " (Mark 14:58//Matt. 26:61).

The temple saying, though distorted by the trial witnesses, certainly originates with Jesus. The evidence converges in a remarkable way on this fact: (1) A variety of witnesses support it (e.g., Mark 15:29//Matt. 27:40; John 2:19; cf. Acts 6:14; Mark

13:2). This variation within the sources indicates that the meaning of the saying is obscure, a fact that in this case speaks not against but in favor of authenticity. (2) In accord with it is the fact that the Jerusalem temple authorities (the Sanhedrin) lead the opposition to Jesus.[78] And in light of Jesus' temple action (Mark 11:15-19), the significance of his word (cf. Amos 7:10-17; Jer. 7:1-15) could easily include a challenge to their own claim of leadership.[79] In confirmation of that possibility, following his action in the temple as reported in John's Gospel, Jesus is confronted by the officials on the issue of authority for his action (2:13-17). What is more, in the response Jesus makes reference to the destruction of the sanctuary and the building of a new sanctuary in three days.

All this imagery says "community." Indeed, even before considering this imagery we find ourselves compelled by the concrete correlates of "the kingdom of God" to posit the ecclesial dimension of the yes that many give to Jesus' proclamation. What the further texts on "temple" or "sanctuary" add is the messianic character and the communitarian character of Jesus' mission. Israel comes to eschatological restoration, not as a disparate scattering of yea-sayers to Jesus, but as an as-yet-ungathered, unorganized community of faith. Jesus' disciples constitute its nucleus.

On the basis of this context we may consider a final esoteric tradition, the last and climactic command of Jesus. This command is to take the bread that he offers and to eat it, to take the cup of wine that he offers and to drink it. The context is the Last Supper, and the command bears on a climactic symbolic act of Jesus reserved for his disciples.

Our argument throughout this section is that the commands of Jesus are not meant as wise sayings directed to all comers but as the charter of messianic Israel. It would be possible to disassociate some of Jesus' moral teaching from the intended ecclesial context, but that context nevertheless stands out as the historic point of reference for all of Jesus' teaching. The Last Supper is among the traditions that are most clearly inseparable from the context of messianic Israel.

Here, according to the Synoptic texts, Jesus makes explicit the covenantal dimension of his mission (Mark 14:24//Matt. 26:28; cf. Luke 22:20). Because there is a clear connection between the Last Supper and the church's worship in the eucharist, it is widely assumed that the Last Supper accounts are fashioned for this purpose (other than Luke 22:15-18). Further, Bultmann supposed that Mark's account was "the cult legend of the Hellenistic circles about Paul."[80] Jeremias, through the demonstration of the Semitisms within Mark's account, rules out that possibility. He shows that the tradition behind the accounts of the Last Supper is formulated in Aramaic (or Hebrew), and that this shines through the Markan account with particular clarity.[81]

Rudolf Pesch presents a most clearly articulated alternative to the views of Bultmann. Taking his stand in the tradition of exegetical and historical study of the eucharistic words inaugurated by Dalman and Jeremias, Pesch clarifies the character of two sets of texts, Mark-Matthew and 1 Corinthians-Luke, by defining clearly their literary genre. The genre of the Markan tradition, as well as of the Matthean tradition dependent on Mark, is historical narrative, originally conceived as part of the passion story. The genre of the tradition in 1 Corinthians 11:23-25 is "liturgical," fashioned for use in the church's worship to explain the origin of the Lord's Supper. Pesch takes Luke's account (the long text) to be a mixed genre, dependent on both Mark 14 and 1 Corinthians 11.[82]

In support of the difference in genre between the Markan and the Pauline accounts, Pesch sets out a range of pertinent considerations. The Markan text (14:22-25) is embedded in the context of the Passover meal of Jesus with his disciples (Mark 14:17, 21, 26). The words on the bread and on the wine are addressed to the twelve. In Mark, narrative traits abound (introductory *kai:* and; narrative *kai edōken:* and he took; the invitation *labete:* take; narrative *kai epion ex autou pantes:* and all of them drank; etc.). Absent from Mark are liturgical traits such as the "remembrance" command (1 Cor. 11:24-25).

The Pauline text, on the other hand, has a different character and represents an independent literary unit. Reference to the original group of the disciples is dropped, yielding to the "you" of the celebrating community. Narrative traits are lacking, whereas the etiological *anamnēsis* (remembrance) is accented. A solemn liturgical notice introduces the text asyndetically, in unconnected fashion (1 Cor. 11:23). The so-called eschatological perspective, which in Mark 14:25 connects the meal situation with the imminent death of Jesus, is missing in Paul, although 1 Corinthians 11:26 does make reference to the past event of Jesus' death and its complementary counterpart, the parousia: "until he comes."[83]

Mark provides a concrete setting, the last Passover meal of Jesus with his disciples: The meal is eaten in the evening, contrasting with other meals eaten in the late afternoon or in the early evening (14:17). Mark indicates that a dish is served before the bread is distributed (14:20). The meal concludes with the singing of a hymn, probably the great Hallel (14:26; Pss. 113-118).[84] Paul, on the other hand, rehearses a tradition that in part, at least, leaves the concrete setting and its original figures behind, thus functioning all the better as a model for liturgical celebration.

As a part of the depiction of the original situation, the elements of the Markan account as a whole are clearly narrative (26 narrative words in 14:22-25). By contrast, the Pauline text is a community-oriented liturgical formulation (23 narrative words, 34 spoken words). There is one imperative in Mark (*labete*) belonging to the historic situation in which Jesus specifically invites the disciples to "take" (and "eat," Matt. 26:26). Two imperatives in Paul envisage the celebrating community (*poieite . . . poieite . . .*: do . . . do . . .). Correspondingly, the phrase "for as often as" (*hosakis gar ean:* 1 Cor. 11:26) evokes the Lord's Supper as repeatable event. Once it is pointed out, this set of contrasts is obviously relevant to and, in fact, reflects and clinches the diversity of genre.

The historicity of the eucharistic words is accordingly placed in a new and far more positive light. Our interest, however, goes beyond historicity to meaning. What is the meaning of Jesus' act of giving the bread and, later, giving the cup to his disciples?

The answer turns on the content and the allusions of the words of institution. Over the bread Jesus spoke the terse words: "Take; this is my body" (Mark 14:22). Thus he signifies to the disciples the gift of himself. The words over the cup fill out or complete "this first saying by making explicit the implicit reference to the forthcoming death of Jesus: his blood is poured out 'for many.' "[85] Jesus designates the bread as "my body" and the third Passover cup as "my blood, covenant-blood, (to be) poured out for many" (my tr. of Mark 14:24//Matt. 26:28; cf. Luke 22:19-20; 1 Cor. 11:24-25). This evokes his coming death under two headings: expiation (the *hyper*/"for" formula probably relates, like the term "many," to Isa. 53), and the sacrifice that seals the covenant (Exod. 24:8; Jer. 31:31).

Jeremias draws the inevitable conclusion:

> If, immediately following his words on the bread and immediately following his words on the wine, Jesus gives the same bread and the same wine to his disciples, this act signifies his giving them a share, by their eating and drinking, in the atoning power of his death.[86]

The point is that the response belongs to this ecclesial context. This response includes the ethical dimension, whether sought by Jesus in his public preaching or in his private transactions with his followers. The ethics of Jesus is aimed toward an eschatological people of God. Messianic ethics, in a word, is the ethos of the messianic community. Whenever the messianic ethics of Jesus is torn from its context in the life of messianic Israel, the church, it becomes ethics that no longer makes real sense. In fact, again and again this ethics has been thus torn asunder from the church. This ethics is a religious and ecclesial teaching. It hinges not on human nature nor on natural law nor on philosophic foundations, but on the mission and destiny of the Jesus of history.

This is perhaps the most telling of all the traits that stamps the ethics of Jesus as uniquely his. If the concrete history and destiny of Jesus were bracketed or severed from the values, injunctions, purposes, and prohibitions that made up his ethics, that ethics would lose its rationale, cohesion, and force. This is an ethics for a specific community, and there can be neither a messianic ethics nor a messianic community without the Messiah.

Conclusion

The aim in this work has been to examine the central significance of the kingdom of God represented in Jesus' eschatological proclamation and mission in relation to ethics. The theology of Ritschl supposed a definite bond between the kingdom of God and ethical action. But the discovery by Weiss of the thoroughly eschatological character of the kingdom of God demolished the structure of theology constructed by Ritschl, refuting Ritschl's ethical-developmental conception of the kingdom.

This posed all the more clearly the question of the relation between eschatology and ethics. But with the evident failure of Ritschl, there was little inclination to take up the question anew; scholars might consider the one with an acknowledgment of the other, but they failed to undertake a direct and comprehensive consideration of eschatology and ethics in their interrelationship.

Important questions are at stake in determining the sources upon which Jesus drew in making his eschatological proclamation and fulfilling his mission. It has therefore been important to understand the variety of eschatological expectations in the Scriptures and in Judaism. The connection between these sources and Jesus has, I hope, illuminated and established more exactly the nature of Jesus' proclamation and mission as stamped by eschatology. In these sources it is already evident that there is a strong link between eschatological promise and appropriate ethical response. The central importance for Jesus of the kingdom of God (and its correlative, the restoration of Israel) is confirmed by the way he begins his mission in relation to John and by the outcome of his proclamation and mission in the formation of the eschatological community around him after the resurrection.

The relation between Jesus' public proclamation and destiny and, correspondingly, the relation between Jesus' destiny and the ethics of discipleship come to light in the esoteric teaching. Just as the understanding of his death is impossible without relation to his life, so also the understanding of his life is impossible without relation to the one for whom he lived, his God and Father, and that for which he lived, the kingdom of God. The death of Jesus is therefore at once related to the eschatological purpose of God and embedded in the social setting of his life and mission. He was condemned as a blasphemous claimant to messiahship, and he was judged to be so dangerous in his influence that he was handed over to the Romans. The inscription on the cross names the political crime. "King of the Jews" is the Roman formulation of "Messiah" as it was established in the Jewish setting. That is, crucifixion is not understood apart from the interaction of Jesus and the Jewish leaders and the Roman officials.

Crucifixion was the result of who Jesus was and how he acted, in the face of the religious and political configurations of power. In this way, Jesus' death had inherent ethical import from the beginning: it was the outcome of his life in response to God in social and political context. Even while dying, instead of words of vengeance, he spoke forgiveness in the fulfillment of love that becomes love of enemies. The formation of disciples within the eschatological community is made possible by and corresponds to this Jesus. Therefore, this community lives by the power of forgiveness, reconciliation out of conflict, creative love in the midst of enmity and evil.

One conspicuous feature of the present investigation has been its constant concern, from beginning to end, with disputed questions about the historical Jesus. The reader may have wondered more than once why a study of the messianic ethics of Jesus has to be burdened by preliminary, nonethical issues: the laborious efforts of scholars to recover the proclamation of Jesus, its eschatological implications, its connection with Jesus' symbolic acts, and its relation to his teachings, the meaning of his career, the authority of his warnings, and the force of his commands and prohibitions.

The fact is that the ethics of Jesus is utterly inseparable from his personal plenipotentiary authority. And the convergent data make us think that this connection between his ethics and his messianic person was entirely conscious on his part. A reasonably accurate comprehension of the ethics of Jesus depends on a reasonably accurate recovery of the whole historical figure that he was. The Schweitzerian and the Harnackian versions of Jesus' ethics are based respectively in a Schweitzerian and a Harnackian reconstruction of the Jesus of history.

A constant concern has accordingly been imposed on us to secure solid historical bases for the understanding of Jesus' ethical teachings, whether in the public forum or in the more intimate circles of his disciples. This has been a more compelling task even than comprehensiveness in the treatment of Jesus' ethics. If the constant attention to historical problems has sometimes been a distraction from ethical issues, it has been a price worth paying for the increased assurance that we have been genuinely in touch with the unique historical figure, Jesus of Nazareth.

The present study, whatever its limits, has sought to exploit a breakthrough in historical research on Jesus: the recovery of his purposes as bearing on the whole people, Israel. The Jesus that emerges here is not the individualist discovered by Bultmann and his followers or by T. W. Manson or Norman Perrin. Rather, Jesus was a man with a mission of eschatological restoration centering on Israel and then encompassing the nations. The fact that not all responded to this mission does not destroy the "ecclesial" character of his encounter with the Israel of his time. Nothing less than the nascent restoration of Israel came into being in those who did respond positively to him. Or, to put the matter more cautiously and exactly, these were the terms in which both he and his followers understood his words, acts, and destiny. The messianic ethics of Jesus survived in history precisely because this understanding of him survived in the Easter community that emerged and followed from his life and death.

In the opening pages of this investigation, I said that the recovery of the messianic ethics of Jesus is not the whole of New Testament ethics. Furthermore, there is required a reflective mediation of New Testament ethics as a whole to the present. Mediation seeks to unite these ethics as represented in the New Testament with the present experience of men and women as they face the future. The process of discernment and mediation within the Christian community of a contemporary Christian ethics therefore stands as a continuing requirement and challenge.

However, the process of discernment and mediation may be restricted or broken off completely for one reason or another. Representatives of the school of "consistent eschatology" (from Albert Schweitzer to Jack Sanders) have insisted on Jesus' ethical teaching as intelligible only in relation to eschatology.[1] Because in this school eschatology was defined as simply imminent event, it could therefore only be understood in terms of failure. From this understanding has issued a fundamental but negative conclusion: Jesus "does not provide a valid ethics for today."[2]

This negative conclusion depends on three interrelated points: (1) The most important of these is the perceived failure of the eschatology of Jesus. Imminent eschatology is constitutive for Jesus. But this eschatology was crushed by his death on the cross as history continued.[3] (2) The ethics of Jesus is impossible. The ethics have their possibility only in the light of the imminent arrival of the kingdom of God. To accept the ethical teaching of Jesus is to cut all ties with the present world, for the kingdom he proclaimed is not of or for this world.[4] In the real world of family, work, and limited resources, the way of Jesus is impossible.[5] With the passing of time and without the fulfillment of eschatological expectation, the ethics are shown to be invalid. (3) Jesus does not provide an ethics usable in modern pluralistic society.[6]

To consider these points in order should help to focus some pertinent issues as well as highlight the larger discussion to which this effort is a contribution. The points Sanders makes are also made by others and deserve to be considered, here in reverse order. Undifferentiated as it stands, the last statement invites a series of questions. What is it about modern society that would make the ethics "unusable"? Is it that society is now so complex that it has moved beyond Jesus' ethics? Is it even a question about having ethics "usable" for society as a whole—and so a problem of control or dominance in society? The original Christian mission, in moving from Judaism to the larger Gentile world, encountered a variegated pluralism and provided ethical coherence and meaning in the lives of many people. And the reality is that in actual human experience it continues to do so today.

Yet the deeper issue for Sanders may be the particular character of the ethics of Jesus. Without accepting Jesus as the beginning for ethics, Sanders still thinks it possible to determine what is "humane" and "right." But what understanding of existence provides content and meaning to these concepts? What he thinks is required is a generalized ethics, an ethics for everyone. The problem is that this turns out to be an abstraction that finally has no real place anywhere. An ethics standing alone and only defining behavior carries no authority in making response to the concrete issues of life. The question about any form of ethics remains pertinent: how are these values determined, and on what ground are they affirmed? In the West they might be Enlightenment values, largely abstracted or derived from the Christian world vision. Some of these values might be particular or "provincial," and others perhaps include more people and places.

In some already achieved ideal world, it might make sense simply to derive ethics from things as they are. What must not be bypassed here is the recognition of evil, even the hopelessness of the world as it stands. To recognize this is at the same time to recognize the limitations of any dominant ethical perspective based on "natural insight" from within that world. There is the alternative of simply accepting the status quo and adapting oneself to the times, but Sanders seems to call for something more than that. The question is, what provides a basis for transcending the present situation as it is?

The kingdom of God points to all-embracing meaning. The renewed community comes into being out of faith in Jesus as the representative of this kingdom. This community therefore represents the character of God's way for Israel and for all creation. Here the general and the particular cannot be alternatives. To begin with Jesus is not to be called to discount either comprehensibility or public significance. His story, as it begins with Abraham, has been around longer and traveled farther than most. It has run through myriad contacts in culture and worldviews. Jesus' impact has created a nearly worldwide communion. His teaching has a wholeness that comprehends politics as well as prayer. Certainly final verification of his teaching can only be anticipated eschatologically, but its enduring relevance over time supports its credibility.

The particularity of Jesus in this case is not bad news but good news worth sharing. This same particularity corresponds to the distinction between the ethics of discipleship dependent on the resources of faith on one hand, and on the other hand, an ethics within the limits of relative fairness and self-preservation. The first is expressive of faith and participation in the renewed community; the second has to do with the field of ethical discourse beyond the borders of faith. This is to emphasize that Jesus' ethics are ecclesial in character, representing in the world the kingdom order to come. This involves a realism about human nature and about the presence and power of evil—and even more clearly, a realism about the presence and power of God to fulfill his purpose. An ethics within the limits of relative fairness may serve as a starting point from which to converse with the larger society. But we need to avoid the mistake of thinking that the highest good of the ethical life can be attained apart from the voluntary response involving the minds and hearts of people.

In stating the impossibility of Jesus' ethics, Sanders singles out the actively generous love of Jesus' ethical teaching as exemplified in the parable of the good Samaritan. Sanders is right in the qualification of this kind of response: "The Samaritan's comportment cannot be possible to every man who, at any time . . . by his own choosing, decides to step into the Samaritan's world."[7] But he is wrong in thinking that this kind of response is meant for some realm other than the present world. It is in the present world that love is opposed and must show itself to be love in the comprehension of certain needs or in confrontation with certain evils (cf. Matt. 13:24-30).

It is true that Jesus' teaching is radical and relativizes all human ties and relationships. And this is done in the light of the coming and already-effective kingdom of God. We cannot expect certain things of all but only as part of the commitment of discipleship: taking the way of unselfish service in hope of the kingdom of God, love for the enemy as a reflection of God's love, forgiving as one has been forgiven. Those who, for the sake of the kingdom, leave behind everything they have, participate in a new family, the community of faith. With this family there are again brothers, sisters, mothers, and children, with "persecutions" (Mark 10:29-30). This happens not in some other world but "now in this age" or time (*nun en tō kairō toutō:* 10:30). Now the reign of God is effective in the creation of renewed community, in the present still marked by suffering. Specifically, the self-forgetful love of the Samaritan has the eschatological community as its horizon. The call is not to a rigorous asceticism; instead, the correlative of this generous love is the sharing community (cf. Mark 10:29-30).

In Jesus' teaching on divorce, there is further evidence for this possibility and this pattern of life in the present defined concretely by participation in the kingdom. This instruction on marriage and divorce supposes healing for "your hardness of heart" in response to God's eschatological initiative (cf. Matt. 19:1-9; 7:17-20//Luke 6:43-45). The response Jesus calls for represents the anticipation of the kingdom of God. That is, the now renewed command of God, "the two shall become one" (Matt. 19:5; Gen. 2:24), does not refer to the ultimate situation on the far side of judgment, when people indeed "neither marry nor are given in marriage" (Matt. 22:30//Mark 12:25//Luke 20:35). Instead, it refers to the time (*kairos*) of fulfillment marked by Jesus' proclamation and mission.

The nature of sin, here sin as divorce, is contrary to the good that God has made possible for men and women in eschatological renewal. But people may refuse or exclude that possibility. The very expression of the prohibition shows that divorce is conceivable. The kingdom becoming effective means new response is possible, but hearts may still be hardened. And because the kingdom in its fullness is still future, divorce is conceivable. This ethics is an ethics of the anticipation of the kingdom of God, who makes possible what "for mortals . . . is impossible" (Mark 10:27).

Thus, the most important issue in Sander's denial of the ethics of Jesus is finally eschatology. If one holds that the eschatology of Jesus is an illusion, then the ethics corresponding to it certainly are invalid. Sanders has taken up the inadequate view of eschatology in the work of Weiss and Schweitzer. They portray Jesus as simply sounding the note of imminence of the end-time, and I have already shown that this fails at crucial points to correspond with the eschatological perspective of Jesus.[8]

Within a more differentiated perspective, it is clear, Jesus held to a near-expectation of the end: "So also, when you see these things taking place, you know that he is near, at the very gates" (Mark 13:29//Matt. 24:33). It is also reasonable to hold that "all these things" to come upon "this generation" in Mark 13:30 are distinguished from "that day" and "that hour" marking the culmination of the kingdom (Mark 13:32). That is, in the eschatological perspective, the judgment of the Lord upon an impenitent people stands in a preparatory relation to the end, but the two events are distinguished in the tradition.

For the prophetic predecessors as well as for Jesus, receiving the word of God did not mean precise or determinate knowledge of the future (cf. Mark 13:32). What is affirmed is the power of God alone to determine the future and the time of the end (cf. Acts 1:7). Jesus' eschatological perspective is best understood in the light of the whole history of prophecy in Israel and promise to Israel. The prophetic word of promise was not repudiated because the expectation for the near future was not immediately fulfilled. Hoping and praying for early fulfillment, Israel learned to entrust that fulfillment to the time of God's own choosing (Hab. 2:2-3). As it turns out, Jesus not only proclaimed the kingdom of God but acted and finally gave himself to enact it. This decisively defines the "kingdom of God" and response to it as that reign of God forms and informs the ethical stance of the messianic community.

Notes

Introduction
1. To Schweitzer, it was clear that nothing could be rescued from the all-encompassing eschatology of Jesus. According to Schweitzer this represented a shattering confrontation of the world-accepting ethic of modern theology and that of Jesus: *Von Reimarus zu Wrede* (Tübingen: Mohr, 1906), tr. by W. Montgomery as *The Quest of the Historical Jesus* (New York: Macmillan, 1968), 402.
2. Cf. Brevard S. Childs, *Biblical Theology in Crisis* (Philadelphia: Westminster, 1970), 124.
3. John H. Yoder, "The Biblical Mandate," in *The Chicago Declaration*, Ronald J. Sider, ed. (Carol Stream, Ill.: Creation House, 1974), 111.
4. Adolf von Harnack, *What Is Christianity?* (Gloucester, Mass.: Peter Smith, 1978), 56, 116.
5. E. F. Scott, *The Ethical Teaching of Jesus* (New York: Macmillan, 1936), 78. See also his *The Crisis in the Life of Jesus* (New York: Charles Scribner's Sons, 1952), 29.
6. Johannes Weiss, *Die Predigt Jesu vom Reiche Gottes* (Göttingen: Vandenhoeck & Ruprecht, 1892); tr. as *Jesus' Proclamation of the Kingdom of God* (London: SCM, 1971), 105, 108.
7. Albert Schweitzer, *Quest*, 402.
8. Albert Schweitzer, *The Mystery of the Kingdom of God* (London, 1914; New York: Schocken Books, 1964), 119.
9. See also the discussion of Marcus J. Borg, *Conflict, Holiness and Politics in the Teaching of Jesus* (New York: Edwin Mellen Press, 1984), 9.
10. Jürgen Moltmann, *Religion, Revolution, and the Future* (New York: Charles Scribner's Sons, 1969). See the chapter "Toward a Political Hermeneutic of the Gospel," 88-93. *New Testament Interpretation: Essays on Principles and Methods*, ed. by I. Howard Marshall (Grand Rapids: Eerdmans, 1977), 55. Paul S. Minear, *To Die and to Live* (New York: Seabury Press, 1977), 79-80.
11. Borg, *Conflict, Holiness and Politics*, 13.
12. Rudolf Bultmann, *Jesus and the Word* (New York: Charles Scribner's Sons, 1958), 38-40.
13. Bultmann, *Jesus*, 52.
14. Bultmann, *Jesus*, 113.
15. Bultmann, *Jesus*, 113.
16. Rudolf Bultmann, *Theology of the New Testament*, tr. by K. Grobel, 2 vols.

(New York: Charles Scribner's Sons, 1951-55), 2:19.

17. Brevard Childs, *Biblical Theology in Crisis*, 128-130.

18. See Robert J. Daly, *Christian Biblical Ethics* (New York: Paulist, 1984), 134-137.

19. Allen Verhey, *The Great Reversal: Ethics and the New Testament* (Grand Rapids: Eerdmans, 1984), 182.

20. The work of David F. Strauss on the life of Jesus, completed in 1836, was notable in the formulation of definite criteria for Gospel criticism. See his work in English *The Life of Jesus Critically Examined*, 4th ed. (London: SCM, 1973). For the more recent discussion, see D. G. A. Calvert, "An Examination of the Criteria for Distinguishing the Authentic Words of Jesus," *New Testament Studies* 18 (1971-72): 209-218; Robert H. Stein, "The 'Criteria' for Authenticity," in *Gospel Perspectives: Studies of History and Tradition in the Four Gospels*, vol. 1, ed. by R. T. France and David Wenham (Sheffield: JSOT Press, 1980), 225-263.

21. See Ben F. Meyer's chapter "Objectivity and Subjectivity in Historical Criticism of the Gospels," in *Critical Realism and the New Testament* (Allison Park, Pa.: Pickwick Publications, 1989). Much of the work is devoted to this and related issues. I made some of these points in my article "Messianic Ethics: Response to the Kingdom of God," *Interpretation* 45 (Jan. 1991): 29-42; used here by permission.

22. See the insightful discussion by Nils A. Dahl, *The Crucified Messiah* (Minneapolis: Augsburg, 1974), 67-69. Now also see Marinus de Jonge, *Jesus, the Servant-Messiah* (New Haven: Yale University Press, 1991), 1-15.

Chapter 1: The Historical Background of the Question

1. Albrecht Ritschl, *Die christliche Lehre von der Rechtfertigung und Versöhnung*, 3 vols. (Bonn: Adolph Marcus, 1870-88).

2. Norman P. J. Metzler, *The Ethics of the Kingdom* (Ann Arbor, Mich.: University Microfilms, 1974), 396f.; Ritschl, *Rechtfertigung*, 2:429-483.

3. Kant's conception was of "an ethical commonwealth under divine moral legislation." See Immanuel Kant, *Religion Within the Limits of Reason Alone* (New York: Harper & Row, 1960), 92.

4. *Rechtfertigung*, chap. 9.

5. Friedrich Schleiermacher, *Christian Faith* (1821; 1880); 1928 ET (English translation) of 1880 ed. by H. R. Machintosh and J. S. Stewart (New York: Harper & Row, 1963), sec. 87, para. 3.

6. *Christian Faith*, 2:361, 363, 425.

7. Richard Rothe, *Still Hours* (London: Hodder and Stoughton, 1886), 239-241, 331-335; Metzler, *Ethics*, 75-76.

8. Schleiermacher, *Christian Faith*, 2:506-508; cf. Metzler, *Ethics*, 68, 72.

9. Metzler, *Ethics*, 73.

10. Metzler, *Ethics*, 72-73.

11. Albrecht Ritschl, *Three Essays* (Philadelphia: Fortress, 1972), 240, 245.

12. Metzler, *Ethics*, 115.

13. Metzler, *Ethics*, 116.

14. Ritschl, *Three Essays*, 236.

15. Ritschl, *Three Essays*, 236.

16. Metzler, *Ethics*, 117.

17. Metzler, *Ethics*, 206.

18. Johannes Weiss, *Die Predigt Jesu vom Reiche Gottes* (Göttingen:

Vandenhoeck & Ruprecht, 1892); ET, *Jesus' Proclamation of the Kingdom of God* (London: SCM, 1971).
    19. As quoted from 2d ed. of Weiss in Metzler, *Ethics*, 206.
    20. Weiss, *Proclamation*, 59.
    21. Weiss, *Proclamation*, 59.
    22. Weiss, *Proclamation*, 76-77; Metzler, *Ethics*, 210.
    23. Weiss, *Proclamation*, 101-103.
    24. Weiss, *Proclamation*, 76-77.
    25. Ritschl, *Three Essays*, 229.
    26. Ritschl, *Three Essays*, 229.
    27. Ritschl, *Three Essays*, 265 (n. 7).
    28. Ritschl, *Rechtfertigung*, 3:12; *Three Essays*, 245.
    29. Ritschl, *Three Essays*, 245.
    30. This means for Ritschl that there is a distinction between the "rules" that govern the person when acting within the scope of his vocation, and those that apply when acting as an individual Christian in intercourse with other people. The primary element in the "ethics of vocation" is patient obedience. See his *Three Essays*, 238, 245, 247, 283 (nn. 161-163).
    31. Ritschl, *Three Essays*, 241.
    32. Ritschl, *Three Essays*, 241. Cf. James Richmond, *Ritschl: A Reappraisal* (London: Collins, 1978), 240-241.
    33. Ritschl, *Rechtfertigung*, 3:267.
    34. Ritschl, *Rechtfertigung*, 3:576.
    35. Metzler, *Ethics*, 181. Metzler notes that "Kant had already called the kingdom of God an invisible reality within the hearts of men" (515, n. 345).
    36. Weiss, *Proclamation*, 82.
    37. Weiss, *Proclamation*, 76.
    38. Weiss, *Proclamation*, 77.
    39. Weiss, *Proclamation*, 84.
    40. Weiss, *Proclamation*, 82, 115.
    41. Weiss, *Proclamation*, 67.
    42. Weiss, *Proclamation*, 68, 73.
    43. Weiss, *Proclamation*, 73.
    44. Weiss, *Proclamation*, 68.
    45. Weiss, *Proclamation*, 78.
    46. Weiss, *Proclamation*, 79.
    47. Weiss, *Proclamation*, 79.
    48. Weiss, *Proclamation*, 94-95.
    49. Weiss, *Proclamation*, 106.
    50. Weiss, *Proclamation*, 108-112.
    51. Weiss, *Proclamation*, 105, 111.
    52. Weiss, *Proclamation*, 52.
    53. Ritschl, *Three Essays*, 230.
    54. Ritschl, *Three Essays*, 258.
    55. Ritschl, *Three Essays*, 258.
    56. Ritschl, *Rechtfertigung*, 3:267.
    57. Weiss, *Proclamation*, 86.
    58. Weiss, *Proclamation*, 86-87.
    59. Weiss, *Proclamation*, 86-87.
    60. Weiss, *Proclamation*, 130.
    61. Ritschl, *Three Essays*, 254.

62. Ritschl, *Three Essays*, 254.

63. Weiss, *Proclamation*, 135. What it means to be liberal here is understood in accord with Enlightenment presuppositions of what is possible and what is not; that is, Christianity is purely a historical phenomenon, and Jesus is to be understood in terms of the critic's own conception of religion as interior experience and ethical ideal. On this basis the eschatological dimension was eliminated from Jesus' teaching.

64. Richard H. Hiers, *Jesus and Ethics: Four Interpretations* (Philadelphia: Westminster, 1968), 32, 38.

65. Adolf von Harnack, *Das Wesen des Christentums* (1899); ET, *What Is Christianity?* (Gloucester, Mass.: Peter Smith, 1978), 6, 38.

66. Harnack, *Christianity*, 52-53.

67. Harnack, *Christianity*, 53.

68. All three citations are from Harnack, *Christianity*, 56.

69. Harnack, *Christianity*, 116.

70. Harnack, *Christianity*, 6.

71. Both citations are from Harnack, *Christianity*, 38.

72. Albert Schweitzer, *Von Reimarus zu Wrede* (Tübingen: Mohr, 1906), tr. by W. Montgomery as *The Quest of the Historical Jesus* (New York: The Macmillan Company, 1968), 238; cf. *The Kingdom of God in 20th-Century Interpretation*, ed. by Wendell Willis (Peabody, Mass.: Hendrickson, 1987), 8-14.

73. Schweitzer, *Quest*, 350.

74. Schweitzer, *Quest*, 351.

75. Schweitzer, *Quest*, 354-355.

76. Schweitzer, *Quest*, 357-358.

77. Schweitzer, *Quest*, 388-390.

78. Schweitzer, *Quest*, 370-371.

79. Schweitzer, *Quest*, 365.

80. Schweitzer, *Quest*, 365-366.

81. Schweitzer, *Quest*, 401.

82. C. H. Dodd, *The Parables of the Kingdom* (New York: Charles Scribner's Sons, 1961), 27.

83. Dodd, *Parables*, 28.

84. Dodd, *Parables*, 28.

85. Dodd, *Parables*, 29.

86. Dodd, *Parables*, 31.

87. Dodd, *Parables*, 34.

88. Dodd, *Parables*, 34.

89. Dodd, *Parables*, 35.

90. Dodd, *Parables*, 37.

91. Dodd, *Parables*, 34.

92. Dodd, *Parables*, 34.

93. Dodd, *Parables*, 83, 39.

94. Dodd, *Parables*, 37.

95. Dodd, *Parables*, 37-38.

96. Dodd, *Parables*, 31.

97. C. H. Dodd, *The Founder of Christianity* (New York: Macmillan, 1970), 84.

98. Dodd, *Founder*, 84-85.

99. Dodd, *Founder*, 85.

100. Dodd, *Founder*, 90.

101. Dodd, *Parables*, 32.
102. Dodd, *Parables*, 79.
103. Dodd, *Parables*, 83-84.
104. Metzler, *Ethics*, 259-260.
105. Metzler, *Ethics*, 261.
106. Rudolf Bultmann, *Jesus and the Word* (New York: Charles Scribner's Sons, 1958), 35-36.
107. Bultmann, *Jesus*, 38.
108. Bultmann, *Jesus*, 39-40.
109. Bultmann, *Jesus*, 40-41.
110. Rudolf Bultmann, *Theology of the New Testament*, tr. by K. Grobel, 2 vols. (New York: Charles Scribner's Sons, 1951-55), 1:4, 7.
111. Bultmann, *Jesus*, 51, 158-159.
112. Bultmann, *Jesus*, 131.
113. Bultmann, *Theology*, 1:19.
114. Bultmann, *Jesus*, 120-132.
115. Bultmann, *Jesus*, 32.
116. Bultmann, *Jesus*, 78, 83.
117. Bultmann, *Jesus*, 77, 92.
118. Bultmann, *Theology*, 1:20.
119. Bultmann, *Jesus*, 113.
120. Bultmann, *Jesus*, 88.
121. Bultmann, *Jesus*, 88.
122. Bultmann, *Jesus*, 88.
123. Bultmann, *Jesus*, 127.
124. Bultmann, *Jesus*, 129.
125. Amos N. Wilder, *Eschatology and Ethics in the Teaching of Jesus* (New York: Harper, 1939), 39.
126. Wilder, *Eschatology*, 40.
127. Wilder, *Eschatology*, 50-51.
128. Wilder, *Eschatology*, 41.
129. Wilder, *Eschatology*, 53.
130. Wilder, *Eschatology*, 58.
131. Wilder, *Eschatology*, 197.
132. Wilder, *Eschatology*, 195.
133. Wilder, *Eschatology*, 199.
134. Wilder, *Eschatology*, 200.
135. Wilder, *Eschatology*, 206-207.
136. Wilder, *Eschatology*, 201.
137. Wilder, *Eschatology*, 153-154.
138. Wilder, *Eschatology*, 199.
139. Wilder, *Eschatology*, 153.
140. Wilder, *Eschatology*, 197.
141. Wilder, *Eschatology*, 166.
142. Wilder, *Eschatology*, 197.
143. Weiss, *Proclamation*, 132.
144. Bultmann, *Theology*, 1:31.
145. Wilder, *Eschatology*, 50.
146. Wilder, *Eschatology*, 50.
147. Richard H. Hiers, *Jesus and the Future* (Atlanta: John Knox, 1981), 107-110.

148. Hiers, *Jesus and Ethics* (Philadelphia: Westminster, 1968), 48-58.
149. Hiers, *Jesus and Ethics*, 155.
150. Hiers, *Jesus and Ethics*, 198-199.
151. Norman Perrin, *Jesus and the Language of the Kingdom* (Philadelphia: Fortress, 1976), 78.
152. Perrin, *Jesus and Language*, 199.
153. Norman Perrin, *Rediscovering the Teaching of Jesus* (London: SCM, 1967), 152-153.
154. Perrin, *Rediscovering*, 152.
155. Ernst Ludwig Dietrich, Šub Šebut: *Die eschatologische Wiederherstellung bei den Propheten* (Giessen: Töpelmann, 1925).
156. Cf. T. W. Manson, *The Teaching of Jesus: Studies in Its Form and Content* (London: Cambridge University Press, 1931); Anton Fridrichsen, et al., *The Root of the Vine* (London: A. C. Black, 1953), 37-62.
157. Joseph Schmitt, "L'Église de Jerusalem, ou la 'Restauration' d'Israël d'après les cinq premier chapitres des Actes," *Recerches de science religieuse* 27 (1953): 209-218.
158. G. B. Caird, *Jesus and the Jewish Nation* (London: Athlone, 1965).
159. Ben F. Meyer, *The Aims of Jesus* (London: SCM, 1979), 127-128, 170-173, 220-222.
160. E. P. Sanders, *Jesus and Judaism* (London: SCM, 1985), 77-119.
161. Gerhard Lohfink, "Die Korrelation von Reich Gottes und Volk Gottes bei Jesus," *Theologische Quartalschrift* 165 (1985): 173-183. See also Gerhard Lohfink, *Jesus and Community* (Philadelphia: Fortress, 1984), 7-26.

Chapter 2: Resources for Jesus' Proclamation and Teaching

1. Gerhard von Rad, "*Basileus* . . . ," in *Theological Dictionary of the New Testament*, ed. by G. Kittel, vol. 1 (Grand Rapids: Eerdmans, 1964), 564ff.; Martin Buber, *Kingship of God* (New York: Harper & Row, 1967), 36-39, 121-128. Martin Buber, in discussion with Gerhard von Rad, brings the issue to focus with primary reference to the Song of the Sea (Exod. 15:1-21) and to the character of the Sinai covenant; see the discussion of the character and date of the song by Frank M. Cross, *Canaanite Myth and Hebrew Epic* (Cambridge, Mass.: Harvard University, 1973), 124-126; David N. Freedman places the origin of the basic formulation of this material before 1200 BCE: *Pottery, Poetry, and Prophecy: Studies in Early Hebrew Poetry* (Winona Lake, Ind.: Eisenbrauns, 1980), 79-81, 216.
2. Millard C. Lind, *Yahweh Is a Warrior* (Scottdale, Pa.: Herald Press, 1980), 50.
3. Lind, *Yahweh*, 51.
4. Rudolf Schnackenburg, *God's Rule and Kingdom* (Montreal: Palm Publishers, 1963), 13.
5. Scholarly opinion is divided on the understanding and origin of the covenant. Still, there are strong arguments to support the view that Exod. 19:3-8 is a reflection of covenant traditions from an early phase of Israel's history. Some scholars have attempted to illuminate the meaning of "covenant" by treaties derived from the Hittite empire (ca. 1500-1200 BCE). These are *suzerainty* treaties between the great king, the *suzerain*, and the lesser monarchs who are his vassals. Of course, even these treaty documents from the Hittites show a variety in form, but they have a number of common elements in particular sequence (i.e., preamble, historical prologue, stipulations, deposition, list of witnesses, curses and blessings).

Exod. 19:3-8 bears covenant formulary marks that first appear in the Hittite suzerainty treaty. The historical prologue is reflected in 19:4, the stipulations in 19:5a, and the blessings in 19:5b-6a. At the same time it is clear that Exod. 19:3-8 is not in detail the text of a covenant. In Josh. 24:1-28, where the covenant is commended and confirmed anew, all the elements of the covenant formulary appear to be represented, some quite fully (historical prologue, stipulations, deposition of the text, and witnesses) and others indicated (the curses and blessings, the preamble): Jon D. Levenson, *Sinai and Zion* (New York: Winston, 1985), 25. God was described to Israel in "covenant" terms (Exod. 19:3-8). The people of the time of Jesus recognized the "theopolitical" nature of this relationship.

6. John Bright refers to the covenant as Israel's acceptance of the lordship of Yahweh. He sees here the origin of the concept of the rule of God over his people, which is the kingdom of God: *A History of Israel* (Philadelphia: Westminster, 1959), 135.

7. Cf. Buber, *Kingship*, 150-151.

8. Buber, *Kingship*, 31. Walther Zimmerli cautions against making a "too close comparison between these treaty formularies" and the covenant of Yahweh with Israel; the caution is appropriate at least to the extent that some of the factors are different in the two settings: Zimmerli, *Old Testament Theology in Outline* (Atlanta: John Knox, 1978), 49-50. Cf. W. L. Moran, "A Kingdom of Priests," in *The Bible in Current Catholic Thought,* ed. by J. L. McKenzie (New York: Herder and Herder, 1962), 7-20, esp. 11-17.

9. Levenson, *Sinai and Zion*, 72.

10. Levenson, *Sinai and Zion*, 72-73.

11. Levenson, *Sinai and Zion*, 72-73.

12. Lind, *Yahweh*, 52.

13. Lind, *Yahweh*, 52, 102; cf. Cross, *Canaanite Myth,* 221.

14. Levenson, *Sinai and Zion*, 97-98.

15. Lind, *Yahweh*, 100.

16. Lind, *Yahweh*, 103.

17. Lind, *Yahweh*, 103.

18. Lind, *Yahweh*, 120.

19. Lind, *Yahweh*, 120.

20. Sigmund Mowinckel, *He That Cometh* (New York: Abingdon, 1954), 24-25. Noteworthy in this context was his study of the theme of kingship in the Psalms.

21. John Gray, *The Biblical Doctrine of the Reign of God* (Edinburgh: T. & T. Clark, 1979), 28-30. Because of the similarities between the ritual of Israel and the Canaanites, Mowinckel concludes that the Israelite festival had developed under the influence of the Canaanite pattern. The more recent careful study of John Gray, in the main, supports Mowinckel in his view that the feast of Tabernacles was the festival of an agricultural community celebrating both the kingship of God (adapted from the Canaanites) and the renewal of the covenant, from Israel's own tradition. Yet insofar as the kingship of God and covenant are shown to be early associated with Israel's own traditions, this will need to be qualified: certain elements may have been derived from foreign sources, but they were then transformed in the service of a new purpose. Mowinckel makes extensive comparisons and shows that it is one thing to note elements Israel took over from alien sources "but quite another what she did with them": 75, 81, 85.

22. Hartmut Gese, *Essays on Biblical Theology* (Minneapolis: Augsburg,

1981), 144. At certain points we would expect parallels of different peoples in the writings dealing with the same general subject matter. With respect to the relation between the divine and creation, Psalm 29 is a case in point. A Canaanite hymn dramatizing the kingship of the god Baal is associated with his activity in rain, snow, and the voice from the clouds in thunder. Gray, *Biblical Doctrine*, 39 (n. 2), translates a fragment of this Canaanite hymn:

> And moreover, may Baal send abundance
> Abundance of moisture with his snow.
> May he send his voice from the clouds,
> His flashing to the earth in lightning.

23. Gray, *Biblical Doctrine*, 42.
24. Gray, *Biblical Doctrine*, 42.
25. Gray, *Biblical Doctrine*, 43.
26. Gray, *Biblical Doctrine*, 43-44.
27. George Eldon Ladd, *The Presence of the Future* (Grand Rapids, Mich.: Eerdmans, 1974), 46-47.
28. Ladd, *Presence*, 48.
29. Claus Westermann, *Elements of Old Testament Theology* (Atlanta: John Knox, 1982), 60.
30. Westermann, *Elements*, 60.
31. Ladd, *Presence*, 48-49.
32. G. R. Beasley-Murray, *Jesus and the Kingdom of God* (Grand Rapids: Eerdmans, 1986), 6.
33. F. F. Bruce, *This Is That: The New Testament Development of Some Old Testament Themes* (Exeter: Paternoster, 1968), 24.
34. Bruce, *This Is That*, 24
35. Mowinckel, *He That Cometh*, 7, 159.
36. Mowinckel, *He That Cometh*, 159, 173. Part of the difficulty is that Mowinckel maintains his position in conjunction with a denial that the prophets developed an eschatology. In order to make his point, he provides a definition of eschatology: the end of the present world order superseded by "another of an essentially different kind," the cataclysmic end of this world followed by the new creation: 125, 159. This definition of eschatology as the end of the present world order superseded by another is, by itself, vague. Mowinckel would himself grant that Deutero-Isaiah hoped for a new order. And if eschatology is understood as a perspective defined by an ultimate horizon, then Amos, at least in this respect, has an eschatology. He saw the end of old Israel in the decisive judgment of God. See further, below.
37. Mayne Saebø, "Messianisms in Chronicles?" *Horizons in Biblical Theology* 2 (1980), 85-109.
38. Gese, *Essays*, 146.
39. Gese, *Essays*, 146-147.
40. Saebø, "Messianisms," 85-109.
41. Gese, *Essays*, 147.
42. Jürgen Moltmann, *The Theology of Hope* (London: SCM, 1967), 129.
43. Moltmann, *Theology*, 128; Westermann, *Elements*, 136.
44. Mowinckel, *He That Cometh*, 256. It certainly appears that Israel pinned its hopes on certain kings in the line of David, only to be disappointed (e.g., Zech. 4:6-9). Every new king must have reminded Israel of the promises made to David. In the events of history, Israelites learned that they must wait on God to send the one worthy to fulfill his purpose.

If the emphasis is on the Messiah as one who would realize the ideals of kingship within the natural course of events in this world, the great expectations embodied in the servant songs properly have no relation to Messianic expectations. According to Mowinckel, the Messiah was not connected to the establishment of the kingdom of God; what was not possible for the Messiah, the servant was to accomplish. This is to say that, with the collapse of the monarchy, messianic hope is enlarged and defined anew. Thus in the Isaiah Targum (52:13-15), the servant is in fact identified as "the Messiah."

45. Mowinckel, *He That Cometh*, 159.
46. Beasley-Murray, *Kingdom*, 22-23.
47. Beasley-Murray, *Kingdom*, 23.
48. Gese, *Essays*, 149-50.
49. E. P. Sanders assembled some of these passages. See "New Temple and Restoration in Jewish Literature," in his *Jesus and Judaism* (London: SCM, 1985), 77-90.
50. Westermann, *Elements*, 126. In the ancient Near Eastern pattern of political authority, the king represented the gods and was above the criticism or judgment of any particular group in society. In Israel, the king was not above judgment.
51. Westermann, *Elements*, 126.
52. Mowinckel, *He That Cometh*, 156-158. According to Mowinckel, there was a correlation between the restoration of Israel and messianic expectation: messianic faith was also faith in the restoration of Israel. Because Mowinckel accepted this correlation, he found it necessary to deny that the prophets developed an eschatology. But why should the restoration of Israel signify the absence of an eschatology? Mowinckel answered: because the restoration of Israel meant "the restoration of the state, the nation, and the monarchy." That is, the restoration of Israel and the work of the Messiah all had their place within the frame of a "natural" course of events. The restoration of Israel and the messianic hope had nothing to do "with a change in the course of the world or an eschatological new creation."
53. Ernst Ludwig Dietrich, *Šub Šebut: Die endzeitliche Wiederherstellung bei den Propheten* (Giessen: Töpelmann, 1925).
54. Dietrich, *Šub Šebut*, 13-28.
55. Mowinckel, *He That Cometh*, 170.
56. Moltmann, *Theology*, 131.
57. Moltmann, *Theology*, 131.
58. Beasley-Murray, *Kingdom*, 47. Quotations of the Pseudepigrapha are from *The Old Testament Pseudepigrapha*, ed. by James H. Charlesworth, 2 vols. (Garden City, N.Y.: Doubleday, 1983-85).
59. Christopher Rowland saw 2 Baruch and 4 Ezra as arising out of the same situation and with similar concerns. He argues convincingly that this was the situation just after the devastation of CE 70 and the issue of what constituted the people of God, those who were finally to be saved: *The Open Heaven* (London: SPCK, 1982), 131, 167-169.
60. Gray, *Biblical Doctrine*, 259; Beasley-Murray, *Kingdom*, 50-51.
61. Geza Vermes, *Jesus the Jew: A Historian's Reading of the Gospels* (Philadelphia: Fortress, 1973), 130.
62. Vermes, *Jesus*, 130.
63. Vermes, *Jesus*, 130.
64. Vermes, *Jesus*, 131.

65. Vermes, *Jesus*, 131.
66. Vermes, *Jesus*, 132; George W. E. Nickelsburg and Michael E. Stone, *Faith and Piety in Early Judaism: Texts and Documents* (Fortress, Philadelphia, 1983), 196-197.
67. Vermes, *Jesus*, 132.
68. Vermes, *Jesus*, 133-134.
69. *The Old Testament Pseudepigrapha*, ed. by Charlesworth, 2:794.
70. This is the rendering of Geza Vermes, *The Dead Sea Scrolls in English* (Harmondsworth: Penguin, 1962).
71. Gese, *Essays*, 148.
72. C. F. D. Moule, *The Origin of Christology* (London: Cambridge University, 1977), 13-14.
73. Gese, *Essays*, 154.
74. Gese, *Essays*, 157-160; Gray, *Biblical Doctrine*, 304-306.
75. E. P. Sanders, *Jesus and Judaism*, 17-90.
76. Bertil Gärtner, *The Temple and the Community in Qumran and the New Testament* (London: Cambridge University, 1965), 18-19.
77. In his allegorical interpretation Philo still bears indirect witness to speculation in the Diaspora on the kingdom of God (cf. *On the Special Laws* 1.207; 4.164; *On Samuel* 2.285; *On Abraham* 261; *On the Life of Moses* 1.190).
78. T. W. Manson, *The Servant Messiah* (London: Cambridge University Press, 1961), 24-25.
79. Westermann, *Elements*, 26.
80. Buber, *Kingship*, 126, 133.
81. Gese, *Essays*, 62.
82. Gese, *Essays*, 176. Westermann sees a distinction between commandments and laws. As to form, the command is addressed directly to the people: "Thou shalt not. . . ." A law, however, has two parts, an assumed situation and a statement of consequences: whosoever does thus and so—this or that will happen to him. The commandments as the direct address of God have their place in worship. The (case) laws were formed in relation to and dependent upon the community forms and their changes. The laws therefore were much more subject to change than the commandments. Laws about slavery became inoperative when slavery was done away with; the law of sacrifices, when the temple was destroyed. On the other hand, the commands like those of the Decalogue have an enduring character. In time "Law" became the primary concept which also included the commandments: Westermann, *Elements*, 175-179.
83. Gese, *Essays*, 185.
84. Buber, *Kingship*, 67-68; Walther Zimmerli, *Old Testament*, 8-9.
85. Zimmerli, *Old Testament*, 7.
86. Moltmann, *Theology*, 115-116.
87. Moltmann, *Theology*, 115-121. God then reveals himself in his name, "which discloses the mystery of his Person to the extent that it discloses the mystery of his faithfulness." And this name is at once a name of promise: God will be present with Israel on the way on which Israel is set, by promise and calling (cf. Exod. 3:12, 14). The promise is one side of the covenant: "God in his freedom binds himself to be faithful to the promise he has given." God gives the command, which corresponds to promise as the other side of the covenant. This created a tension between the time of the promises being issued and their coming to fulfillment, thereby creating freedom for response or obedience. For Israel on the way to Canaan, the promise pointed the goal and the command pointed the way.

88. Patrick D. Miller has extensively studied this correspondence pattern between sin and judgment. A dramatic early example of this is David's sin of murder and adultery. David's misuse of royal power means that his office will be under continual threat and danger. Because David had Uriah killed with the sword, the "sword shall never depart from your house" (2 Sam. 12:10). Because he took Uriah's wife, David himself will experience this (2 Sam 12:11). Evil (*ra'*) leads to evil (*ra'*). The evil of David's sin leads to the evil (punishment) of God's judgment: Miller, *Sin and Judgment in the Prophets* (Chico, Calif.: Scholars Press, 1982), 82-83.

89. Miller, *Sin and Judgment*, 102, 127.

90. Gese, *Essays*, 80-81.

91. Gese, *Essays*, 83-84.

92. H. H. Rowley, *The Relevance of Apocalyptic* (London: Lutterworth, 1963), 38-39.

93. J. A. T. Robinson, *Jesus and His coming* (London: SCM, 1957), 94.

94. Rowland, *The Open Heaven*, 26-29.

95. Ladd, *Presence*, 96.

96. Ladd, *Presence*, 96.

97. Rowland, *The Open Heaven*, 145. Also see note 59, above. As we have noted, the relation between eschatology and ethical response is basically the same in 1 Enoch and 4 Ezra. E. P. Sanders sees 4 Ezra as exceptional in the literature representing Jewish thought on salvation and the keeping of the law. He argues that in this work, the covenant has collapsed and salvation is not by mercy but by merit. In making the point that people will be judged according to their deeds, 4 Ezra evidently presents this emphasis. The point seems to be that a few righteous people have the "good works stored up" to earn final salvation. Yet Ezra, in the same passage, included himself among those who have sinned and who must depend on the mercy of God (8:31-33). The righteous are few, but they include the repentant righteous. Thus, there may be a difference in emphasis, but on the key points with which we are concerned, this work stands in continuity with other Jewish literature. Cf. E. P. Sanders, *Paul and Palestinian Judaism* (London: SCM, 1977), 409, 420-422.

98. Ladd, *Presence*, 97. Also see note 97, above. For a discussion of questions on the unity and teaching in 4 Ezra see E. P. Sanders, *Paul and Palestinian Judaism*, 409-418.

99. What can the "restoration of Israel" mean in this restricted view? Lou H. Silberman sees that ethical response has been severely limited or reduced in this work, but he ascribes this to the circumstances in which it was written. See "The Human Deed in a Time of Despair: The Ethics of Apocalyptic," in *Essays in Old Testament Ethics* (New York: Ktav Publishing House, 1974), 191-202.

100. Weiss states that when the kingdom comes, "God will destroy this old world which is ruled and spoiled by the devil, and create a new world": *Die Predigt Jesu vom Reiche Gottes* (Göttingen: Vandenhoeck & Ruprecht, 1892); ET, *Jesus' Proclamation of the Kingdom of God* (London: SCM, 1971), 130.

101. Albert Schweitzer, *Von Reimarus zu Wrede* (Tübingen: Mohr, 1906), tr. by W. Montgomery as *The Quest of the Historical Jesus* (New York: The Macmillan Company, 1968), 367.

102. Schweitzer, *Quest*, 321, 368.

103. Schweitzer, *Quest*, 254.

104. See the pertinent discussion of T. Francis Glasson, "Schweitzer's Influence—Blessing or Bane?" in the work edited by Bruce Chilton, *The Kingdom of*

God in the Teaching of Jesus (Philadelphia: Fortress, 1984), 107-120. The "rock" on which the pre-Christian dating for the Similitudes rested was largely the identification of "kings and the mighty" as Maccabean princes and the Sadducees who supported them. But the reference is almost certainly to Gentile oppressors (cf. 1 Enoch 46:7; 63:4-7). As for the meager historical references in the work, they, along with other evidence, point to a post-Christian date. See discussions of the issue in Beasley-Murray, *Kingdom*, 63-68; E. P. Sanders, *Paul and Palestinian Judaism*, 347-48; *The Old Testament Pseudepigrapha*, ed. by Charlesworth, 1:6-7.

105. David Wenham, "The Kingdom of God in Daniel," *The Expository Times* 98, no. 5 (Feb. 1987): 132-134; cf. Jeremias, *New Testament Theology* (London: SCM, 1971), 98-99, 205.

106. Wenham, "Kingdom," 132-134; Donald Juel, *Messianic Exegesis: Christological Interpretation of the Old Testament in Early Christianity* (Philadelphia: Fortress, 1987), 169.

107. Wenham, "Kingdom," 132-134.

Chapter 3: The Kingdom of God and the Proper Response

1. Bruce Chilton, "Introduction," in *The Kingdom of God in the Teaching of Jesus*, ed. by Bruce Chilton (Philadelphia: Fortress, 1984), 2-3.

2. David Flusser, *Jesus* (New York: Herder and Herder, 1969); Joachim Jeremias, *New Testament Theology* (London: SCM, 1971).

3. Morton Smith, *Jesus the Magician* (New York: Harper & Row, 1982); Marcus J. Borg, *Jesus: A New Vision: Spirit, Culture, and the Life of Discipleship* (San Francisco: HarperSanFrancisco, 1988).

4. Gustaf Dalman, *The Words of Jesus* (Edinburgh: T. & T. Clark, 1902), 98-101.

5. Ernst Ludwig Dietrich, *Šub Šebut: Die endzeitliche Wiederherstillung bei den Propheten* (Giessen: Töpelmann, 1925).

6. See George B. Caird's essay, "Jesus and Israel: The Starting Point for New Testament Christology," in Robert F. Berry and Sarah A. Edwards, eds., *Christological Perspectives* (New York: Pilgrim, 1982), 58-68.

7. Adolf von Harnack, *What Is Christianity?* (Gloucester, Mass.: Peter Smith, 1978), 16-17.

8. Harnack, *Christianity*, 16-17.

9. R. Bultmann, *The History of the Synoptic Tradition* (Oxford: Basil Blackwell, 1963), 205.

10. Ernst Käsemann, *New Testament Questions of Today* (London: SCM, 1969), 56, 101.

11. Norman Perrin, *Rediscovering the Teaching of Jesus* (London: SCM, 1967), 39.

12. Norman Perrin, *Jesus and the Language of the Kingdom* (Philadelphia: Fortress, 1976), 198-199.

13. Perrin, *Language*, 58-60. The first difficulty with Perrin's exposition of "kingdom of God" is this: He makes Jesus' teaching relative to the kingdom to depart from an apocalyptic understanding of time, not to involve the end of time, and to yield no guidance as to the manner and time of consummation. What then is left of his original assertion that the kingdom of God is an apocalyptic concept in the teaching of Jesus? A second and more serious problem is the distinction he makes between steno-symbols and tensive symbols, identifying apocalyptic reference to "kingdom of God" as an instance of the first, and Je-

sus' use as an instance of the second. Consider the imaginative use of symbol to represent redemption by the Lamb in Revelation 5, or the expression of redemption through the image of combat, the portrayal of the parousia in Revelation 19, and the symbols used to describe the city of God in Revelation 21:9—22:5. To describe these representations of God's redemptive interventions as "steno-symbols" is hardly accurate.

14. Perrin, *Language*, 40.
15. Perrin, *Language*, 198-199.
16. E. P. Sanders, *Jesus and Judaism* (London: SCM, 1985), 91-95.
17. G. B. Caird, *Jesus and the Jewish Nation* (London: Athlone, 1965), 7.
18. Ben F. Meyer, *The Aims of Jesus* (London: SCM, 1979), 117.
19. Meyer, *Aims*, 118.
20. Meyer, *Aims*, 118.
21. Caird, *Jesus and the Jewish Nation*, 7; Meyer, *Aims*, 118. There are points of comparison between the summons of the Baptist and the self-understanding and purposes of other groups. E.g., the exiles returning from the land of Babylon saw "the remnant of Israel in themselves as those who had survived the judgment. The Baptist assembled the remnant of Israel to the extent that he sponsored a public rite to signify the decision of repentance. Though the remnant, like contemporary remnant groups such as the Essenes, was thereby assembled in advance of the judgment, unlike them it did not exist as a separate organized community. It was distinctive in remaining genuinely open to all Israel": Meyer, *Aims*, 120.
22. Meyer, *Aims*, 122; cf. John A. T. Robinson, *The Priority of John* (London: SCM, 1985), 137.
23. Meyer, *Aims*, 123.
24. Bultmann, *Synoptic Tradition*, 246.
25. Josephus, *The Jewish War* 18.116-119; available in *Works of Josephus*, 10 vols., Loeb Classical Library (Cambridge: Harvard University Press, 1926-65). Josephus, for his own purposes, appears to downplay certain features of John's proclamation. But he does say that Herod had him killed because he feared the influence of John with the people.
26. The text of Luke 16:16 is secondary at least in form. See W. G. Kümmel, " 'Das Gesetz und die Propheten gehen bis Johannes'—Lukas 16,16 in Zusammenhang der heils geschichtlichen Theologie der Lukasschriften," in *Verborum Veritas* (Wuppertal: Brockhaus, 1970), 279-301; see esp. 288-300. In substance, the historicity of the saying gains probability from multiple attestation of Jesus' affirmation of the eschatological new age opening with John. See Jeremias, *New Testament Theology*, 46-47. The key to this text is whether the word *heōs/mechri* is to be taken inclusively or exclusively. The emphasis is different in Matthew 11:13 and Luke 16:16, but fundamentally the two are compatible. Cf. G. R. Beasley-Murray, *Jesus and the Kingdom of God* (Grand Rapids: Eerdmans, 1986), 94.
27. Beasley-Murray, *Kingdom*, 94.
28. Beasley-Murray, *Kingdom*, 95.
29. Meyer, *Aims*, 128.
30. Gerhard Lohfink, *Jesus and Community* (Philadelphia: Fortress, 1984), 7-9.
31. To be sure, according to Matthew 3:2, John also announces that the kingdom is near. In John's message, however, the dominant reference is to judgment (Matt. 3:7-10//Luke 3:7-9). Jesus alludes to a difference of emphasis re-

flected in conduct (Matt. 11:12-19//Luke 7:31-35).

32. N. T. Wright, "Jesus, Israel and the Cross," *Society of Biblical Literature: 1985 Seminar Papers* (Atlanta: Scholars Press), 75-95.

33. Beasley-Murray, *Kingdom*, 121.

34. Jeremias, *The Parables of Jesus* (London: SCM, 1963), 101.

35. Caird, *Jesus and the Jewish Nation*, 10.

36. Bultmann thinks that Luke 13:1-5 is probably a formulation of the church. He has difficulty because it is hard to identify it with a specific interest of the church and rule against authenticity on the basis of the principle of dissimilarity. He therefore allows that it could easily contain "historical reminiscence": *Synoptic Tradition*, 55. While Luke 13:1-5 cannot be identified with a specific incident on the basis of other sources, examination of the background provides reason for accepting the episode as historical: I. Howard Marshall, *The Gospel of Luke* (Grand Rapids: Eerdmans, 1978), 52-53.

37. Wright, "Jesus, Israel," 81. The coherence of these predictions with Jesus' eschatological proclamation has come to be more clearly recognized. Cf. Caird, *Jesus and the Jewish Nation*, 11; E. P. Sanders, *Jesus and Judaism*, 71-73.

38. Caird, *Jesus and the Jewish Nation*, 11; Wright, "Jesus and Israel," 81-82.

39. Meyer, *Aims*, 138-39.

40. For a fuller discussion, see James H. Charlesworth, *Jesus Within Judaism* (New York: Doubleday, 1988), 136-138.

41. The historicity of the twelve in Jesus' public career is secured by a convergence of criteria: (1) discontinuity: the ascription of Judas Iscariot to "the twelve"; (2) multiple attestation, such as triple tradition, e.g., Mark 6:7-13//Matt. 10:1, 9-14//Luke 9:1-6; matter common to Matthew and Luke, e.g., Matt. 19:28 //Luke 22:30; and special traditions, e.g., Luke 8:1-3; John 6:67-71; (3) multiform tradition, such as story, logion, and faith-formula in 1 Cor. 15:5. On these criteria, see my discussion in the Introduction. Cf. Beasley-Murray, *Kingdom*, 276.

42. Meyer, *Aims*, 154.

43. On the historicity of this text, opinions are divided; I side with the majority view, well expressed by J. Jeremias, *Jesus' Promise to the Nations* (Philadelphia: Fortress Press, 1982). In particular, there is no clear reason to deny a reference to the inclusion of a Gentile. E. P. Sanders, *Jesus and Judaism*, 220, argues that, since Matt. 8:12 is a Matthean addition, Matt. 8:11 is to be seen as a reference to the dispersion. But the antithetic parallelism of the clauses tells in favor of the authenticity of this logion as a whole: see G. R. Beasley-Murray, *Kingdom*, 169-170.

It is important to note the fact that this favorable word from Jesus on Gentile participation in eschatological salvation by no means stands alone. Much is indicated by Jesus' condemnation of Chorazin, Bethsaida, and Capernaum for failing to make response to his proclamation that would have been accepted by Tyre, Sidon, or Sodom, if they had been offered a like opportunity (cf. Matt. 11:21-24//Luke 10:13-15). Similarly, Jesus refers to the condemnation that the Ninevites and the Queen of Sheba will utter at the judgment, since they gave heed to the word delivered by Jonah and Solomon (cf. Matt. 12:41-42//Luke 11:31-32).

In this pericope (Matt. 8:5-13), the reference to Gentiles participating in the feast of the kingdom is a fitting climax to the account of a Gentile who has come and the meaning of his faith. For a discussion of the unity of the passage, see Eduard Schweizer, *The Good News According to Matthew* (Altanta: John Knox,

1975), 213-214. The text insofar as it supposes the eschatological pilgrimage of the nations, stands in conspicuous discontinuity with the church of the world mission.

44. Beasley-Murray, *Kingdom*, 173.

45. For *makarios* with a singular subject, see Matt. 16:17; 24:46; Ps. 1:1, LXX. Further, with reference to all of the Gospel Beatitudes, scholars differ on which edition, Matthew's or Luke's, is more original. There is general agreement that the basic form and content of the Beatitudes goes back to Jesus. In Matt. 5:3-10 the first eight Beatitudes form a composite description. These Beatitudes constitute a single poetic structure, each sentence formed to parallel the others, each contributing to the meaning of the whole. Each beatitude clarifies and reinforces the others. For example, those who enter the kingdom (5:3, 10) are certainly the same as the "children of God" (5:9): Paul S. Minear, *Matthew: The Teacher's Gospel* (New York: Pilgrim, 1982), 46-47.

Matt. 5:3-4, 6//Luke 6:20-21 are acknowledged by form critics to be the earliest of the Beatitudes, and their authenticity is strongly affirmed. On this see W. D. Davies and Dale C. Allison, *The Gospel According to Saint Matthew* (Edinburgh: T & T Clark, 1988). Cf. Werner Grimm, *Weil ich dich Liebe: Die Verkündigung und Deuterojesaja* (Frankfurt: Herbert Lang Bern, 1976), 68-69.

46. Beasley-Murray makes the point that the Beatitudes set forth the prospect of future glory. This is not to negate the kingdom coming into effect in the present. Thus the emphasis is that when the kingdom which has become effective with its representative comes in its fullness, it is the "poor" who will receive it: *Kingdom*, 162-163.

47. My purpose here is not to deal with the historicity of each beatitude in the Matthean tradition, but to make the point that the Beatitudes evoke an eschatological pattern to which the appropriate response is thankful and singlehearted acceptance. See below. See also Beasley-Murray, *Kingdom*, 162.

48. Schweizer, *Matthew*, 81. The beatitude is a specific genre in both Greek and Jewish contexts (e.g., Ps. 1:1; Prov. 8:34; Dan. 12:12; Ps. of Sol. 4:23; 17:44; 18:16). Early Christians made extensive use of it (e.g., Rom. 14:22; Matt. 5:3-12; John 20:29; Rev. 14:13; 16:15; 22:7).

49. J. Jeremias, *Sermon on the Mount* (Philadelphia: Fortress, 1963), 27.

50. Jeremias, *Sermon on the Mount*, 26-27.

51. The text of Mark 1:14-15 is secondary in form: it is Mark's own summary, as we have observed. Yet it is historical in substance: Jesus did proclaim the imminence of the kingdom of God. Both John and Jesus make a proclamation and issue a call to repentance. But the distinctive note in Jesus' speech and action begins to emerge; the accent for Jesus falls on the fulfillment of time, the kingdom of God, and acceptance (in trust) of this good news: cf. Vernon K. Robbins, *Jesus the Teacher* (Philadelphia: Fortress Press, 1984), 28-30.

"Repentance" derived its meaning from the proper response to the proclamation: see below. The precise form "Believe the gospel/good news" is probably Markan or pre-Markan. On later Hebrew and Aramaic, see Rudolf Pesch, *Das Markusevangelium* (Freiburg-Basel-Wien: Herder, 1977), 1:103. Respecting repentance in the Jewish perspective, hear Rabbi Levi from the third century: "If the Israelites would but repent for one day they would be redeemed, and the son of David would come immediately": see Jack P. Lewis, *The Gospel According to Matthew*, Living Word Commentary (Austin: Sweet, 1976), 1:74.

52. Paul S. Minear, *Commands of Christ* (New York: Abingdon, 1972), 23-24.

53. Minear, *Commands*, 25.
54. Minear, *Commands*, 21-28.
55. Minear, *Commands*, 24-26.
56. Jeremias, *Theology*, 119. E. P. Sanders, *Jesus and Judaism*, 203-204. Sanders reviews or criticizes Jeremias. He notes that there is very little material in which Jesus calls Israel to repent. Material that so portrays Jesus, he regards as Lucan (Luke 15:7, 10; 19:1-9).
57. Stephen Westerholm, *Jesus and Scribal Authority* (Lund: CWK Gleerup, 1978), 132.
58. E. P. Sanders, *Jesus and Judaism*, 206.
59. George F. Moore, *Judaism in the First Centuries of the Christian Era* (Cambridge: Harvard University Press, 1927), 1:507; J. Behm, "Metanoeō, metanoia," in *Theological Dictionary of the New Testament*, ed. by G. Kittel, vol. 4 (Grand Rapids: Eerdmans, 1967), 989-999.
60. C. G. Montefiore, *Rabbinic Literature and Gospel Teachings* (London: Macmillan, 1930), 391. *The Lord's Prayer and Jewish Liturgy*, ed. by Jakob J. Petuchowski and Michael Brocke (New York: Seabury, 1978). Petuchowski (50-51), in discussing the Eighteen Benedictions, says the prayer may well go back to the prerabbinic period and was already used by the priests in the Jerusalem Temple.
61. Bruce D. Chilton, *The Glory of Israel: The Theology and Provenience of the Isaiah Targum* (Sheffield: JSOT, 1983), 37-46. In this Targum he sees reflected important elements of theology "from just prior to the destruction of the Temple until the beginning of the Bar Kochba revolt," with further developments in the Amoraic period: Chilton, 12.
62. Chilton, *The Glory of Israel*, 40-44.
63. George Eldon Ladd, *The Presence of the Future* (Grand Rapids, Mich.: Eerdmans, 1974), 110.
64. E. P. Sanders, *Jesus and Judaism*, 92-93.
65. Rudolf Pesch, *Das Markusevangelium*, 1:102. Aloysius M. Ambrozic calls attention to the important point in this connection: the perfect tense of the verb *peplērōtai* (fulfilled) in Mark 1:15a precedes its subject and thus emphasizes completed action: *The Hidden Kingdom: A Redactional Critical Study of the References of the Kingdom of God in Mark's Gospel* (Washington D.C.: The Catholic Biblical Association of America, 1972), 21.
66. "The time is fulfilled" (*peplērōtai ho kairos*, Mark 1:15); "In order that what was spoken might be fulfilled" (*hina plērōthē to rhēthen*, Matt. 4:14, 17); "Today this scripture has been fulfilled in your hearing" (*sēmeron peplērōtai hē graphē hautē en tois ōsin humōn*, Luke 4:21).
67. Meyer, *Aims*, 132.
68. Marcus J. Borg, *Conflict, Holiness and Politics in the Teaching of Jesus* (New York: Edwin Mellen Press, 1984), 110-111.
69. Meyer, *Aims*, 162. To say, as does G. F. Moore, that Jesus called for repentance in the same way and to the same purpose as the Jewish teachers of the law, is therefore completely inadequate: *Judaism*, 1:518-519. On Jesus' table fellowship with sinners, now also see John Dominic Crossan, *The Historical Jesus: The Life of a Mediterranean Jewish Peasant* (San Francisco: HarperSanFrancisco, 1991).
70. Leander E. Keck, *A Future for the Historical Jesus* (Nashville: Abingdon, 1971), 222.
71. Cf. Bultmann, *History of the Synoptic Tradition*, 54, 118.

72. Edward Schillebeeckx, *Jesus: An Experiment in Christology* (New York: Seabury, 1979), 196. The historicity of Jesus' reception by those who knew him and his parents is established on the basis of discontinuity with earliest Christianity.

73. Schillebeeckx, *Jesus*, 196-197.

74. That is to say no more or less than that Jesus, in accord with his purpose, expected faith but allowed for the refusal of faith. Jesus expected faith, and on certain occasions is amazed at the lack of faith (Mark 4:40; 6:6). Specifically, forgiveness is bound both to faith and to repentance (e.g., Mark 2:5; Luke 15:7, 10). The faith Jesus calls for is actualized and completed in the repentance that carries a person into a new relationship (cf. Mark 10:52; Luke 17:11-19). If faith and repentance are interdependent, this means that the call for one tacitly includes the other. Which is called for in a particular case will depend on the standpoint of those addressed: those outside and uninvolved are directed to repent (e.g., Mark 6:12; Luke 13:3); those already involved are called to faith (e.g., Mark 5:36; Luke 7:50). Thus the focus of each term may be distinct, but the substantial correspondence between the two terms also becomes evident.

75. Meyer, *Aims*, 159. Pesch underscores the point that Jesus' eating with sinners (e.g., Mark 2:15-17) is part of the fabric of what we know about Jesus' activity. Further, it is also confirmed out of the charges of the opponents: *Markusevangelium*, 1:167.

76. Meyer, *Aims*, 159; Joachim Jeremias, *Die Abendmahlsworte Jesu*, 3d ed. (Göttingen: Vandenhoeck & Ruprecht, 1960), tr. by N. Perrin as *The Eucharistic Words of Jesus* (New York: Charles Scribner's Sons, 1966), 232; cf. John Dominic Crossan, *The Historical Jesus*.

77. Meyer, *Aims*, 159-160. Yet it is clear that "clean" and "unclean" cannot be equated with righteous and unrighteous: see E. P. Sanders, *Jesus and Judaism*, 177-188.

78. Jeremias, *New Testament Theology*, 134-151.

79. Heinz Schürmann, *Traditionsgeschichtliche Untersuchungen zu den synoptischen Evanglien* (Düsseldorf: Patmos-Verlag, 1968), 146.

80. T. W. Manson, *The Teaching of Jesus: Studies of Its Form and Content* (London: Cambridge University Press, 1931), 163; R. Bultmann, *History and Eschatology*, The 1955 Gifford Lectures (Edinburgh: University Press, 1957), 31. Cf. Norman Perrin, *Rediscovering the Teaching of Jesus*, 67: "The victory of God is resulting not in the restoration to a state of purity of the land Israel and its people, but in the restoration to wholeness of a single disordered individual. The experience of the individual, rather than that of the people as a whole, has become the focal point of the eschatological activity of God."

81. A. Oepke, *Das neue Gottesvolk in Schrifttum, bildender Kunst und Weltgestaltung* (Gütersloh: Mohr, 1950), 165-167.

82. See Rudolf Schnackenburg, *God's Rule and Kingdom*, tr. by John Murray (Freiburg: Herder, 1963; Montreal: Palm Publishers, 1963), 222-223.

83. T. W. Manson's emphasis on the present overlooks the fact that the present participation in the kingdom is characterized by anticipation of the kingdom in consummation: *The Teaching of Jesus*, 163, 173. John W. Bowman, *Prophetic Realism and the Gospel* (Philadelphia: Westminster, 1955), 200-202.

84. The moral struggle is over, though the values that the ethics had expressed within the limitations of history endure, sublated by eternal life.

85. C. H. Dodd in *The Parables of the Kingdom* (New York: Charles Scribner's Sons, 1961), 148-149, makes the point that the parable of the wheat and

the weeds has its own emphasis, but he has great difficulty in giving a coherent interpretation of this parable. He, of course, equates the coming kingdom with the harvest that is already realized in the work of Jesus. He may not be completely off track in relating the question in the parable about the weeds to the presence of many sinners in Israel. This being the case, how can his interpretation be that the kingdom of God has come (in fullness)? In the parable, this question of what to do about the weeds can only come before the harvest. But in Dodd's framework, the question and answer remain mysterious because harvest has come. The attempt to identify the coming reign of God with one element in the parable here most visibly fails.

86. Beasley-Murray, *Kingdom*, 133.
87. Beasley-Murray, *Kingdom*, 134.
88. Perrin, *Language*, 89.
89. Perrin, *Language*, 134.
90. Thus Allen Verhey, who highlights the accent in Matthew on fulfillment of the law, sets Matthew and Mark in contrast at this point: Mark presents freedom from the law, whereas Matthew teaches that the law holds. One must agree that the accent falls differently even within a single Gospel, depending on the point that is being made; this is not only to be expected but true of the two different Gospel accounts. To say the least, careful attention to both differences and appropriate coherence seems important for the sake of proper interpretation. See his *The Great Reversal: Ethics and the New Testament* (Grand Rapids: Eerdmans, 1984), 83-87.
91. Eduard Schweizer in his book *Matthew* suggests that the material as it now stands in Matthew has been developed from three sayings of Jesus "which may have belonged together from the very outset as defining his attitude." Similarly, Davies and Allison see dependence of this tradition at key points on Jesus (particularly well grounded are Matt. 6:4, 7-8, 9-13, 14-15). Yet much of the content and form of the sayings on almsgiving and fasting, because of its "finely balanced structure" and "patently catechetical character," is taken to be of post-Easter origin. On these premises one can well acknowledge the editorial work of Matthew (or his predecessor) and still hold to dominical origin: "balance" does not point away from Jesus. W. D. Davies and Dale C. Allison, *Matthew*, 574-575. If the material has been reformulated, Paul Minear provides some cogent arguments for accepting in substance the authenticity of this teaching: *Commands*, 66-68.
92. Ben F. Meyer from a piece on "Jesus Christ" to be published in the *Anchor Bible Dictionary* (New York: Doubleday).
93. Meyer, "Jesus Christ."
94. The connection between Jesus' proclamation of the kingdom coming with blessing for the poor in the Beatitudes also has ties to Isa. 61:1-2. See Davies and Allison, *Matthew*, 443.
95. Gerhard Lohfink, *Jesus and Community*, 14-15.
96. Lohfink, *Jesus and Community*, 88.
97. Graham N. Stanton, *The Gospels and Jesus* (New York: Oxford University Press, 1989), 202.
98. John H. Yoder, *The Original Revolution* (Scottdale, Pa.: Herald Press, 1977), 51; W. D. Davies, *The Setting of the Sermon on the Mount* (London: Cambridge University Press, 1966), 240-241.
99. Borg, *Conflict, Holiness and Politics*, 129.
100. The use of the word *perfect* in Matt. 5:48 has been much controverted. It

does create serious difficulties if it is interpreted as a call to absolute flawlessness of character so as to leave no room for growth. The OT background is Deut. 18:13 ("be blameless," *tamin, teleios*) and Lev. 19:2 ("be holy as I . . . am holy"). The emphasis is whole-hearted devotion to the imitation of God. The term refers to what is whole, intact, undivided (cf. 1 Kings 8:61; 11:4; 15:3-4). See Eduard Schweizer, *Matthew*, 135.

101. See K. M. Campbell, "The New Jerusalem in Matthew 5:14," *Scottish Journal of Theology* 31 (1978), 335-363.

Chapter 4: Jesus' Messianic Mission

1. T. W. Manson, *The Teaching of Jesus: Studies of Its Form and Content*, 2d ed. (London: Cambridge University Press, 1935), 4-6, 13-17.

2. Respecting the historicity of the pre-Easter designation of Jesus as Messiah, the following data are relevant:

(1) According to John 6:15, a Galilean crowd intended to make Jesus a "king." This tradition gains in plausibility from contemporary research on messianic movements in the late second-temple period. See R. A. Horsley and J. S. Hanson, *Bandits, Prophets, and Messiahs* (Minneapolis: Winston, 1985).

(2) The riddle on the new sanctuary (Mark 14:58//Matt. 26:61), the historicity of which is generally acknowledged, implies a royal, messianic function.

(3) Jesus' proclamation of the kingdom of God was clearly God's last word to Israel. The envoy of God is accordingly equipped with plenipotentiary authority, as indicated by Jesus' use of "Amen" and the emphatic "I" (*egō*); this is personal rather than scriptural authority. Matt. 4:23; 9:35; cf. 11:5 take "proclamation" to be a messianic function (cf. Qumran's Melchizedek text: 11QMelch 18).

(4) Further data, suggesting a claim to messiahship, derive from the passion story: the answer to the high priest (Mark 14:62//Matt. 26:64); the purple cloak, the crown of thorns, the *titulus* or inscription on the cross.

(5) The confession of Caesarea Philippi is followed by the exchange between Jesus and Peter. This exchange, indeed, implies at least high status for Jesus. Moreover, in the Synoptic tradition, the exchange is firmly located as the follow-up on the confession. In Luke the two are combined in a single pericope. Cf. Bultmann, *The History of the Synoptic Tradition* (Oxford: Basil Blackwell, 1963), 258. See also Jeremias, *Theology of the New Testament* (New York: Charles Scribner's Sons, 1951), 32.

3. Cf. C. F. D. Moule, "Mark 4:1-20 Yet Once More," *Neotestamentica et Semitica* (Edinburgh: T & T Clark, 1969), 99-101.

4. Moule, *Neotestamentica et Semitica*, 106. See also the discussion on the parables, above.

5. Martin Hengel, "That Jesus Did Send Forth the Disciples Can Hardly Be Doubted in Principle," in *The Charismatic Leader and His Followers* (Edinburgh: T. & T. Clark, 1981), 73-74.

6. Paul S. Minear reviewed these distinctions between hearers relative to Jesus' teaching in the Synoptics carefully. See his "Audience Criticism and Markan Ecclesiology," in *Neue Testament und Geschichte*, ed. by Heinrich Baltensweiler and Bo Reicke (Tübingen: J. C. B. Mohr, 1972), 77-89; "The Disciples and the Crowds in Matthew," *Anglican Theological Review*, Supp. ser., 1974:28-44; and "Jesus' Audiences According to Luke," *Novum Testamentum* 16 (1974): 81-109.

7. One may find Minear's basic presentation convincing without neces-

sarily accepting his precise delineation of these groups of hearers. The boundaries of the two groups, disciples and crowds, seem not to be as firm as he makes them. Note that "disciple" is used to refer to people beyond the twelve and that "crowd" can refer to others than people sympathetic to Jesus. The crowd is indeed most often a reference to people sympathetic to Jesus, but to speak of them as "committed believers" is going too far and makes it difficult to preserve the distinction between "crowd" and "disciples." The relation of the crowd to Jesus is not settled; among them are those who cease to follow and those who come forward to become disciples (cf. Matt. 8:18-22).

8. Manson, *Teaching*, 19; cf. J. Arthur Baird, *Audience Criticism and the Historical Jesus* (Philadelphia: Westminster, 1969), 11-16.

9. Manson, *Teaching*, 320-327. Even if it is clear that not all the words appearing as indices for each category are equally significant, still the number of definite words specific to each of the three categories is impressive.

10. See James H. Charlesworth, *Jesus Within Judaism* (New York: Doubleday, 1981), 9-24; Graham N. Stanton, *The Gospels and Jesus* (London: Oxford University Press, 1989), 17-18, 156-158.

11. Stanton, *Gospels*, 18; Ben F. Meyer, *The Aims of Jesus* (London: SCM, 1979), 82-83. The greater part of the material which the Synoptic tradition represents as esoteric calls from itself for such a context; thus, it is difficult, if not impossible, to imagine esoteric traditions, such as the prophecy of the destruction of the temple or the eucharistic words, as ever having had a place in "public" tradition. The issue, then, is not primarily one of "setting." It is directly an issue of historicity itself. When Jesus taught that the temple would be destroyed, he certainly reserved this teaching to his disciples, regardless of whether the details of the setting of Mark 13 and parallels are secondary.

At the same time, Jesus evidently said something about the temple in the public domain that became the basis of the testimony at his trial (Mark 14:58//Matt. 26:61) and the mockery beneath the cross (Mark 15:29//Matt. 27:40). This testimony and mockery (with distortion) most likely has its source in the enigmatic saying of Jesus reported in John 2:19, which cannot but remain obscure to his hearers. It is occasioned by the demand for a sign to establish Jesus' authority for the action of cleansing the temple (John 2:14-18). In support of the character and historicity of this saying, there is another equally disconcerting and enigmatic saying, the words on the "sign of Jonah" (Matt. 12:39; Luke 11:29), also in response to the demand for a sign. That Jesus made some such statement about the temple is confirmed by the testimony at the trial and the mockery at the cross.

The saying is conditional, "destroy this temple," followed by the main assertion, "and in three days I will raise it up (again)." Eschatologically, the temple was expected to have significance not only for Israel but for the whole world (cf. Isa. 2:2-4; 28:16; 51:3). The temple, always associated with community, by Jesus' time could directly signify believing community (cf. Isa. 28:16; 1QS 5.5f.; 8.7-10; 9.3-6; 1QH 6.25-28). To unbelief, Jesus would offer no sign but the "temple" identified with and coming into being out of the climactic events of his mission —Jesus and his renewed community. Therefore, what in John 2:19 is enigmatic and conditional in character is turned into open statement by Jesus in his teaching to the disciples.

Our conclusion, then, is that the historicity of esoteric traditions should be established. There is, however, no need to reconstruct specific settings for such traditions. The Synoptists have already done this for us. Cf. E. E. Ellis, "Present and Future Eschatology in Luke," *New Testament Studies* 12 (1964-65): 27-41.

12. Moule, *Birth of the New Testament* (London: Adam & Charles Black, 1981), 10.

13. E. P. Sanders, *Jesus and Judaism* (London: SCM, 1985), 14, makes this point in dependence on Berger Gerhardsson, "Der Weg der Evangelienstradition," in *Das Evangelium und die Evangelien* (Tübingen: Mohr, 1983), 79-102. As part of the evidence in making this point, Gerhardsson notes the fact that in Acts we become aware that the author knows the life and work of Jesus; but the writer does not cite detail from that knowledge in Acts, so we might neglect to recognize his full and detailed knowledge of Jesus' teaching and work. Again, the author of 1 John at the least was well aware of the Johannine form of the Jesus tradition, if he was not himself the evangelist. Yet he does not once explicitly cite a word from Jesus; but it was clearly fundamental for him (2:7, 24; 3:11): Gerhardsson, 81.

14. Sanders, *Jesus*, 14.

15. Sanders, *Jesus*, 14.

16. His primary interest is to examine the place of audience identification in terms of the redactional work of each of the Synoptics. In the process he shows that the audience tradition is part of the whole fabric of the Gospel material. There are differences on this point between the Gospels: Luke is less definite at times in his audience identifications than Matthew and Mark. But this does not destroy their coherence in this respect. See also E. P. Sanders and Margaret Davies, *Studying the Synoptic Gospels* (London: SCM, 1989), 123-137.

17. Vernon K. Robbins is convincing in making the point that the best hope for comprehensive understanding of Jesus' teaching "lies in methods which preserve and appreciate the fields of discourse which early Christians used to transmit the settings, action, and speech of Jesus." And he continues by making the observation that, "unfortunately, traditional methods have exercised great violence on the fields of discourse which bring Jesus' parables and sayings to us." Referring to source, form, and redaction criticism, Robbins notes that they "cut the sayings and parables out of their contexts." Since situations and actions provide the contextual field in which sayings and stories have meaning, to take them out of this field is not only to remove them from their context but also to reconstruct the data of the saying or parable itself.

Through the use of what he terms the "criterion of pragmatic relations," Robbins develops a pattern of analysis in which he identifies extant contextual fields of discourse as part of a larger network of communication; later parts of the network emerged through some kind of bridging with the earlier network. See Robbins, "Pragmatic Relations as a Criterion for Authentic Sayings," *Focus and Facets Forum* 1 (3 August 1985): 35-62.

Even on the presupposition that *context* is generally secondary, this would not provide license for the effort to determine the original meaning of a saying in isolation from the context. The editorial pattern not only reveals the intention of the Gospel writer but may well also point to the meaning of the saying in the earlier tradition from which it was derived. The immediate context therefore remains a matter of crucial importance.

18. David Daube, *The New Testament and Rabbinic Judaism* (London: The Athlone Press, 1956), 142ff. Morton Smith makes much the same point. He cites Paul's reference to "the wisdom of God in a mystery" that he speaks to the mature (1 Cor. 2:1-6). He also refers to the parallel distinction recognized by the Tannaim between material suitable for public teaching and that reserved for se-

cret teaching: Mishnah Hagigah 2:1; available in *The Mishnah*, tr. by Herbert Danby (London: Oxford University Press, 1933), 212-213; cf. Talmud. See Smith, *Tannaitic Parallels and the Gospels* (Philadelphia: Society of Biblical Literature, 1968), 155-156; and Joachim Jeremias, *New Testament Theology* (London: SCM 1971), 255-257.

Jeremias goes on to make the point that esoteric teaching was both prevalent and important in the Judaism of Jesus time. It was a crucial element of the Qumran community, and it was present as the reason for the gathering of groups of disciples in other branches of Judaism. One aspect of the character of apocalyptic writings seems to be that it is reserved for an in-group.

19. William Wrede, *The Messianic Secret* (London: Cambridge, 1971). For a concise review of Wrede's position, see Martin Hengel, *Studies in the Gospel of Mark*, tr. by John Bowden (London: SCM, 1985), 41-45.

20. See J. A. Fitzmyer, "Further Light on Melchizedek from Qumran Cave 11," *Journal of Biblical Literature* 86 (1967): 25-41; reprinted in his *Essays on the Semitic Background of the New Testament* (Chico, Calif.: Scholars Press, 1974), 246-267, esp. 248ff.

21. On the royal entry, see the parallel addressed by Richard A. Horsley and J. S. Hanson, *Bandits, Prophets, and Messiahs* (Minneapolis: Winston, 1985), 110-117, 256-257. For the cleansing, it is clear that in Israel the establishing, maintenance, and reform of cult was historically a royal prerogative in Israel as in Mesopotamia.

22. See N. A. Dahl, "The Crucified Messiah," in *The Crucified Messiah and Other Essays* (Minneapolis: Augsburg, 1974), 10-36.

23. Marinus de Jonge, "The Earliest Christian Use of *Christos:* Some Suggestions," in *New Testament Studies* 32 (1986): 321-343.

24. Horsley, *Bandits*.

25. Meyer, *Aims*, 188.

26. Horsley, *Bandits*, 256-257.

27. Horsley, *Bandits*, 98-102, 108-110.

28. M. de Jonge, "The Earliest Christian Use of *Christos*."

29. Dietrich Bonhoeffer, *Ethics* (New York: Macmillan, 1955), 80.

30. To interpret Jesus' response to the confession, "You are the Christ," as a negative is not only alien to Mark as a whole it also overlooks the progression from Mark 8:27-30 to 8:31-33. The first text anticipates the content of the second; the second text interprets and completes the first. On the meaning and authenticity of these texts see Meyer, *Aims*, 190, 215-219. Cf. Stanton, *Gospels*, 223.

31. See the cautious discussion of these texts in Joseph A. Fitzmyer, *The Gospel According to Luke (X-XXIV)* (New York: Doubleday, 1985), 993-997. The concise parabolic language strongly supports the authenticity of these sayings.

32. Albert Schweitzer, *Von Reimarus zu Wrede* (Tübingen: Mohr, 1906), tr. by W. Montgomery as *The Quest of the Historical Jesus* (New York: Macmillan, 1968), 388-390.

33. Rudolf Bultmann, *Das Verhältnis der urchristlichen Christusbotschaft zum historischen Jesus*, Sitzungsberichte der Heidelberger Akadamic der Wissenschaften, Phil-his. Klasse, 1960, Z. Abhandlung, 3. Aufl. (Heidelburg, 1962), 12.

34. The debate is well represented in the two essays, one by Anton Vögtle, "Todesankündigungen und Todesverständnis Jesu," and one by Rudolf Pesch,

"Das Abendmahl und Jesu Todesverständnis," both in *Der Tod Jesu: Deutungen im Neuen Testament*, ed. by K. Kertelge, Quaestiones Disputatae 74 (Freiburg: Herder, 1976): 51-113, 137-187.

35. Vögtle, "Todesankündigungen," 67-76.

36. Vögtle, "Todesankündigungen," 113; cf. Fiedler, "Sünde und Vergebung im Christentum," *Concilium* 10 (1974), 568-571.

37. Pesch, "Das Abendmahl," 181-182.

38. Pesch, "Das Abendmahl," 183-184.

39. That the text is a post-Easter product cannot be assumed from the imagery of the cross. That imagery was commonplace in Palestinian Judaism. The text of Mark 8:34//Matt. 16:24//Luke 9:23 envisages the moment when the condemned man takes the *patibulum* or yoke on his shoulder and turns to face the howling mob from which he is now cast out. The rabbis (Babylonian Talmud Sanhedrin 85a) considered the condemned man to be already dead. Anyone who strikes him is free of punishment. In the Gospel text this outcast is proposed as the paradigm of discipleship. Hence, the relevance to historicity of the index of originality. Cf. Martin Hengel, *Studies in the Gospel of Mark*, 42.

40. Hengel, *The Charismatic Leader*.

41. Hans-Dieter Betz, *Nachfolge und Nachahmung Jesu Christi im Neuen Testament* (Tübingen: Mohr, 1967).

42. Ernest Best, *Following Jesus: Discipleship in the Gospel of Mark* (Sheffield: JSOT, 1981), 37-40.

43. Martin Hengel has given thorough consideration to the relation between disciple and master in the Jewish and Hellenistic world, and the points here presented sum up part of his exposition: *The Charismatic Leader*, 42-57.

44. Best, *Following Jesus*, 37; William L. Lane, *The Gospel According to Mark* (Grand Rapids: Eerdmans, 1974), 307.

45. Robert P. Meye, *Jesus and the Twelve: Discipleship and Revelation in Mark's Gospel* (Grand Rapids, Mich.: Eerdmans, 1968), 123. On Matt. 16:24//Mark 8:34//Luke 9:23, some make much of the aorist tense of *aratō ton stauron*, "take up their cross," to indicate a single action and thus a single act of martyrdom. But attention should also be directed to the present imperative of *akoloutheitō*, "let them ... follow," implying a period of discipleship after taking up the cross. Cf. Best, *Following Jesus*, 38-39.

46. Jeremias, *The Parables of Jesus* (London: SCM, 1962), 218-219.

47. See Yoder, *The Politics of Jesus* (Grand Rapids: Eerdmans, 1972), 58-61; Cf. Sanders, *Jesus and Judaism*, 294-295.

48. Jeremias, "Die älteste Schicht der Menschensohn-Logien," *Zeitschrift für die neutestamentliche Wissenschaft und die Kunde der älteren Kirche* 58 (1967): 159-172, esp. 167.

49. Meyer, *Aims*, 211-213.

50. Yoder, *Politics*, 45.

51. E. J. Tinsley, *The Imitation of God in Christ* (London: SCM, 1960), 31.

52. Stanley Hauerwas, *The Peaceable Kingdom* (Notre Dame: Notre Dame University Press, 1983), 78.

53. C. F. D. Moule, *The Origin of Christology* (London: Cambridge, 1977), 10-22. The use of *gar*, "for," in Mark 8:35 shows that 8:35 is closely bound to 8:34 and explains it. After *heneken*, "for the sake of," in 8:35: *emou kai*, "for my sake," is lacking in some important manuscripts but present in others; both Matt. 16:25 and Luke 9:24 have it but lack *kai tou euaggeliou*, "and for the sake of the gospel." The last phrase is probably an interpretative addition by Mark. Cf. Best,

Following Jesus, 40; Ralph P. Martin, *Mark: Evangelist and Theologian* (Grand Rapids: Zondervan, 1972, 1986), 24-28.

A new argument for the historicity of Mark 10:45//Matt. 20:28 has been offered by Peter Stuhlmacher, "Vicariously Giving His Life for Many, Mark 10:45 (Matt. 20:28)," in *Reconciliation, Law, and Righteousness* (Philadelphia: Fortress, 1986), 16-29. Stuhlmacher's treatment shows that the saying (1) does not derive from eucharistic tradition, though it does parallel the eucharistic words in part. (2) It draws on Isa. 43:3-4 and on Isa. 53:11-12, but, above all, has its distinctiveness from the reversal of the situation in Dan. 7:14 where "all peoples, nations, and languages" serve the "one like a son of man" (RSV). Here the Son of man serves them by making himself their ransom.

54. A contrast between "physical life" and "spiritual life" is not intended. Consistency in the meaning of *psychē*, "life," throughout Mark 8:35 seems required by the use of the pronouns for it in the second half of each contrast. And it can have this consistency only if it is given the fullest possible meaning as true or essential life: Best, *Following Jesus*, 41.

55. J. L. Houlden reviews this material on Christology and discipleship in Mark and concludes that there is a "paucity of ethical material." The small amount of ethical content which Mark does present derives from nonethical interests: Christology and the kingdom of God. But does the evidence that is cited for this judgment not simply show that the ethics is theological rather than autonomous? See Houlden, *Ethics and the New Testament* (London: Penguin, 1973), 41-42.

56. Yoder, *Politics*, 47.

57. Note the supporting evidence of the social relevance of this "minority" community: the formation of a group of disciples comprised of both former Zealots and former publicans, the representative number twelve, and the mission of the twelve, which is the source of Herod's first concern and perplexity about Jesus (Luke 9:7-9).

58. C. H. Dodd, *The Interpretation of the Fourth Gospel* (London: Cambridge University Press, 1968), 393. The view that John *restricts* love to members of the community is finally an argument from silence. Even in the call to be a community of love, others beyond the community are not left out of concern (John 13:35b). Love is thus not confined to disciples, but it is defined in the community of disciples. Cf. John A. T. Robinson, *The Priority of John* (London: SCM, 1985), 334-336.

59. Bultmann refers to this on one hand as a reformulation and expansion of a dominical saying, and on the other as a "Christian construction": *Tradition*, 141, 147. But the teaching is in coherence with what we know from Jesus; Bultmann's claim is unsupported.

60. Jeremias, *Theology*, 192-194. On the authenticity and historicity of this saying, see the fairly full discussion by I. Howard Marshall in *The Gospel of Luke* (Grand Rapids: Eerdmans, 1978), 867-868. There is some reason to hold to a dominical origin of this saying, but it has a broken textual history.

61. Joachim Jeremias, "The Lord's Prayer in the Light of Recent Research," in *The Prayers of Jesus*, Studies in Biblical Theology, no. 6 (London: SCM, 1967), 92, 103.

62. This statement is strongly aligned in content with other teaching on discipleship. It may be a reformulation but in substance comes from Jesus. See Fitzmyer, *Luke*, 1061.

63. Fitzmyer sums up the statement from Luke: "Only the person who is ca-

pable of a radical and painful decision, to set all natural, human relations behind the connection with Jesus (cf. 9:59-62; 8:19-21; 11:27-28) and to give up life itself in martyrdom, can really become a disciple of Jesus": *Luke*, 1062.

64. Paul Minear discusses with real insight the rationale for persecution on the basis of John 16:1-3. See his *John: The Martyr's Gospel* (New York: Pilgrim, 1984), 24-30.

65. Yoder, *Politics*, 128, 46-47.

66. This is an example of teaching common to John and the Synoptics and represented by different vocabulary (so that literary dependence is inherently improbable); yet they are clearly the same teaching. The variety of forms supports both the authenticity and importance of this teaching (cf. Matt. 10:39; 16:25; Mark 8:35; Luke 9:29; 17:33). Cf. C. H. Dodd, *Historical Tradition in the Fourth Gospel* (London: Cambridge, 1963), 335-365.

67. Robert C. Tannehill, *The Sword of His Mouth* (Philadelphia: Fortress, 1975), 99-101.

68. Minear, *John*, 129-130.

69. Tannehill, *Sword*, 101.

70. Dan Otto Via, *The Ethics of Mark's Gospel—In the Middle of Time* (Philadelphia: Fortress, 1985), 81.

71. Meyer, *Aims*, 185-186, 188.

72. G. R. Beasley-Murray, *Jesus and the Kingdom of God* (Grand Rapids: Eerdmans, 1986), 181-184. In this Qumran text there is reference to the gates of death, the city built on rock, and the securely bolted doors.

73. Meyer, *Aims*, 180; Betz, *Jesus*, 90.

74. Betz, *Jesus*, 90.

75. Though the historicity of Matt. 16:17-19 has been repeatedly questioned, Ben Meyer shows evidence that strongly supports both its substantial historicity and its placement in the Caesarea Philippi scene. All the Gospels, not only Matthew, are in agreement that Simon received the name Peter from Jesus (Mark 3:16; Luke 6:14; John 1:42). In Mark and Luke the significance of this datum is left altogether unexploited. "It received neither special accent nor thematic development. The only way in which this lack of emphasis, whether on the name itself or on its bestowal, can affect the judgment of the critic is to support a verdict of historicity." Similarly in John 1:42, where the original Aramaic, *Kephas*, "Cephas," is given, its force is supposed but not highlighted or developed.

All this provides strong warrant for the conclusion that Jesus in fact gave Simon the completely new name. Furthermore, if the basis for the giving of the new name offered by Matt. 16:17-19 is not accepted, what alternative explanation has ever made this act even minimally plausible? Furthermore, the character and importance of the role of "Cephas" is highly esteemed in other texts and accords exceedingly well with the voice of the Matthean text: this is true in passages that are pre-Pauline (1 Cor. 15:5), Pauline (Gal. 1:18; 2:9, 11, 14; 1 Cor. 1:12; 3:22; 9:5; 15:5), and post-Pauline. See Meyer, *Aims*, 186.

76. The historicity of Jesus being handed over to Pilate on the basis of certain determinations made by the Jewish leaders, is hardly to be questioned. Cf. A. E. Harvey, *Jesus and the Constraints of History* (London: Duckworth, 1982), 25-26. If the Gospels report preliminary proceedings and not fundamentally a trial, then Jewish tradition about procedure at such trials is of less relevance (Mishnah Sanhedrin 4-5). Yet certain basic information in such a case would certainly soon be in the public realm. See Betz, *Jesus*, 87-88.

77. First, Mark 14:61-62 cannot be easily set aside as a later Christian reflection on the significance of Jesus. Observe the careful avoidance of the name of God through use of the phrases "the Blessed" and "right hand of Power." This points to traditional Jewish usage rather than Christian confessional formulas. See Stanton, *Gospels*, 262; Betz, *Jesus*, 89; Meyer, *Aims*, 180. There is question about precisely what could form the basis for a charge of blasphemy. Rabbinic evidence indicates that it was necessary to have pronounced the divine name (Mishnah Sanhedrin 7.5); Philo and probably Josephus, who furnish evidence for the first century, show that the basis for the charge was more inclusive. See A. E. Harvey, *Jesus on Trial: A Study in the Fourth Gospel* (London: SPCK, 1976), 77-81.

78. See K. Schubert, "Biblical Criticism Criticised: With Reference to the Markan Report of Jesus's Examination Before the Sanhedrin," in *Jesus and the Politics of His Day*, ed. by Ernst Bammel and C. F. D. Moule (London: Cambridge University Press, 1984), 385-402, esp. 396.

79. Meyer, *Aims*, 180; Betz, *Jesus*, 89-90; Bertil Gärtner, *The Temple and the Community in Qumran and the New Testament* (London: Cambridge, 1964), 115-122.

80. Rudolf Bultmann, *Theology of the New Testament*, tr. by K. Grobel, 2 vols. (New York: Charles Scribner's Sons, 1951-55), 1:148-149.

81. Joachim Jeremias, *The Eucharistic Words of Jesus* (London: SCM, and New York: Charles Scribner's Sons, 1966), 173-203.

82. Rudolf Pesch, *Das Abendmahl und Jesu Todesverständnis* (Freiburg: Herder, 1978), 21-34.

83. Pesch, *Abendmahl*, 31-34.

84. See also Stanton, *Gospels*, 257.

85. Stanton, 258.

86. J. Jeremias, *Die Abendmahlsworte Jesu*, 3d ed. (Göttingen: Vandenhoeck & Ruprecht, 1964), 224-225. N. Perrin's translation in *The Eucharistic Words of Jesus* (London: SCM, 1966), 133, differs slightly.

Conclusion

1. Jack T. Sanders, *Ethics in the New Testament* (Philadelphia: Fortress, 1975).

2. Sanders, *Ethics*, 29.

3. Sanders, *Ethics*, 29.

4. Sanders, *Ethics*, 9.

5. Sanders, *Ethics*, 8-9.

6. Sanders, *Ethics*, 20, 45.

7. Sanders, *Ethics*, 8.

8. For fuller discussion of the character of Jesus' eschatology, see Ben Wiebe, "The Focus of Jesus' Eschatology," in *Self-Definition and Self-Discovery in Early Christianity: A Study in Changing Horizons*, ed. by Thomas Robinson and David Hawkin (New York: Edwin Mellen Press), 1990.

Bibliography

Ambrozic, A. M. *The Hidden Kingdom: A Redactional Critical Study of the References of the Kingdom of God in Mark's Gospel.* Catholic Biblical Quarterly Monograph Series, 2. Washington. 1972.

Baird, J. Arthur. *Audience Criticism and the Historical Jesus.* Philadelphia: Westminster, 1969.

Barrett, C. K. "The Background of Mark 10:45." In *New Testament Essays: Studies in Memory of Thomas Walter Manson,* ed. by A. J. B. Higgins, 1:1-18. London: S.P.C.K., 1972.

_____. *Jesus and the Gospel Tradition.* Philadelphia: Fortress, 1968.

Beare, Francis W. *The Earliest Records of Jesus.* New York: Abingdon, 1962.

Beasley-Murray, G. R. *The Coming of God.* London: Paternoster Press, 1983.

_____. *Jesus and the Kingdom of God.* Grand Rapids: Eerdmans, 1986.

Behm, J. "Metanoeō, Metanoia." In *Theological Dictionary of the New Testament,* ed. by G. Kittel, vol. 4. Grand Rapids: Eerdmans, 1967.

Best, Ernest. *Following Jesus: Discipleship in the Gospel of Mark.* Sheffield: JSOT, 1981.

Betz, Hans-Dieter. *Nachfolge und Nachahmung Jesu Christi im Neuen Testament.* Tübingen: J. C. B. Mohr, 1967.

Bonhoeffer, Dietrich. *Ethics.* New York: Macmillan, 1955.

Borg, Marcus J. *Conflict, Holiness and Politics in the Teaching of Jesus.* Lewiston, N.Y.: Edwin Mellen Press, 1984.

Bornkamm, Günther. *Jesus of Nazareth.* Tr. by Irene and Fraser MeLusky with James M. Robinson. New York: Harper & Row, 1959.

Borsch, F. H. *The Christian and Gnostic Son of Man.* Studies in Biblical Theology, 2nd ser., no 14. London: SCM, 1970.

Bowman, John W. *Prophetic Realism and the Gospel.* Philadelphia: Westminster, 1955.

Bright, John. *A History of Israel.* Philadelphia: Westminster, 1959.

Bruce, F. F. *This Is That: The New Testament Development of Some Old Testament Themes.* Exeter: Paternoster, 1976.

Buber, Martin. *Kingship of God.* Tr. by Richard Scheimann. New York: Harper & Row, 1967.

Bultmann, Rudolf. *Exegetica: Aufsätze zur Erforschung des Neuen Testaments.* Ed. by E. Dinkler. Tübingen: J. C. B. Mohr, 1967.

——————. *History and Eschatology*. The 1955 Gifford Lectures. Edinburgh: University Press, 1957.

——————. *The History of the Synoptic Tradition*. Tr. by John Marsh. Oxford: Basil Blackwell, 1963.

——————. *Jesus and the Word*. Tr. by L. P. Smith and E. H. Lantero. New York: Charles Scribner's Sons, 1958.

——————. *Theology of the New Testament*. Tr. by K. Grobel. 2 vols. New York: Charles Scribner's Sons, 1951-55.

——————. *Das Verhältnis der urchristlichen Christusbotschaft zum historischen Jesus*. Sitzungsberichte der Heidelberger Akademic der Wissenschaften, Phil-his. Klasse, 1960, Z. Abhandlung, 3. Aufl. Heidelburg, 1962.

Caird, George B. "Jesus and Israel: The Starting Point for New Testament Christology." In *Christological Perspectives*, ed. by Robert F. Berry and Sarah A. Edwards. New York: Pilgrim, 1982.

——————. *Jesus and the Jewish Nation*. London: Athlone, 1965.

Calvert, D. G. A. "An Examination of the Criteria for Distinguishing the Authentic Words of Jesus." *New Testament Studies* 18 (1971-72): 209-218.

Campbell, K. M. "The New Jerusalem in Matthew 5.14." *Scottish Journal of Theology* 31 (1978): 335-363.

Cassidy, Richard J. *Jesus, Politics, and Society: A Study of Luke's Gospel*. New York: Orbis Books, 1978.

Charlesworth, James H. *Jesus Within Judaism*. New York: Doubleday, 1988.

——————, ed. *The Old Testament Pseudepigrapha*. 2 vols. Garden City: Doubleday, 1983-85.

Childs, Brevard S. *Biblical Theology in Crisis*. Philadelphia: Westminster, 1970.

Chilton, Bruce D. *The Glory of Israel: The Theology and Provenience of the Isaiah Targum*. JSOT Suppl. ser., no. 23. Sheffield: JSOT, 1983.

——————. *God in Strength: Jesus' Announcement of the Kingdom*. Freistadt: Verlag F. Plochl, 1979.

——————. *The Kingdom of God in the Teaching of Jesus*. Philadelphia: Fortress, 1984.

Cranfield, C. E. B. "Thoughts on New Testament Eschatology." *Scottish Journal of Theology* 35 (1982): 497-512.

Crenshaw, James L., and John T. Willis. *Essays in Old Testament Ethics*. New York: Ktav, 1974.

Cross, Frank M. *Canaanite Myth and Hebrew Epic*. Cambridge: Harvard University, 1973.

Crossan, John Dominic. *The Historical Jesus: The Life of a Mediterranean Jewish Peasant*. San Francisco: HarperSanFrancisco, 1991.

Dahl, Nils A. *The Crucified Messiah and Other Essays*. Minneapolis: Augsburg, 1974.

Dalman, Gustaf. *The Words of Jesus*. Edinburgh: T. & T. Clark, 1902.

Daly, R. J. *Christian Biblical Ethics*. New York: Paulist Press, 1984.

——————. "The Eucharist and Redemption: The Last Supper and Jesus' Understanding of His Death." *Biblical Theological Bulletin* (1981): 21-27.

Daube, R. David. *The New Testament and Rabbinic Judaism*. London: The Athlone, 1956.

Davies, W. D., and Dale C. Allison. *The Gospel According to Saint Matthew*. Edinburgh: T & T Clark, 1988.

Davies, W. D. *The Setting of the Sermon on the Mount.* London: Cambridge University Press, 1966.

de Jonge, Marinus. "The Earliest Christian Use of *Christos:* Some Suggestions." *New Testament Studies* 32 (1986): 321-343.

_____. *Jesus, the Servant-Messiah*. New Haven: Yale University Press, 1991.
Dietrich, Ernst Ludwig. *Sub Šebut: Die endzeitliche Wiederherstellung bei den Propheten*. Biheft 40 of *Zeitschrift für die alttestamentliche Wissenschaft*. Giessen: Töpelmann, 1925.
Dodd, C. H. *Gospel and Law*. New York: Columbia University Press, 1951.
_____. *Historical Tradition in the Fourth Gospel*. London: Cambridge University Press, 1963.
_____. *The Interpretation of the Fourth Gospel*. London: Cambridge University Press, 1968.
_____. *The Parables of the Kingdom*. New York: Charles Scribner's Sons, 1961.
Dunn, James D. G. *Christology in the Making*. London: SCM, 1980.
Ellis, E. E., "Present and Future Eschatology in Luke." *New Testament Studies* 12 (1964-65): 27-41.
Fiedler, P. "Sünde und Vergebung im Christentum." *Concilium* 10 (1974): 568-571.
Fitzmyer, Joseph A. "Further Light on Melchizedek from Qumran Cave 11." *Journal of Biblical Literature* 86 (1967): 25-41; also in *Essays on the Semitic Background of the New Testament*. Chico, Calif.: Scholars Press, 1974: 246-276.
_____. *The Gospel According the Luke (X-XXIV)*. New York: Doubleday, 1985.
Flusser, David. *Jesus*. New York: Herder, 1969.
Freedman David N. *Pottery, Poetry, and Prophecy: Studies in Early Hebrew Poetry*. Winona Lake, Ind.: Eisenbrauns, 1980.
Fridrichsen, Anton, et al., *The Root of the Vine*. London: A. C. Black, and New York: Philosophical Library, 1953.
Gärtner, Bertil. *The Temple and the Community in Qumran and the New Testament*. London: Cambridge University Press, 1964.
Gerhardsson, Berger. "Der Weg der Evangelienstradition." In *Das Evangelium und die Evangelien*. Tübingen: Mohr, 1983.
Gese, Hartmut. *Essays on Biblical Theology*. Minneapolis: Augsburg, 1981.
Glasson, T. Francis. "Schweitzer's Influence—Blessing or Bane?" In *The Kingdom of God in the Teaching of Jesus*, ed. by Bruce Chilton. Philadelphia: Fortress, 1984.
Gray, John. *The Biblical Doctrine of the Reign of God*. Edinburgh: T. & T. Clark, 1979.
Grimm, Werner. *Weil ich dich Liebe: Die Verkündigung Jesu und Deuterojesaja*. Frankfurt: Herbert Lang Bern, 1976.
Harnack, Adolf von. *What Is Christianity?* Tr. by Thomas B. Saunders. Gloucester, Mass.: Peter Smith, 1978.
Harvey, A. E. *Jesus and the Constraints of History*. London: Duckworth, 1982.
_____. *Jesus on Trial: A Study in the Fourth Gospel*. London: SPCK, 1976.
Hauerwas, Stanley. *The Peaceable Kingdom*. Notre Dame: University Press, 1983.
Hengel, Martin. *The Atonement*. Tr. by John Bowden. London: SCM Press, 1981.
_____. *The Charismatic Leader and His Followers*. Tr. by James C. G. Grieg. Edinburgh: T. & T. Clark, 1981.
_____. *Property and Riches in the Early Church*. Tr. by John Bowden. Philadelphia: Fortress Press, 1974.
_____. *Studies in the Gospel of Mark*. Tr. by John Bowden. London: SCM, 1985.
Henry, Carl F. H. "Jesus as the Ideal of

Christian Ethics." In *Christian Personal Ethics*. Grand Rapids: Eerdmans, 1957.

Hiers, Richard H. *Jesus and Ethics: Four Interpretations*. Philadelphia: Westminster, 1968.

―――――. *Jesus and the Future*. Atlanta: John Knox, 1981.

Hooker, Morna D. *The Son of Man in Mark*. Montreal: McGill University, 1967.

Horsley, Richard A., and J. S. Hanson. *Bandits, Prophets, and Messiahs*. Minneapolis: Winston, 1985.

Houlden, J. L. *Ethics and the New Testament*. London: Penguin, 1973.

Hunter, Archibald M. "The Sermon and Its Interpreters." In *A Pattern for Life*. Philadelphia: Westminster, 1965.

Jeremias, Joachim. *Die Abendmahlsworte Jesu*. 3d ed. Göttingen: Vandenhoeck & Ruprecht, 1964. Tr. by N. Perrin as *The Eucharistic Words of Jesus*. London: SCM, 1966.

―――――. "Die älteste Schicht der Menshensohn-Logien." *Zeitschrift für die neutestamentliche Wissenschaft und die Kunde der älteren Kirche* 58 (1967): 159-172.

―――――. *Jesus' Promise to the Nations*. Philadelphia: Fortress Press, 1982.

―――――. "The Lord's Prayer in the Light of Recent Research." In *The Prayers of Jesus*. Studies in Biblical Theology, no. 6. London: SCM, 1967.

―――――. *New Testament Theology*. London: SCM, 1971.

―――――. *The Parables of Jesus*. London: SCM, 1962.

―――――. *The Sermon on the Mount*. Philadelphia: Fortress, 1963.

Jonge, Marinus de. *See* de Jonge

Josephus. *Works of Josephus*. 10 vols. Tr. by H. St. J. Thackeray, R. Marcus, A. Wikgren, and L. H. Feldman. Loeb Classical Library. Cambridge: Harvard University Press, and London: William Heinemann, 1926-1965.

Juel, Donald. *Messianic Exegesis: Christological Interpretation of the Old Testament in Early Christianity*. Philadelphia: Fortress, 1987.

Kant, Immanuel. *Religion Within the Limits of Reason Alone*. New York: Harper & Row, 1960.

Käsemann, Ernst. *New Testament Questions of Today*. London: SCM, 1969.

Keck, Leander E. *A Future for the Historical Jesus*. Nashville: Abingdon, 1971.

Kelber, Werner H. *The Kingdom in Mark: A New Place and a New Time*. Philadelphia: Fortress, 1974.

Kim, Seyoon. *The Son of Man as the Son of God*. Grand Rapids: Eerdmans, 1983.

Kümmel, Werner G. " 'Das Gesetz und die Propheten gehen bis Johannes'—Lukas 16,16 in Zusammenhang der Lukasschrifter." In *Verborum Veritas* (G. Stählin Festscrift). Ed. by O. Böcker and H. Haacker. Wuppertal: Brockhaus, 1970.

―――――. *The Theology of the New Testament*. Tr. by J. E. Steely. Nashville: Abingdon, 1973.

Ladd, George Eldon. *The Presence of the Future*. Grand Rapids: Eerdmans, 1974.

Lane, William L. *The Gospel According to Mark*. Grand Rapids: Eerdmans, 1974.

Levenson, Jon D. *Sinai and Zion*. New York: Winston, 1985.

Lewis, Jack P. *The Gospel According to Matthew*. Vol. 1. Living Word Commentary. Austin: Sweet, 1976.

Lind, Millard C. *Yahweh Is a Warrior*. Scottdale: Herald Press, 1980.

Lindars, Barnabas. *The Gospel of John.* London: Marshall, Morgan and Scott, 1972.
_____. *Jesus Son of Man.* Grand Rapids: Eerdmans, 1983.
Lohfink, Gerhard. *Jesus and Community.* Tr. by John P. Galvin. Philadelphia: Fortress, 1984.
_____. "Die Korrelation vom Reich Gottes und Volk Gottes bei Jesus." *Theologische Quartalschrift* 165 (1985): 173-183.
Maddox, Robert. *The Purpose of Luke-Acts.* Edinburgh: T. & T. Clark, 1982.
Manson, T. W. *The Servant Messiah.* London: Cambridge University Press, 1961.
_____. *The Teaching of Jesus.* London: Cambridge University Press, 1931; 2d ed., 1935.
Marshall, I. Howard. *The Gospel of Luke.* Grand Rapids: Eerdmans, 1978.
_____. *New Testament Interpretation: Essays on Principles and Methods.* Grand Rapids: Eerdmans, 1977.
Martin, Ralph P. *Mark: Evangelist and Theologian.* Grand Rapids: Zondervan, 1972, 1986.
Metzler, Norman P. J. *The Ethics of the Kingdom.* Ann Arbor: University Microfilms, 1974.
Meye, Robert P. *Jesus and the Twelve: Discipleship and Revelation in Mark's Gospel.* Grand Rapids: Eerdmans, 1968.
Meyer, Ben F. *The Aims of Jesus.* London: SCM, 1979.
_____. *Critical Realism and the New Testament.* Allison Park, Pa.: Pickwick, 1989.
Miller, Patrick D. *Sin and Judgment in the Prophets.* Chico, Calif.: Scholars Press, 1982.
Minear, Paul S. "Audience Criticism and Markan Ecclesiology." In *Neue Testament und Geschichte*, ed. by Heinrich Baltensweiler and Bo Reicke. Tübingen: J. C. B. Mohr, 1972.
_____. *Commands of Christ.* New York: Abingdon, 1972.
_____. "The Disciples and the Crowds in Matthew." *Anglican Theological Review*, Suppl. ser., 1974:28-44.
_____. "Jesus' Audiences According to Luke." *Novum Testamentum* 16 (1974): 81-109.
_____. *John: The Martyr's Gospel.* New York: Pilgrim, 1984.
_____. *Matthew: The Teacher's Gospel.* New York: Pilgrim, 1982.
_____. "Some Archetypal Origins of Apocalyptic Prediction." In *Horizons in Biblical Theology* 1 (1979).
_____. *To Die and to Live.* New York: Seabury, 1977.
Moltmann, Jürgen. *The Crucified God.* London: SCM, 1974.
_____. *The Experiment Hope.* Philadelphia: Fortress, 1975.
_____. *The Future of Creation.* Tr. by Margaret Kohl. Philadelphia: Fortress, 1979.
_____. *The Theology of Hope.* Tr. by James W. Leitch. London: SCM, 1967.
Montefiore, C. G. *Rabbinic Literature and Gospel Teachings.* London: Macmillan, 1930.
Moore, George F. *Judaism in the First Centuries of the Christian Era.* Vol. 1. Cambridge: Harvard University Press, 1927.
Moran, W. L. "A Kingdom of Priests." In *The Bible in Current Catholic Thought*, ed. by J. L. McKenzie. New York: Herder, 1962.
Moule, C. F. D. *Birth of the New Testament.* London: Adam & Charles Black, 1981.
_____. "Mark 4:1-20 Yet Once More." In *Neotestamentica et Semitica*, ed. by E. Earle Ellis and Max Wilcox. Edinburgh: T & T Clark, 1969.
_____. *The Origin of Christol-*

ogy. London: Cambridge University Press, 1977.

Mowinckel, Sigmund. *He That Cometh*. Tr. by G. W. Anderson. New York: Abingdon, 1954.

Oepke, A. *Das neue Gottesvolk in Schrifttum, bildender Kunst und Weltgestaltung*. Gütersloh: Mohn, 1950.

Pannenberg, Wolfhart. *Basic Questions in Theology*. 2 vols. Philadelphia: Fortress, 1970.

———. "Can Christianity Do Without an Eschatology?" In the collection *The Christian Hope*. London: SPCK, 1970.

Perrin, Norman. *Jesus and the Language of the Kingdom*. Philadelphia: Fortress, 1976.

———. *The Kingdom of God in the Teaching of Jesus*. London, SCM, 1963.

———. *Rediscovering the Teaching of Jesus*. New York: Harper & Row, 1967.

Pesch, Rudolf. "Das Abendmahl und Jesu Todesverständnis." In *Der Tod Jesu: Deutungen im Neuen Testament*. Ed. by K. Kertelege. Quaestiones Disputatae 74. Freiburg: Herder, 1976:137-187.

———. *Das Abendmahl und Jesu Todesverständnis*. Freiburg: Herder, 1978.

———. *Das Markusevangelium*. Freiburg-Basel-Wien: Herder, 1977.

Petuchowski, Jakob J., and Michael Brocke, eds. *The Lord's Prayer and Jewish Liturgy*. New York: Seabury, 1978.

Philo. *Works of Philo*. 12 vols. Tr. by F. H. Colson, Ralph Marcus, and G. Whitaker. The Loeb Classical Library. Cambridge: Harvard University Press, and London: William Heinemann, 1949-1962.

Rad, Gerhard von. *"Basileus."* In *Theological Dictionary of the New Testament*, ed. by G. Kittel, vol. 1. Grand Rapids: Eerdmans, 1964.

Ritschl, Albrecht. *Three Essays*. Tr. by Philip Hefner. Philadelphia: Fortress, 1972.

Robbins, Vernon K. *Jesus the Teacher*. Philadelphia: Fortress Press, 1984.

———. "Pragmatic Relations as a Criteron for Authentic Sayings." *Foundations and Facets Forum* 1, no. 3 (1985).

Robinson, John A. T. *The Priority of John*. London: SCM, 1985.

Rothe, Richard. *Still Hours*. Tr. by Jane T. Stoddart. London: Hodder and Stoughton, 1886.

Rowland, Christopher. *The Open Heaven*. London: SPCK, 1982.

Rowley, H. H. *The Relevance of Apocalyptic*. London: Lutterworth, 1963.

Saebø, Mayne. "Messianisms in Chronicles?" *Horizons in Biblical Theology* 2 (1980): 85-109.

Sanders, E. P. *Jesus and Judaism*. London: SCM, 1985.

———. *Paul and Palestinian Judaism*. London: SCM, 1977.

———. *The Tendencies of the Synoptic Tradition*. London: Cambridge University Press, 1969.

Sanders, Jack T. *Ethics in the New Testament: Change and Development*. Philadelphia: Fortress, 1975.

Schillebeeckx, Edward. *Jesus: An Experiment in Christology*. New York: Seabury, 1979.

Schleiermacher, Friedrich, *Christian Faith* (German 1st ed., 1821; 2d ed., 1880). Tr. of 2 ed. by H. R. Macintosh and J. S. Stewart (1928). New York: Harper & Row, 1963.

Schmitt, Joseph. "L'Eglise de Jerusalem, ou la 'Restauration' d'Israël d'après les cinq premier chapitres des Actes." *Recerches de science religieuse* 27 (1953): 209-218.

Schnackenburg, Rudolf. *God's Rule*

and Kingdom. Tr. by John Murray. Freiburg: Herder, 1963; Montreal: Palm Publishers, 1963.
_____. *The Moral Teaching of the New Testament.* Tr. by J. Holland-Smith and W. J. O'Hara. Montreal: Palm, 1965.
Schrage, Wolfgang. *Ethik des Neuen Testaments.* Gottingen: Vandenhoeck and Ruprecht, 1982.
Schubert, K., "Biblical Criticism Criticized: With Reference to the Markan Report of Jesus' Examination Before the Sanhedrin." In *Jesus and the Politics of His Day,* ed. by Ernst Bammel and C. F. D. Moule, 385-402. London: Cambridge University Press, 1984.
Schürmann, Heinz. *Traditionsgeschichtliche Untersuchungen zu den synoptischen Evanglien.* Düsseldorf: Patmas-Verlag, 1968.
Schweitzer, Albert. *The Mystery of the Kingdom of God.* Tr. by W. Lowrie. London: 1914.
_____. *Von Reimarus zu Wrede.* Tübingen: Mohr, 1906. Tr. by W. Montgomery as *The Quest of the Historical Jesus.* New York: The Macmillan Company, 1968.
Schweizer, Eduard. *The Good News According to Matthew.* Tr. by David E. Green. Atlanta: John Knox, 1975.
Scott, E. F. *The Ethical Teaching of Jesus.* New York: Macmillan, 1936.
_____. *The Crisis in the Life of Jesus.* New York: Charles Scribner's Sons, 1952.
Sigal, Phillip. *The Halakah of Jesus of Nazareth According to the Gospel of Matthew.* Lanham, Md.: University Press of America, 1986.
Silberman, Lou H. *Essays in Old Testament Ethics.* Ed. by James L. Crenshaw and John T. Willis. New York: Ktav, 1974.
Smith, Morton. *Tannaitic Parallels to the Gospels.* Philadelphia: Society of Biblical Literature, 1968.
Sparks, H. F. D., ed. *The Apocryphal Old Testament.* Oxford: Clarendon, 1984.
Stanton, Graham N. *The Gospels and Jesus.* Oxford: University Press, 1989.
Stein, Robert H. "The 'Criteria' for Authenticity." In *Gospel Perspectives: Studies of History and Tradition in the Four Gospels,* vol. 1. Ed. by R. T. France and David Wenham. Sheffield: JSOT Press, 1980.
Stendahl, Krister. *Paul Among Jews and Gentiles.* Philadelphia: Fortress, 1976.
Strauss, David F. *Life of Jesus Critically Examined.* London: SCM, 1973.
Stuhlmacher, Peter. *Reconciliation, Law, and Righteousness.* Philadelphia: Fortress, 1986.
Talbert, Charles H. *Reading Luke: A Literary and Theological Commentary on the Third Gospel.* New York: Crossroad, 1982.
Tannehill, Robert C. *The Sword of His Mouth.* Philadelphia: Fortress, 1975.
Tinsley, E. J. *The Imitation of God in Christ.* London: SCM, 1960.
Vermes, Geza. *Jesus the Jew: A Historian's Reading of the Gospels.* Philadelphia: Fortress, 1973.
_____. *The Dead Sea Scrolls in English.* Middlesex, England: Penguin, 1962.
_____. "The Use of Bar Nash/Bar Nasha in Jewish Aramaic." In *Post-Biblical Jewish Studies.* Leiden: E. J. Brill, 1975.
Via, Dan Otto. *The Ethics of Mark's Gospel—In the Middle of Time.* Philadelphia: Fortress, 1985.
_____. *The Parables: Their Literary and Existential Dimension.* Philadelphia: Fortress, 1967.
Vielhauer, P. "Gottesreich und Mens-

chensohn in der Verkündigung Jesu." In *Aufsatze zum Neuen Testament*. München: Kaiser Verlag, 1965.

Vögtle, Anton. "Todesankündigungen und Todesverständnis Jesu." In *Der Tod Jesu: Deutungen im Neuen Testament*. Ed. by K. Kertelege. Quaestiones Disputatae 74. Freiburg: Herder, 1976:51-113.

von Rad, G. *See* Rad, Gerhard von.

Weiss, Johannes. *Die Predigt Jesu vom Reiche Gottes*. Göttingen: Vandenhoeck & Ruprecht, 1892. Tr. by R. H. Hiers and D. L. Holland as *Jesus' Proclamation of the Kingdom of God*. London: SCM, 1971.

Wenham, David. "The Kingdom of God in Daniel." *The Expository Times* 98, no. 5 (Feb. 1987).

Verhey, Allen. *The Great Reversal: Ethics and the New Testament*. Grand Rapids: Eerdmans, 1984.

Westerholm, Stephen. *Jesus and Scribal Authority*. Lund: CWK Gleerup, 1978.

Westermann, Claus. *Elements of Old Testament Theology*. Tr. by Douglas W. Stott. Atlanta: John Knox, 1982.

Wiebe, Ben. "The Focus of Jesus' Eschatology." In *Self-Definition and Self-Discovery in Early Christianity: A Study in Changing Horizons*, ed. by David Hawkins and Thomas Robinson. Lewiston, N.Y.: Edwin Mellen Press, 1990.

_____. "Messianic Ethics: Response to the Kingdom of God." *Interpretation* (Jan. 1991): 29-42.

Wilder, Amos. *Eschatology and Ethics in the Teaching of Jesus*. New York: Harper & Brothers, 1939.

Willis, Wendell, ed. *The Kingdom of God in 20th-Century Interpretation*. Peabody, Mass.: Hendrickson Publishers, 1987.

Wrede, William. *The Messianic Secret*. London: Cambridge University Press, 1971.

Wright, N. T. "Jesus, Israel and the Cross." In *Seminar Papers*, Society of Biblical Literature. Atlanta: Scholars Press, 1984.

Yoder, John H. "The Biblical Mandate." In *The Chicago Declaration*, ed. by Ronald J. Sider. Carol Stream, Ill.: Creation House, 1974.

_____. *He Came Preaching Peace*. Scottdale, Pa.: Herald Press, 1986.

_____. "The Political Axioms of the Sermon on the Mount." In *The Original Revolution*. Scottdale, Pa.: Herald Press, 1971.

_____. *The Politics of Jesus*. Grand Rapids: Eerdmans, 1972.

_____. *The Priestly Kingdom: Social Ethics as Gospel*. Notre Dame: Notre Dame University Press, 1984.

Zimmerli, Walther. *The Old Testament and the World*. London: SPCK, 1976.

_____. *Old Testament Theology in Outline*. Tr. by David E. Green. Atlanta: John Knox, 1978.

Index of Ancient Sources

OLD TESTAMENT

Genesis
2:24 173
49:10 65

Exodus
2:23-25 83
3:12 184
3:13-15 82
3:14 184
3:15-17 83
3:16-17 83
3:22 60
4:22 154
7:4 57
12-15 58
13:17-22 57
15:1-21 .... 57, 180
15:3 57
15:13 57
15:18 57
17 59
19-24 58
19:3-8 ...... 58, 180-181
19:6 57-58
20:1-6 82
20:1-17 58
20:2 82
20:4-6 84
23:16 60
24:8 166

Leviticus
19:2 .... 82, 193

19:18 132
19:33-34 83
25 128

Numbers
23:21 .... 57-58, 82
24:7 81
24:17 77

Deuteronomy
1:30-33 57
6:5 132
8:6 154
10:12 154
10:15-19 154
11:22 154
15:2 128
15:13-15 83
16:13-15 60
17:18-20 59
18:13 193
18:18-19 78
28:47-48 84
30:11 20
30:14 20
33:2 62
33:5 .... 57-58, 62

Joshua
24:1-28 181

Judges
4:14 59
8:23 58

1 Samuel
8-12 59
8:4-22 59
8:8 59
8:10-20 59
8:19b-20 58
9:1—10:16 59
9:16 59
10:17-19 59
10:17-27 59
10:18-19 59
10:25 60
11:1-13 59
11:14—12:25 59
12:8-12 59
12:14-15 60
12:16-19 59
13:8-14 59
15:22 82

2 Samuel
7 59
7:4-7 59
7:4-17 64
7:11-14 78
7:12-14a 161
7:13 162
7:13-14 144
7:14 ... 59, 66, 144, 162
7:16 .... 66, 162
12:10 185
12:11 185
23:5 161

209

1 Kings
8:61 193
9:4-5 59
11:4 193
11:26–12:16 59
15:3-4 193

1 Chronicles
17:12-13 144
28:5 68

Ezra
3:12 74

Job
42:10 71

Psalms
1:1 189
2:7 .... 144, 161
14:7 72
18:3-19 62
18:4 146
29 60
29:3-4 60
29:8 60
29:10 60
29:11 60
32:6 146
34:9 79
41:9 120
42:7 146
65 60
65:5 60-61
65:6-8 61
65:9-13 60
66:12 146
67 62
67:3 62
67:4 63
67:5 62
67:6-7 62
89:3-5 161
89:20-29 161
89:20-37 64
89:27 .... 144, 161
96:10-13 61
97:1 64
98:8-9 61
99:1 64
110:1-4 78
110:3 .... 144, 161
113-118 165
126:1 72
126:4 72
132:11-18 64
145:11-13 61

Proverbs
8:34 189

Isaiah
2:1-5 88
2:2-4 .... 84, 194
2:2-5 67
2:40 106
2:51 106
3:10 84
9:5-11 161
9:7 67
11 76-77
11:1-5 .... 68, 79
11:1-10 .... 65, 67
11:3-5 67
11:4 68
11:10 67-68
25:1-9 73
25:6-9 106
28:16 .... 161, 194
29:18-19 92
30:27-28 146
33:22 64
35:5-6 92
40:2 72
40:9 81
40:9-10 69
40:11 105
42:1-4 .... 67, 155
42:1-9 88
42:3-4 68
42:9-10 73
43:3-4 198
43:18-19 73
44:23 72
45:14 106
45:23-24 106
49:1-6 .... 67, 155
49:5-6 .... 68, 70
49:6 68
49:8 110
49:9-13 72
49:10 110
49:13 110
50:4-9 .... 67, 155
51:3 194
52:7 116
52:7-9 103
52:7-10 .... 53, 92
52:8-9 105
52:10 106
52:13—53:12 .... 67, 155
53 166
53:4-8 69
53:8 72
53:11-12 .... 69, 155, 198
55:3 68
56:1 84
56:1-8 70
56:6-7 72
56:7 106
60:3-14 70
60:13 70
61:1-2 ..... 92, 109-110, 128, 192
61:1-3 53
62:2 73
65—66 74
66:18-24 70
66:22 74

Jeremiah
1:16 113
2:13 113
2:17 113
2:19 113
3:12-14 113
3:19-22 113
5:7 113
5:19 .... 84, 113
6:19 84
7:1-15 163
22:16 154
23:5-6 .... 65, 72
29:14 71
30:2-3 72
30:18 71
30:18-22 69
31:23 71
31:31 166
31:31-34 84
33:6-11 70

33:7 71	7:21-22 74	**Zechariah**
33:9 72	7:25-27 80	4:6-9 182
33:10-18 72	7:27 .... 74, 79, 89, 91	4:14 79
33:11 71-72	9:7 87	6:12-13 .... 144, 161
33:14-18 .... 65, 78	9:14 87	9:9 81
33:26 71	9:17-19 87	9:9-10 .... 66, 69
34:8-17 128	12:1-2 76	
36:3 113	12:2-3 76	**NEW TESTAMENT**
36:7 113	12:12 189	
48:47 71		**Gospels** 105
49:6 71	**Hosea**	
49:39 71	3:4-5 65	**Matthew**
	7:10-13 58	3:1 99
Ezekiel	10:12 84	3:1-6 101
16:53 71		3:2 .... 99, 115, 187
21:26 127	**Amos**	3:3 115
21:27 65	1:2—2:3 63	3:7 103
34:11-16 72	3:1-5 63	3:7-10 .... 118, 187
34:12-14 105	3:2 63	3:9 99
34:23-24 .... 66, 72	5:6-9 63	3:11 101
36:25-28 84	5:18-20 63	3:11-12 100
37:1-14 73	7:10-17 163	4:12 100
37:14 83	7:12-13 59	4:14-17a 116
37:21-23 72	9:7 63	4:17 .... 94-95, 115,
37:24-28 .... 66, 72	9:11 72	119, 190
40-48 78	9:11-15 69	4:23 .... 95, 103, 115-
40—43 72	9:14 72	116, 193
40—48 78		4:23-25 110
	Micah	4:25 139
Daniel	4:1-2 72	5:3 .... 94, 109
1:8-20 87	4:1-4 .... 72, 84	5:3-4 189
2 91	4:1-7 71	5:3-10 189
2:21 88	4:2-3 72	5:3-12 .... 108, 189
2:35 91	5:2-4 .... 65, 67, 72	5:4 109
2:44 .... 89, 91	5:4 105	5:6 .... 109, 189
2:44-45 74	6:6-8 20	5:8 .... 109, 126
2:45 91		5:11 109
3:1-26 87	**Habakkuk**	5:11-12 109
4:27 87	2:2-3 174	5:14 ...... 110, 134, 193
5:25-28 88	3:3 62	5:19 94
6:6-23 87	3:10-13 62	5:21 132
6:26-27 88		5:21-26 132
7 .... 75, 79, 89, 91	**Zephaniah**	5:22 133
7:9-14 .... 74, 79	3:16-20 70	5:23 131
7:11-27 87		5:24-26 133
7:13-14 .... 76, 80, 91	**Haggai**	5:39-42 133
7:14 .... 74, 79, 88, 91,	1:1-2 144	5:42 128
198	2:3 74	5:43-48 133
7:17 89	2:20-23 144	5:44 157
7:18 74		5:45 133
7:21 91		5:46 132

5:48 192
6:1-6 126
6:3-6 134
6:4 192
6:7-8 192
6:8 130
6:9-13 192
6:12 ...... 110, 128, 131, 157
6:14-15 .... 128, 192
6:15 110
6:16-18 126
6:17-18 126
6:19-24 129
6:24 152
6:25-33 129
6:32 130
6:33 95
6:117-18 134
7:17-20 173
7:28 .... 115, 139
8:1 139
8:5-13 188
8:11 ... 94, 97, 107, 188
8:11-12 106
8:12 .... 94, 107, 188
8:18-22 139
8:19 150
8:21-22 150
9:2 119
9:8 139
9:11-13 120
9:12 118
9:12-13 118
9:33 139
9:35 .... 95, 103, 193
9:35—10:16 138
10:1 188
10:1-4 105
10:1-23 39
10:9-14 188
10:34-39 152
10:35 134
10:37-39 134
10:38 .... 150, 153
10:42 134
11:2-3 124
11:3 101
11:3-6 128
11:5 .... 103, 193
11:5-6 92

11:6 111
11:7-15 101-102
11:9-10 102
11:10 101
11:12 .... 102, 124
11:12-13 .... 101, 116
11:12-19 188
11:13 187
11:14 101
11:18 115
11:19 .... 115, 120
11:21-24 .... 119, 188
11:25-27 .... 111, 118
12:15 139
12:18 41
12:23 139
12:25-28 32
12:28 .... 41, 124-125
12:38-42 119
12:39 194
12:41-42 188
13:11 .... 94, 126
13:11-13 138
13:15-16 137
13:16-17 111
13:19 94
13:24-30 .... 103, 124, 172
13:25 124
13:28 124
13:30 125
13:31 94
13:38 94
13:47-50 103
13:58 120
14–15 131
14:13 139
15:22-28 119
15:28 119
15:31 139
16:13-23 136
16:13-28 135
16:16 151
16:16-19 162
16:16-20 144
16:17 189
16:17-19 .... 161, 199
16:18 160-161
16:19 94
16:21 145
16:21-23 144

16:22 150
16:24 ...... 93, 149-151, 197
16:24-27 149
16:24-28 134
16:25 .... 154, 159, 197
16:25-26 158
17:10-13 101
17:22-23 149
18:3-4 127
18:6 134
18:15-18 158
18:23-25 128
18:23-35 157
18:35 110
19:1-9 173
19:1-12 .... 122, 134
19:5 173
19:10 134
19:14 .... 108, 134
19:28 .... 105, 188
20:1-16 120
20:16 127
20:17-19 149
20:20-23 146
20:20-24 135
20:20-28 149
20:25-28 155
20:28 .... 154, 198
21:9 139
21:11 139
21:21-32 117
21:23 116
21:26 139
21:28-32 ...... 116, 118, 120
21:31 .... 118, 127
21:31-32 117
21:32 .... 100, 118
21:46 139
22:1-10 104
22:15-22 126
22:30 .... 123, 173
22:31-32 97
22:34-40 .... 132, 156
22:37-40 126
23:8-10 140
23:8-11 130
23:9 130
23:12 127
23:23-24 117

23:29-39 146
23:34-35 104
23:34-36 106
24:14 .... 95, 115
24:33 174
24:46 189
26:13 115
26:26 165
26:28 ... 155, 157, 164, 166
26:29 94
26:59-66 162
26:61 .... 143-144, 162, 193-194
26:63-64a 144
26:64 193
27:40 .... 143, 162, 194
28:5-10 131

Mark
1:1 141
1:4 99
1:6 115
1:14 100
1:14b 116
1:14-15 .... 41, 55, 116-117, 189
1:15 .... 41, 92, 94-95, 103, 107, 111-112, 116-117, 119, 190
1:15a 190
1:15b 116
1:18 150
1:21-22 115
1:38 93
1:40-44 103
1:40-45 140
2:5 .... 119, 191
2:5-12 ... 103, 115, 140
2:7-12 137
2:11 119
2:12 139
2:13 139
2:14 150
2:15-17 191
2:16-17 120
2:17 118
2:18-20 115-116
2:19-20 143
2:23-28 140
2:25-28 143

3:8-9 139
3:13-19 .... 105, 138
3:14-15 150
3:16 .... 160, 199
3:22-27 143
3:31-35 130
3:32 129
3:32-34 139
3:32-35 129
4:1 139
4:1-2 139
4:9 93
4:10 139
4:10-20 136
4:11 .... 94, 138
4:11-12 138
4:26 94
4:30 94
4:34 136
4:40 191
4:41 137
4:61 162
5:12:41 138
5:21 139
5:24 138
5:27 138
5:30-31 138
5:36 .... 119, 191
6:1 150
6:2-6 119
6:5-6 120
6:6 191
6:7 106
6:7-13 188
6:12 .... 119, 191
6:34-45 139
7 142
7:8-13 118
7:14 139
7:17 139
7:17-23 136
7:25-30 119
7:33 139
7:37 139
8:1-2 139
8:11-13 119
8:18 137
8:27 .... 142, 144
8:27-29 137
8:27-30 .... 142, 144-145, 196

8:27-33 136
8:27-38 135
8:29 .... 142, 144, 151
8:30-31 143
8:31 145
8:31-33 . 144-145, 196
8:32 150
8:34 .... 93, 139, 149-151, 197
8:34-9:1 134
8:34-38 149
8:35 .... 154, 197-198
9:11 142
9:11-13 101
9:18-24 119
9:30-32 149
9:31 143
9:35 127
9:35-37 140
9:42 134
9:43-49 146
10:1 139
10:1-2 139
10:1-12 .... 122, 133
10:6-9 20
10:27 174
10:28 150
10:29-30 .... 129-130, 173
10:29-31 129
10:30 173
10:32 150
10:32-34 149
10:35-36 152
10:35-40 .... 146, 152
10:35-41 135
10:35-44 149
10:35-45 149
10:38 142
10:38-39 143
10:42-43 130
10:42-45 155-156
10:45 .... 35, 154, 198
10:45a 155
10:45b 155
10:46 139
10:46-52 119
10:52 191
11:9 139
11:15-19 163
11:18 139

11:25 130	3:1ff. 99	9:23-26 149
11:30 100	3:7 103	9:23-27 134
11:32 .... 102, 139	3:7-9 .... 118, 187	9:24 .... 154, 197
12:1-9 148	3:8 .... 99, 102	9:43-45 149
12:12 139	3:19 100	9:57 150
12:13-17 126	4:16-21 .... 92, 115	9:59-60 150
12:25 .... 123, 173	4:18-19 128	9:61 150
12:25-26 39	4:18-21 53	10:1 106
12:28-34 .... 132, 156	4:19 116	10:13-15 .... 119, 188
12:29-34 126	4:21 .... 111, 116, 190	10:21-22 118
12:35-37 139	4:43 .... 93, 128	10:22-24 130
12:37 139	5:20 119	10:23-24 137
12:41-44 131	5:30-32 120	10:25-28 .... 132, 156
13 .... 98, 194	5:31 118	10:27-28 126
13:1-31 104	6:14 .... 160, 199	10:38-42 131
13:2 163	6:20 94	10:42 131
13:11 94	6:20-21 189	11:4 157
13:14 92	6:20-23 108	11:20 41
13:29 174	6:27-28 133	11:29 194
13:30 174	6:28 157	11:29-32 119
13:32 174	6:29-30 133	11:31-32 188
14:3-9 131	6:31-36 133	11:49-51 .... 104, 106
14:6-8 131	6:32 132	12:15-21 129
14:6-9 131	6:35 133	12:31 .... 33, 95
14:17 164-165	6:35-36 123	12:32 .... 92, 105, 130
14:20 165	6:43-45 173	12:49 152
14:21 164	7:18-23 128	12:49-50 .... 143, 146
14:22 165	7:19 101	12:51-53 152
14:22-24 140	7:21 109	12:53 134
14:22-25 164-165	7:22 111	12:57-59 133
14:23 157	7:22-23 92	13:1-5 .... 104, 188
14:24 .... 155, 164, 166	7:24-27 101	13:3 191
14:25 .... 94, 149, 165	7:24-28 102	13:6-9 104
14:26 164-165	7:31-35 188	13:18 94
14:55-64 162	7:33 115	13:28 107
14:58 .... 143-144, 162, 193-194	7:34 120	13:28-29 106
14:61-62.55, 149, 200	7:39-40 131	13:29 94
14:61-62a 144	7:41-43 120	13:30 127
14:62 .... 92, 162, 193	7:50 191	13:34-35 104
14:64 162	8:1-3 .... 130, 188	14:11 127
15:11 138	8:10 94	14:15-24 104
15:15 138	8:25 137	14:24 127
15:26 55	9:1-6 188	14:26 152
15:29 .... 143, 162, 194	9:7-9 198	14:26-27 134
15:32 55	9:10 138	14:27 .... 153, 158
15:40-41 130	9:18-21 144	14:28-33 153
	9:18-22 136	15:1-32 .... 117, 120
Luke	9:18-27 135	15:5 120
1—23 141	9:20 151	15:7 190-191
2:30 53	9:22 144-145	15:9-10 120
	9:23 .... 149-151, 197	15:10 190-191

Index of Ancient Sources   215

Reference	Page(s)
15:32	121
16:1-8	104
16:16	95, 101, 116, 187
17	98
17:3	132, 158
17:3-4	157
17:4	132
17:11-19	191
17:20-21	44, 104
17:23-24	44
18:14	127
18:31-34	149
19:1-9	190
19:1-10	103
19:8	120
19:41-44	104
20:20-26	126
20:35	123, 173
22:15-18	164
22:19-20	157, 166
22:20	164
22:24-27	149
22:25	158
22:26	157
22:27	154, 156
22:28	105
22:30	105, 188
22:70-71	144
23:34	157
24	141
24:4-12	131

John

Reference	Page(s)
1:9	110
1:18	118
1:42	160, 199
2:13-17	163
2:14-18	194
2:19	143, 162, 194
3:22—4:3	93
3:26	100
3:34-35	118
4:7-27	131
6:15	135, 145, 152, 193
6:51c	155
6:60	152
6:61-65	136
6:66	152
6:67-71	188
8:12	110
11:1-44	131
11:17-27	131
12:1-8	131
12:3-8	131
12:23-24	136, 159
12:23-26	149
12:24	159
12:24-25	159
12:25-26	159
13:1-13	156
13:1-17	156
13:34	156
13:34-35	156
13:35	157
13:35b	198
14:1-7	136
15:20	158
16:1-3	199
20:11-18	131
20:29	189

Acts

Reference	Page(s)
1:7	174
2:42	21
6:14	143, 162
7:46-50	144
10:36-38	53
15:6-21	21
15:15-16	144
15:16-17	162
15:28-29	21

Romans

Reference	Page(s)
8:15-16	130
12:2	20
14:22	189

1 Corinthians

Reference	Page(s)
1:12	199
2:1-6	195
3:16	162
3:22	199
9:5	199
11:23	165
11:23-25	164
11:24-25	164, 166
11:26	165
15:5	188, 199

Galatians

Reference	Page(s)
1:18	199
2:9	199
2:11	199
2:14	199

1 Peter

Reference	Page(s)
2:4-10	162

1 John

Reference	Page(s)
2:7	195
2:24	195
3:11	195

Revelation

Reference	Page(s)
5	187
14:13	189
16:15	189
19	187
21:9—22:5	187
22:7	189

APOCRYPHA

4 Ezra (2 Esdras)

Reference	Page(s)
	74-75, 79, 87-89, 183, 185
3:27	87
3:30	87
4:26-32	88
5:4-12	91
5:28	87
7:11-14	88
7:20-25	88
7:28-33	90
7:28-34	75
7:45-61	88
7:5	88
7:50	87
7:63	114
8:1-3	88
8:31-33	185
13:9-13	79
13:32	79
13:35-40	79
13:37	79
13:52	90

1 Maccabees

Reference	Page(s)
2:23ff	133

Sirach
5:5-7 114
17:24-26 114
24:22-23 114

PSEUDEPIGRAPHA

Assumption of Moses
10:1 75
10:7 75
10:8-10 75
10:8-9 75

2 Baruch
.... 75, 89-90, 183
36-40 75
40:3 .... 75, 90
74:2-3 75

1 Enoch
.... 89, 185
1-36 85
2:1 86
5:1-2 86
6 86
9:11 86
9:5 86
12:3 86
22:14 86
25:7 86
37-71 90
46:7 186
48:10 79
52:4 79
62:2-5 90
63:4-7 186
81:5ff. 86
89:58 86
89:71 86
89:75 86

Jubilees
.... 75
21:23 114
23:26 114
23:27 75
23:30-32 75

Psalms of Solomon
.... 76-77, 86, 89
3:7-8 113

3:8 113
4:23 189
8:28 80
9:6-8 113
11:2 80
14:1-2 113
16:11 113
17 .... 74, 76-77
17:21 80
17:23-36 77
17:24 80
17:26 80
17:31 80
17:44 189
18 76
18:16 189
18:6 76
18:8 76

Testaments of the Twelve Patriarchs 78

T. of Joseph
6:6 113

T. of Judah
15:4 113
17:5-6 78
21:1-4 78
22:2-3 78
24:1-6 78

T. of Levi
18:2-5 78

T. of Reuben
1:9 113
6:10-12 78
6:5-12 78

T. of Simeon
7:1-2 78

QUMRAN

CD (Cairo Damascus Document)
15.5-7 114
15.7-11 89
16.1-3 114

19.16 114
5.4-7 80

4QFlor (Florilegium from Cave 4)
1.10-13 78
1-13 .... 143-144, 161

1QH (Hymn Scroll)
3.19-23 76
3.28-36 76
5.34 76
6.23-28 161
6.24-27 76
6.25-28 194
7.8-9 161
8.5-9 76

1QM (War Scroll)
1.13-15 76
1.5 76
2.1-3 80
5.1-2 78
12.7-15 88
13.1-2 78
14.9-10 88
17.2 107
18.1-11 88

1QS (Manual of Discipline)
4.7-9 75
5.2-7 80
5.5f. 194
5.8-10 89
8.2-6 80
8.4-10 80
8.7-10 194
8.9-10 80
9.10-11 78
9.11 76
9.3-6 194
11.7-11 80

11QMelch (Melchizedek text)
18 193

RABBINICAL WRITINGS

Mishnah Hagigah
2.1 196

Mishnah Sanhedrin
4-5 199
7.5 200

TARGUMS

Targum Isaiah
1:16-18 114
1:3 114
8:18 114
17:11 114
42:14 114
52:13-15 183
57:19 114

JOSEPHUS 200

The Jewish War
18.116-119 187

PHILO 184, 200

On Rewards and Punishments
162-172 81
163-165 81
168 81
94-97 81

On Abraham
261 184

On the Life of Moses
1.190 184

On Samuel
2.285 184

On the Special Laws
1.207 184
4.164 184

Author Index

Allison, Dale C., 189, 192
Ambrozic, Aloysius M., 190

Baird, J. Arthur, 194
Beasley-Murray, G. R., 122, 182-183, 186-189, 192, 199
Behm, J., 190
Best, Ernest, 197-198
Betz, Hans-Dieter, 150, 197, 199-200
Bonhoeffer, Dietrich, 145, 196
Borg, Marcus J., 95, 175, 186, 190, 192
Bowman, John W., 122, 191
Bright, John, 181
Brocke, Michael, 190
Bruce, F. F., 182
Buber, Martin, 180-181, 184
Bultmann, Rudolf, 16, 18-19, 44-46, 50, 52-54, 97, 122, 147, 164, 169, 175, 179, 186-188, 190-191, 193, 196, 198, 200

Caird, George B., 53, 97, 180, 186-188
Calvert, D. G. A., 176
Campbell, K. M., 193
Charlesworth, James H., 183, 188, 194
Childs, Brevard S., 175-176
Chilton, Bruce D., 114, 185-186, 190
Cross, Frank M., 180
Crossan, John Dominic, 190-191

Dahl, Nils A., 143-144, 176, 196
Dalman, Gustaf, 96, 164, 186
Daly, Robert J., 176
Daube, David, 195
Davies, Margaret, 195

Davies, W. D., 189, 192
de Jonge, Marinus, 143-145, 176, 196
Dietrich, Ernst Ludwig, 53, 71, 96, 180, 183, 186
Dodd, C. H., 40-44, 48, 50-51, 122, 147, 178-179, 191, 198-199
Ellis, E. E., 194

Fiedler, Peter, 147-148
Fitzmyer, Joseph A., 196, 198
Flusser, David, 95, 186
France, R. T., 176
Freedman, David N., 180
Fridrichsen, Anton, 180

Gärtner, Bertil, 184, 200
Gerhardsson, Berger, 195
Gese, Hartmut, 67, 181-185
Glasson, T. Francis, 185
Gray, John, 181-183
Grimm, Werner, 189

Hanson, J. S., 143, 193, 196
Harnack, Adolf von, 15, 17, 36-38, 49, 54, 97, 169, 175, 178, 186
Harvey, A. E., 199-200
Hauerwas, Stanley, 197
Hengel, Martin, 144, 150, 193, 197
Hiers, Richard H., 51-52, 178-180
Horsley, Richard A., 143, 193, 196
Houlden, J. L., 198

Jeremias, Joachim, 95, 110, 121-122, 164, 166, 186-191, 193, 196-198, 200

Author Index

Juel, Donald, 186

Kant, Immanuel, 26-27, 176
Käsemann, Ernst, 98, 186
Keck, Leander E., 190
Kümmel, Werner G., 121-122, 187

Ladd, George Eldon, 182, 185, 190
Levenson, Jon D., 181
Lind, Millard C., 180-181
Lohfink, Gerhard, 54, 180, 187, 192

Manson, T. W., 16, 81, 121-122, 139, 169, 180, 184, 191, 193-194
Marshall, I. Howard, 175, 188, 198
Martin, Ralph P., 198
McKenzie, J. L., 181
Metzler, Norman P. J., 176, 179
Meye, Robert P., 197
Meyer, Ben F., 13, 53, 97, 176, 180, 187-188, 190-192, 194, 196-197, 199-200
Miller, Patrick D., 185
Minear, Paul S., 139, 142, 175, 189, 193, 199
Moltmann, Jürgen, 175, 182-184
Montefiore, C. G., 190
Moore, George F., 190
Moran, W. L., 181
Moule, C. F. D., 184, 193, 195, 197
Mowinckel, Sigmund, 72, 181-183

Nickelsburg, George W. E., 184

Oepke, A., 122, 191

Perrin, Norman, 16, 52-54, 98, 122, 169, 180, 186-187, 191-192
Pesch, Rudolf, 147-149, 164, 189-190, 196-197, 200
Petuchowski, Jakob J., 190

Rad, Gerhard von, 180
Richmond, James, 177
Ritschl, Albrecht, 15, 25-32, 34-36, 44, 49, 167, 176-178
Robbins, Vernon K., 189, 195
Robinson, John A. T., 85, 185, 187, 198
Rothe, Richard, 26-27, 176
Rowland, Christopher, 85, 183, 185

Rowley, H. H., 185

Saebø, Mayne, 182
Sanders, E. P., 54, 80, 97, 141, 180, 183-188, 190-191, 195
Sanders, Jack A. T., 170-172, 174, 200
Schillebeeckx, Edward, 191
Schleiermacher, Friedrich, 26-27, 176
Schmitt, Joseph, 53, 97, 180
Schnackenburg, Rudolf, 121-122, 180, 191
Schubert, K., 200
Schürmann, Heinz, 121, 191
Schweitzer, Albert, 15, 17-18, 38-40, 43-46, 50-52, 54, 89-91, 122, 147, 169-170, 174-175, 178, 185, 196
Schweizer, Eduard, 188-189, 192-193
Scott, E. F., 17, 175
Silberman, Lou H., 185
Smith, Morton, 95, 186, 195-196
Stanton, Graham N., 192, 194, 196, 200
Stein, Robert H., 176
Stone, Michael E., 184
Strauss, David F., 176
Stuhlmacher, Peter, 198

Tannehill, Robert C., 199
Tinsley, E. J., 197

Verhey, Allen, 176, 192
Vermes, Geza, 76, 183-184
Via, Dan Otto, 199
Vögtle, Anton, 147-149, 196-197

Weiss, Johannes, 15, 17-18, 26, 29-30, 32-40, 43-45, 48-50, 54, 89, 91, 110-111, 167, 174-179, 185
Wenham, David, 176, 186
Westerholm, Stephen, 190
Westermann, Claus, 182-184
Wiebe, Ben, 176, 200
Wilder, Amos N., 25, 36, 47-51, 179
Wrede, William, 143, 196
Wright, N. T., 188

Yoder, John H., 175, 192, 197-199

Zimmerli, Walther, 83, 181, 184

Subject Index

Apocalyptic, 29-30, 38, 47, 74-75, 79, 85-86, 89-90, 98
   eschatology of, 85, 89-90, 95
   moral, 20

Baptism, 146

Community. *See under* Jesus; Kingdom of God
Covenant, 57-58
   Davidic, 59, 64-66, 78
   eschatological, 70
   Israel, and, 57, 71
   judgment, 63, 71
   law, and, 113
   new, 84, 148, 157, 164, 166
   relationship of, 58
   repentance of, 114
   repentance, and, 113
   restoration of, 70
   Sinai, 82

Disciples, 150
   cross of the, 151, 153
Discipleship, 19, 149
   cross of, 158

Eschatology, 15, 18-20, 38, 40, 84. *See also under* Kingdom of God; Jesus; Resurrection
   ethics of, 82, 85-87
   Jesus teaching of, 19
Eschaton, 27
Ethics, 15, 17, 19, 82, 85. *See also under* Kingdom of God; Scriptures
   biblical, 20, 82
   Christian, 20
   decisions, 19
   human response, 25-26
   insight, 20
   messianic, 20
   moralization of, 16
   situation, 15
   specific content, 18
Evil, 32, 46, 124, 168
   age of, 86, 88
   end of, 125
   powers of, 31, 48, 124-125
   response, human ethical, 124
   Satan, 30, 33, 37, 75
   spirits of, 32

Faith, 119, 133, 172-173
   repentance, 119
Forgiveness, 128, 131, 147, 157-158, 168
   debt, of, 128-129
   sin, of, 128
Freedom, 83

Gentiles, 75, 106, 119
   present and future of, 107
God, 20-21, 27-28, 34, 71, 73-74, 76, 82-83, 86-87, 118, 126-127
   faith of, 125
   faithfulness of, 83, 104
   father, as, 130
   forgiveness of, 131
   grace of, 16, 104, 110, 125
   history, in, 87-88

Subject Index 221

holy, as, 82
initiative of, 16, 29, 43, 103, 107-112, 114-115, 117, 120, 125, 129, 173
judgment of, 71
king, as, 56-60
kingship and the world, 61
kingship of, 33, 60, 63, 74, 82, 92, 103, 105
love of, 34, 43, 147
mercy of, 118
people of, 21
promise of, 83
redemption of, 28, 57, 62, 83
righteousness of, 34, 115
will of, 34, 38, 46, 86-87, 117, 129-130
world, and the, 60
Gospels, 115
   authenticity of, 22, 24
   criteria/criticism of, 22-24, 97-98, 137, 139-142
   historical criticism of, 22
   historicity of, 23-24
   narratives about Jesus, as, 141-142

Heaven, 75
Hell, 75
Hope, 87. *See also* Eschatology; Israel

Israel, 69, 84, 97, 104-106, 119, 146, 153-154, 161, 163
   covenant of, 84
   eschatological restoration of, 53, 63, 69, 71-74, 78, 80-81, 89-92, 94, 96, 100, 102-107, 116, 119-120, 124, 134, 144, 153-154, 160, 163, 169
   eschatology, 72-73
   imitation of God, called to, 154
   nations, and the, 55-56, 70, 72-75, 77, 80-81
   redemption of, 139
   twelve tribes of, 105

Jerusalem, 70-71, 73-74, 76-77, 79, 84
Jesus, Christ/Messiah, 22, 26, 32, 56, 64, 69, 75-76, 79, 81, 90, 116-117, 119, 132, 135, 144-145, 147, 154-155, 160, 163
   acts of, 102, 104-105, 107-108, 115, 119, 128, 135
   children, and, 134
   church of, 20, 22, 29, 54
   church, and, 122
   community of, 21, 35, 99, 126-127, 132-134, 140, 153, 156, 160, 162-164, 166, 168-169, 173
   community, and, 129-130
   cross of, 158
   Davidic king, 72-73, 77-78, 81
   Davidic kingdom, 80
   death of, 34-35, 39, 50-51, 135-136, 142-150, 153, 155, 157, 159, 162, 165-166, 168
   disciples of, 22, 105, 109-111, 115, 130, 136, 138, 142, 144, 150-151, 153, 155-156, 163, 168
   discipleship of, 48, 93, 149-150, 152, 154, 168
   enemies, love of, 168
   eschatological mission of, 21
   eschatology of, 122
   esoteric teaching of, 135-138, 142-146, 149, 154, 160, 162
   ethics of, 40, 49, 166, 169-172, 174
   expectation of, 66-67
   faith, 120
   forgiveness, and, 113, 123
   imitation of, 155
   Israel, and, 121-122, 146, 148, 152-153, 169
   king, as, 155
   kingdom of, 68-69, 79-80
   Last Supper, 32
   law, and the, 46, 108, 113
   life of, 26, 38, 168
   Lord, as, 140-141
   love of, 172
   message of, 16
   messiahship, 63, 136-137, 143-146, 149, 151-152, 162, 169
   messianic kingdom, 75
   ministry of, 51, 100, 102
   mission of, 18, 21, 32, 54, 63, 68, 73, 92, 95, 99, 102-104, 106, 110, 115, 117, 119, 121, 124-125, 128, 130, 135, 138, 142-144, 148, 151, 155, 158, 161-163, 169
   opponents of, 139
   parousia, 17, 51, 165
   possessions, and, 129
   present and future of, 98, 119

222   Messianic Ethics

priest, as, 77-78
proclamation of, 15, 25-26, 29-30, 32, 37, 49, 51, 54, 69, 73, 89-99, 102-105, 107-112, 115-122, 128
public ministry of, 22
purpose of, 135, 138, 144, 152, 169
redemption of, 28
response, ethical, 121
restoration of, 21
resurrection of, 34, 141, 145, 147
sacrifice, existence of, 148
servant, as, 155
sinners, and, 103, 107, 113, 118, 120, 123, 125, 131, 146
social order, and, 120, 128, 134, 170
Son of God, 30, 144
Son of man, 32, 39, 47
storyteller, as, 22
teaching of ethics, 122
teaching of, 19, 21-22, 26, 29-30, 32, 34-35, 37-38, 40, 43-44, 46, 48, 52, 54, 89, 93, 95, 97, 102, 107-108, 110, 112-113, 122, 126, 135, 139, 151-152, 173
teaching on community, 17
teaching on conflict, 16
teaching on ethics, 17, 19, 122-124
teaching on justice, 16
teaching on liberation, 16
teaching on poverty, 16
twelve disciples, 39, 105-107, 138
women, and, 131, 133
John the Baptist, 32, 95, 99-102, 116-117
  disciples of, 115
  eschatological prophet, 99
  Israel, and, 100
  Jesus, and, 100-102
  ministry of, 101-102
  mission of, 102, 115
  proclamation of, 99
  prophet of judgment, 99-100
Jubilee, 128-129
  year of, 128
Judgment, 73-76, 80, 84, 98, 101-104, 106, 118, 121, 125, 127, 131, 146, 174
  Israel, and, 100
Justice, 72, 83

Kingdom of God, 15, 18-19, 25-26, 28-37, 50, 54-55, 61, 73-76, 79, 81, 90-92, 94-96, 98, 101-109, 111-112, 116-118, 124-126, 129, 133-134, 136, 138, 145, 147-149, 154-155, 160, 163, 173-174
  centrality of, 55, 136
  community of, 28, 30, 33, 43, 47, 53-54, 84, 89, 129-131. *See also under* Jesus
  contemporary Judaism, 41
  context of, 99
  definition of, 61, 94, 96
  end, the, 18, 25, 27, 32, 34-35, 39-40, 48, 50. *See also under* Eschatology
  eschatological, 18, 41
  eschatological drama, 44
  eschatological restoration of, 106
  ethics of, 27-28, 30-31, 34, 36, 38-39, 43-44, 48-49, 127, 167, 170, 174. *See also* Ethics
  future, as, 29, 45
  future of, 37, 40
  highest good, 26-28, 44
  history, in, 25, 44
  importance of, 29
  individual experience, 17, 28, 42, 45
  initiative of, 62
  inward reality, 37, 43, 53
  Israel, and, 97-99, 123
  Jesus, and, 48, 51, 123, 146-147
  Judaism, and, 56
  judgment, 44
  law, and the, 123
  mission of, 18, 47
  nature of, 17
  opponents of, 139
  power of, 123
  presence of, 40
  present and future of, 30, 32-37, 39-42, 44-45, 47-48, 50, 52, 76, 88, 108, 110, 116, 122-124
  proclamation of, 29, 56
  redemption of, 34
  repentance of, 48
  salvation of, 73
  Son of man, 44
  symbolic, 42, 52, 98
  women, and, 130-131

worldly reality, as other, 17

Last Supper, 163-165
Law, 114, 116
  sinners, and, 115
Liberal theology, 36, 50
  eternal, 159
  losing of, 159
  saving of, 159
Love, 18-19, 31-32, 37-38, 46, 132, 156
  command of, 126, 132, 156-157
  enemies, of, 110, 133
  neighbor, of, 28, 31

Messiah, 75-77
Moral reason, 26

Passover,
  meal of, 164
Patriarchy, 130
Peace, 71, 83-84, 88, 103, 108-109, 152
Peacemakers, 133
Pharisees, 139
Prayer, 76-77, 96, 114, 128

Reconciliation, 131-132, 134
Repentance, 35, 39, 43, 46, 93, 99, 101-102, 104, 106, 111-119, 126, 133, 157-158
  faith, and, 112
Response and faith, 107
Response, human ethical, 15, 17-21, 25, 27-29, 31, 33, 35-36, 38, 40, 45-46, 48-49, 82, 93, 105, 107, 109, 111-112, 115, 117-119, 121-127, 129, 132-133, 136-138, 149, 152-154, 156, 158-160, 166, 172-173. *See also* Love
  beatitudes, 108
  expected, 93
  individualistic, 16
  Israel, and, 100
  teaching of, 107
Resurrection, 74-75. *See also* Eschatology
Righteous, the, 117-118, 121, 127

Salvation, 73, 76, 84, 88, 92, 95, 98, 102, 105, 109-111, 116, 119, 147-148
  Israel, of, 82
Scriptures, 20-21
  ethics/morality, 20-21. *See also* Ethics
Sin, 16, 84, 113-115, 117-118
Sinners, 127, 132, 148
  divorce, 173
  forgiveness of, 34, 84, 87, 115, 119, 131-133, 136, 157-158
  guilt of, 35
Son of man, 79-80, 87, 90
Soul, 38

Temple, 74, 78, 80-81, 104, 143-144, 161-163
Trust, 87

Violent revolution, 17

The Author

Ben Wiebe attended Freed-Hardeman College (Henderson, Tennessee) and earned a B.A. at Abilene (Texas) Christian University, an M.Div. at Toronto School of Theology, and an M.A. and a Ph.D. at McMaster University (Hamilton, Ontario).

For fourteen years, Wiebe has served as a minister in Church of Christ congregations in Toronto, Edmonton, Thunder Bay, and Hamilton, where he now resides. He has been writing and teaching part-time at McMaster University and at Wilfrid Laurier University (Waterloo, Ontario).

Wiebe's work has appeared in journals such as *Restoration Quarterly* and *Interpretation*, and in the book *Self-Definition and Self-Discovery in Early Christianity: A Study in Changing Horizons*, edited by David Hawkins and Thomas Robinson (Edwin Mellen Press). He is a member of the Canadian Society of Biblical Studies and a board member of the International Bible Correspondence School, chiefly serving Africa and India.

Ben Wiebe was born in Mexico, and since 1953 Canada is home for him. He is married to Patti Mann, and they are the parents of Paul, Carrie, and Stephen. With his family he is part of the Stoney Creek Church of Christ, where he teaches in the adult education program and is one of the pastors.